Ready® Common Core

K Reading INSTRUCTION
Teacher Resource Book

Advisors

Crystal Bailey, Math Impact Teacher, Eastern Guilford Middle School, Guilford County Schools, Gibsonville, NC

Leslie Blauman, Classroom Teacher, Cherry Hills Village Elementary, Cherry Creek School District, Cherry Hills Village, CO

Max Brand, Reading Specialist, Indian Run Elementary, Dublin City School District, Dublin, OH

Kathy Briguet, Retired Curriculum Coordinator for K–12 Literacy, Forest Lake Area Schools, Forest Lake, MN; Adjunct Instructor, Reading Instruction in the Elementary Grades, University of Minnesota, Minneapolis, MN

Helen Comba, Supervisor of Basic Skills & Language Arts, School District of the Chathams, Chatham, NJ

Cindy Dean, Classroom Teacher, Mt. Diablo Unified School District, Concord, CA

Randall E. Groth, Ph.D., Associate Professor of Mathematics Education, Salisbury University, Salisbury, MD

Jennifer Geaber, Kingston Hill Academy Charter School, South Kingstown, RI

Bill Laraway, Classroom Teacher, Silver Oak Elementary, Evergreen School District, San Jose, CA

Susie Legg, Elementary Curriculum Coordinator, Kansas City Public Schools, Kansas City, KS

Sarah Levine, Classroom Teacher, Springhurst Elementary School, Dobbs Ferry School District, Dobbs Ferry, NY

Nicole Peirce, Classroom Teacher, Eleanor Roosevelt Elementary, Pennsbury School District, Morrisville, PA

Donna Phillips, Classroom Teacher, Farmington R-7 School District, Farmington, MO

Kari Ross, Reading Specialist, MN

Sunita Sangari, Math Coach, PS/MS 29, New York City Public Schools, New York, NY

Shannon Tsuruda, Classroom Teacher, Mt. Diablo Unified School District, Concord, CA

Mark Hoover Thames, Research Scientist, University of Michigan, Ann Arbor, MI

Acknowledgments

Project Managers: Diane Arnell, Martha Goodale, Claudia Herman, Maura Wolk
Cover Designer & Illustrator: Julia Bourque

Book Designer: Mark Nodland
Director–Product Development: Daniel J. Smith
Vice President–Product Development: Adam Berkin

ISBN 978-0-7609-8716-2
©2014—Curriculum Associates, LLC
North Billerica, MA 01862

Table of Contents

Unit 5: Integration of Knowledge and Ideas in Literature

Unit 6: Integration of Knowledge and Ideas in Informational Text

Projectables

Ready® Common Core Program Overview

Ready® Common Core is an interactive read-aloud program built to teach the Common Core State Standards (CCSS) for Reading. The main focus of the program is the CCSS Reading Literature and Informational Text strands. Other Reading and ELA standards are integrated throughout the lessons. The components of the program are described below.

Built for the Common Core. Not just aligned.

Student Instruction

Ready Common Core Student Book includes thoughtful, text-based activities that encourage students to apply and practice the CCSS. Lessons follow a repetitive, predictable structure that supports emergent readers and scaffolds student learning. Each time students complete a lesson, they have independently applied a new skill.

Features

 Built with brand-new content

 Uses a research-based gradual-release instructional model

 Employs higher-rigor questions, requiring students to cite text-based evidence to support answers

 Includes award-winning trade books from a wide range of genres

 Embeds thoughtful professional development

Teacher Resource Book, Trade Book Collection, and Teacher Toolbox

Ready Common Core Teacher Resource Book supports teachers with strong professional development, step-by-step lesson plans, and developmentally appropriate best practices for implementing the CCSS.

Ready Common Core Trade Book Collection includes nine high-quality literature and informational texts from a variety of genres. These rich, complex texts are the vehicle for teaching and modeling the standards. See page A11 for a listing of the trade books and Projectables.

The online **Ready** Teacher Toolbox gives teachers access to a host of multilevel resources, such as PDFs of the Student Book and Teacher Resource Book lessons, instructional support, online lessons, and lessons for prerequisite skills. (See pages A16–A17 for more.)

i-Ready® Diagnostic

Built on the Common Core and integrated with the **Ready** program, **i-Ready Diagnostic** helps teachers track student growth, pointing teachers toward the correct **Ready** lessons to use for remediation. See page A18 for details. (**i-Ready** sold separately.)

A6

Supporting the Implementation of the Common Core

The Common Core State Standards (CCSS) were developed to make sure that by the time students graduate from high school, they are college- and career-ready. Therefore, the creators of the standards started with the expectations they had for students at the end of 12th grade and worked down to kindergarten. As a result of this backward design approach, the CCSS are more rigorous than most current standards. The creators of the standards want students at every grade to be creative and critical readers and writers. At the end of each grade, students are expected to independently read and comprehend increasingly complex text. Not only are most current textbooks lacking alignment to the CCSS, they also lack the levels of complex text identified in the CCSS. *Ready® Common Core* is here to help.

Using *Ready* to Support the Transition to the Common Core

As a Supplement to a Textbook

Your classroom textbook may not have been developed for the Common Core. It may not have all the resources you need to meet these challenging standards. In addition, the passages in textbooks often do not reflect the levels of text complexity required by the Common Core, and the activities and questions do not reflect the rigor of the standards. By supplementing with *Ready*, you'll be able to address all of these gaps and deficiencies.

With a Balanced Literacy/ Reading Workshop Curriculum

Because every standard in *Ready Common Core* has been addressed with clear, thoughtful pedagogy, you can use *Ready* as the main structure of an interactive read aloud program. Any other materials aligned to the Common Core can be woven into the curriculum.

With *i-Ready® Diagnostic*

If you are an *i-Ready* subscriber, you can administer the *i-Ready Diagnostic* as a cross-grade-level assessment to pinpoint instructional needs and address them with *Ready Common Core*. For more on this, see page A18.

Helpful Resources for the Transition to the Common Core

http://www.corestandards.org/
The main website for the Common Core. Here you'll find the full text of the standards, plus frequently asked questions and resources.

http://www.smarterbalanced.org/ and http://www.parcconline.org
The testing consortia creating Common Core assessments for future implementation.

http://www.ascd.org/common-core-state-standards/common-core.aspx
A helpful list of all of ASCD's resources on the Common Core, as well as a link to ASCD's free EduCore digital tool, which was funded by a grant from the Bill & Melinda Gates Foundation. A repository of evidence-based strategies, videos, and supporting documents that help educators transition to the Common Core.

http://www.reading.org/resources/ResourcesByTopic/CommonCore-resourcetype/CommonCore-rt-resources.aspx
Links to helpful articles about the Common Core from *Reading Today Online*.

http://www.engageny.org/
Hosted by the New York State Education Department (NYSED), this site features curriculum resources and professional development materials to support the transition to the Common Core.

Answering the Demands of the Common Core with *Ready*®

THE DEMANDS OF THE COMMON CORE	HOW *READY*® DELIVERS
High-Quality Texts: It's important that students are exposed to well-crafted texts that are worth reading closely and exhibit exceptional craft and thought or provide useful information. The Common Core State Standards (CCSS) Appendix B provides text exemplars that reflect the rigor and quality required by the CCSS.	The nine trade books in **Ready** were carefully chosen to match the rigor and quality of read aloud text in Appendix B. The list includes award-winning and renowned authors and illustrators Tomie dePaola, Kevin Henkes, Leo and Diane Dillon, and Edward Lear as well as information books from the highly regarded Let's-Read-and-Find-Out Science series. See page A9 for more information about text complexity.
Read Aloud Texts: Students can gain comprehension skills by listening to texts being read that are of higher complexity than what they can normally read.	**Ready** offers Read Aloud lessons in which teachers read the texts and then unpack the key details step by step, giving students access to concepts and vocabulary beyond what they could manage independently.
Wide Range of Genres; Emphasis on Nonfiction: Students must read a true balance of authentic literary and informational texts. Success in college and the real world requires that students master the skills needed to read a variety of informational texts.	The trade books and Projectables in **Ready** encompass a range of genres and text types, including realistic fiction, folktale, fantasy, poetry, science, biography, and procedural and persuasive text. See page A11 for a list of the trade books and Projectables.
Intentional, Close Reading: Careful, close readings of complex texts teach students how to gather evidence and build knowledge.	Each **Ready** Teacher Resource Book lesson includes Close Reading activities in which teachers prompt students with higher-level text-dependent questions, and then lead students to closely examine words and pictures to find the answers. See more on page A10.
Text-Based Evidence: Students' interpretations and comprehension of the text must be supported by the words in the text.	**Ready** Turn and Talk activities require students to back up their answers with evidence directly from the text. Instruction throughout the Teacher Resource Book reinforces the importance of quoting from the text to substantiate interpretations.
Building Content Knowledge: Students should view reading as an opportunity to learn new information.	The informational trade books in **Ready** relate to grade-appropriate science and social studies content. Students deepen their knowledge of the content in Read Aloud Student Book pages by drawing representations of concepts and key details.
Integrated ELA Instruction: It's important that teachers use the texts as a source of rich language arts instruction, as opposed to isolated skill instruction.	**Ready** lessons provide students with consistent contextualized opportunities for speaking and listening in response to a text. Foundational Reading and Language standards are addressed in activities that draw on words taken directly from the trade books.

The Importance of Complex Read Aloud Text

Why Emphasize Complex Text?

Research has shown that the complexity levels of the texts in current classrooms are far below what is required for college- and career-readiness. A major emphasis of the Common Core State Standards (CCSS) is for students to encounter appropriately complex texts at each grade level in order to develop the mature language skills and conceptual knowledge they need for success in school and life. Instructional materials should meet this challenge with rich and rigorous texts at each grade level.

How do I Introduce Complex Text to K–1 Students?

At grades K–1, rich, interactive read aloud text is an important part of the curriculum. Students at these levels can listen to and comprehend much more complex material than they can read independently. The CCSS provide the following information about read aloud text:

> "Read-aloud selections should be ... at levels of complexity **well above what students can read on their own**." (Coleman & Pimentel, Revised Publishers' Criteria, 2012, p. 5)

> "Children in the early grades (particularly K–2) should participate in **rich, structured conversations** with an adult in response to the written texts that are read aloud, orally **comparing and contrasting** as well as **analyzing** and **synthesizing**, in the manner called for by the Standards." (Common Core State Standards, 2010, p. 33)

> "By reading a story or nonfiction selection aloud, teachers allow children to experience written language **without the burden of decoding**, granting them access to content that they may not be able to read and understand by themselves. Children are then **free to focus their mental energy on the words and ideas presented in the text**, and they will eventually be better prepared to tackle rich written content on their own." (Common Core State Standards, 2010, Appendix A)

Read Aloud Trade Books in *Ready*®

Given the CCSS emphasis on read aloud text, *Ready Common Core* bases standard instruction on high-quality trade books that are read aloud. The trade book selections were influenced by the read-aloud exemplars listed in CCSS Appendix B. Not only do the trade books align with the complexity levels of these exemplars, but they also draw on the same, or comparable, authors and series, including Tomie DePaola, Kevin Henkes, Claire Llewellyn, Wendy Pfeffer, Patricia Lauber, and the Let's-Read-and-Find-Out Science series. See a complete list of the trade books on page A11.

Close-Up on Close Reading

What Is Close Reading?

According to PARCC, "[Research] links the close reading of complex text—whether the student is a struggling reader or advanced—to significant gains in reading proficiency." (PARCC, 2011) The purpose of close reading is to unpack the meaning in a text by examining and interpreting the author's choices. Although this seems like a highly sophisticated practice, even emerging readers can begin to understand that authors choose their words carefully, organize their sentences thoughtfully, and make intentional decisions about the placement of words, pictures, and other features.

Close Reading Instruction in *Ready® Common Core*

Every *Ready Common Core* Teacher Resource Book lesson features Close Reading activities (see below). Through these activities, teachers model and guide students to apply close reading strategies to specific sections of the read aloud text. Key features of a Close Reading activity include the following:

Multiple readings: The instructional design of *Ready* requires multiple readings of the text. Students first explore a text through Read Aloud Lessons, which focus on literal comprehension of key details. Then, in Focus Lessons, students revisit the text while applying specific CCSS Reading Literature or Informational Text standards. The Close Reading feature in every lesson guides students to reread the text a third time, zooming in on specific words, phrases, and illustrations to make inferences, analyze the author's purpose, or find evidence to support a claim about the text.

Text-dependent questions: "The purposes of text-dependent questions are to prompt rereading, encourage the use of textual evidence to support answers, and deepen comprehension using the analytic processes." (Fisher, Frey, & Lapp, 2012) In *Ready* Close Reading activities, students answer a range of questions from literal to inferential (e.g. *Why do you think the author chose this word? What is the story's message?*) To answer such questions, students must revisit the text and choose precise details in the words and pictures and use them to defend their ideas.

Text-based discussion: Each *Ready* Close Reading activity allows students to develop and use academic and domain-specific language while engaging in focused talk around one aspect of the text. Open-ended questions allow students the opportunity to make claims, defend them with text evidence, and respectfully discuss conflicting ideas, all resulting in a deeper understanding of the text.

1 Teachers define the goal for students so they can look and listen with a purpose in mind as a small portion of the text is revisited. Often this goal is a strategy that good readers utilize during close reading.

2 Teachers give targeted prompts that lead students to a key understanding about the text or the author's intentions. Students must always use text evidence to answer questions directly or support their interpretations.

3 Teachers close the activity by helping students "connect the dots" between the ideas highlighted in the prompts in order to achieve a deeper understanding of the text.

1 Close Reading

- Tell children they can also use picture clues to compare and contrast characters. Display page 9. Help children find Chrysanthemum. Ask:

  What do you notice about Chrysanthemum's name? *(It does not fit in the box.)*

2 **Is that the same as or different from the other kids?** *(different; their names are shorter and fit in the box)*

  How does Chrysanthemum's face look? *(worried and sad)*

  Is that the same as or different from the other kids? *(different; the other kids are laughing)*

3 - Discuss how the picture clues emphasize how Chrysanthemum's name is different from the rest of her classmates' names.

Trade Books and Projectables in *Ready*®

The Common Core emphasizes the importance of selecting rigorous, high-quality texts that reward students for their work. To encourage students to dig deeply during their readings of texts, **Ready** focuses instruction on a set of popular, well-respected trade books, both literature and informational text. Chosen for their range of genres as well as their text complexity, these trade books offer ample opportunities for close reading and practicing Common Core skills. In addition, Projectables, short text selections, provide extra genre and skill support. Located at the end of the Teacher Resource Book (see pages 163–167) and as PDFs in the Teacher Toolbox, Projectables are designed to be displayed with lessons that feature specific skills. The following chart shows the genre of each text, and the **Ready** lessons in which each title appears.

Trade Books and Projectables	Genre	*Ready*® Lessons
*Jamaica's Blue Marker** by Juanita Havill	Realistic Fiction	A, 1, 3, 4, 11, 15
*The Art Lesson** by Tomie dePaola	Realistic Fiction	B, 1, 2, 11
*Chrysanthemum** by Kevin Henkes	Fantasy	C, 2, 5, 15
*Stone Soup** by Marcia Brown	Folktale	D, 3, 9, 10, 14
*Why Mosquitoes Buzz in People's Ears** by Verna Aardema	Folktale	E, 4, 9, 11, 14
*Red-Eyed Tree Frog** by Joy Cowley	Informational Text: Narrative Nonfiction	F, 6, 8, 12, 13
What's It Like to Be a Fish? by Wendy Pfeffer	Informational Text: Science	G, 6, 7, 8, 13, 18
What Lives in a Shell? by Kathleen Weidner Zoehfeld	Informational Text: Science	H, 7, 13, 16, 18
*America's Champion Swimmer** by Gertrude Ederle	Informational Text: Biography	I, 12, 16, 17
Projectable 1: "The Owl and the Pussy-Cat" by Edward Lear	Poem	10
Projectable 2: How to Make Play Dough	Procedural Text: Recipe	10
Projectable 3: "Eat Better!" by Linda Gold	Persuasive Text: Nutrition	17

*Since this book does not have page numbers, we identified page numbers to reference in the student and teacher lessons. In **Ready**, page 1 is considered the first right-hand page opposite the inside front cover of the trade book (see sample below) regardless of whether or not this page includes text.

page 1

Using *Ready® Common Core*

The easy-to-use Teacher Resource Book contains best-practice instructional techniques to help you teach each new Common Core reading standard effectively. Much more than just an answer key to the **Ready** Student Book, this resource has the embedded professional development you'll need to teach students research-based strategies to conquer the challenges of reading complex text. Using the read aloud trade books as the vehicle to drive instruction, the **Ready** program enables you to help students develop proficiency in each Common Core reading standard by reading and revisiting these engaging, authentic literary and informational texts—utilizing a proven-effective, gradual-release approach that builds student confidence.

Teacher Resource Book

Get professional development right when you need it—while you're teaching a new standard. Proven-effective teaching strategies and tips throughout the Teacher Resource Book help you transition to the more rigorous standards, and every lesson plan gives you an easy-to-use set of tools to coordinate the trade books with the instruction presented in the **Ready** program.

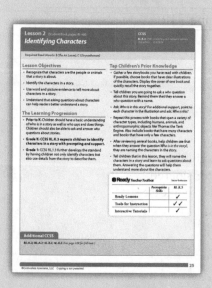

Trade Books

Provide students with the opportunity to apply Common Core reading standards throughout nine high-quality, authentic texts spanning a range of genres, topics, and text types.

Student Instruction Book

Provide rigorous instruction on every Common Core reading standard. First, students listen to each trade book and answer questions to demonstrate understanding. Then, they explore key components of each standard in relation to the trade book text and answer questions using text-based evidence.

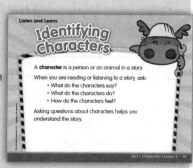

Teacher Toolbox

Differentiate instruction with the online Teacher Toolbox. It has a host of multilevel resources to help teachers introduce a new concept.

Year-Long Pacing Guide for Kindergarten

The pacing guide below shows how **Ready Common Core** fits into the curriculum throughout the year. Each "week" is based on three days of Lesson instruction at 30 minutes per day, leaving time for teachers to revisit or reinforce concepts as needed.

Week	*Ready® Common Core Instruction*
1	Read Aloud Lesson A: *Jamaica's Blue Marker*
2	Read Aloud Lesson B: *The Art Lesson*
3	Lesson 1: Asking Questions
4	Read Aloud Lesson C: *Chrysanthemum*
5	Lesson 2: Identifying Characters
6	Read Aloud Lesson D: *Stone Soup*
7	Lesson 3: Identifying Setting
8	Read Aloud Lesson E: *Why Mosquitoes Buzz in People's Ears*
9	Lesson 4: Identifying Events
10	Lesson 5: Retelling Stories
11	Read Aloud Lesson F: *Red-Eyed Tree Frog*
12	Read Aloud Lesson G: *What's It Like to Be a Fish?*
13	Lesson 6: Asking Questions
14	Read Aloud Lesson H: *What Lives in a Shell?*
15	Lesson 7: Main Topic
16	Lesson 8: Describing Connections
17	Lesson 9: Unknown Words
18	Lesson 10: Types of Texts
19	Lesson 11: Authors and Illustrators
20	Read Aloud Lesson I: *America's Champion Swimmer*
21	Lesson 12: Unknown Words
22	Lesson 13: Parts of a Book
23	Lesson 14: Story Words and Pictures
24	Lesson 15: Comparing Characters
25	Lesson 16: Words and Pictures
26	Lesson 17: Identifying Reasons
27	Lesson 18: Comparing Two Books

Teaching with *Ready® Common Core*

To support teachers in effectively introducing the read aloud text as well as teaching the Common Core State Standards, **Ready Common Core** contains two types of lessons: Read Aloud Lessons and Focus Lessons. Learn more about each type of lesson here.

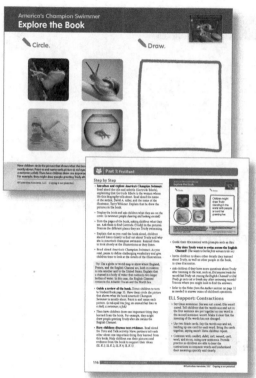

Read Aloud Lessons

Read Aloud Lessons provide a comprehensive introduction to each trade book in the program. After a brief review of critical vocabulary and new concepts, teachers read the entire book aloud. Over the next two days, teachers revisit the book in smaller chunks, calling students' attention to the key details needed to comprehend and ultimately retell the text. This introduction prepares students to dig deeper into the key details, craft and structure, and integration of knowledge and ideas in each text as they proceed through each Focus Lesson.

Literature Read Aloud Lessons guide students to identify the characters and key events in the beginning, middle, and end of a story.

Informational Text Read Aloud Lessons guide students to identify the main topic and key details in a text.

Suggested Daily Pacing

The models below show how to pace a Read Aloud Lesson over a period of three days. The optional features give you the flexibility to make the best choices for your allotted instructional time.

Ready Common Core Read Aloud Lesson

	Day 1 (30 minutes)		Day 2 (30 minutes)		Day 3 (30 minutes)
Teacher Resource Book	**Introduction: Critical Vocabulary and New Concepts**	**Part 1: First Read**	**Part 2: Reread for Meaning**	**Part 3: Reread for Meaning**	**Part 4: Reread for Meaning** **Retell the Text**
Student Book Literature Lesson OR Informational Lesson		**Characters**	**In the Beginning**	**In the Middle**	**At the End**
		Explore the Book	**Key Details**	**Key Details**	**Key Details**
Optional Teacher Resource Book Features		**ELL Support**	**Tier Two Vocabulary**	**Tier Two Vocabulary**	**Integrating Foundational Skills** **Additional Activities**

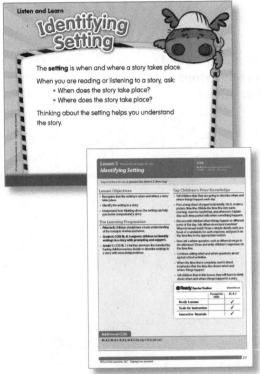

Focus Lessons

Each **Ready** Focus Lesson targets a specific CCSS Reading Literature or Informational Text standard. Through a gradual release of responsibility, teachers model the habits of active readers and guide students to practice these habits—first with guidance and then independently. Each lesson includes the following components:

- **Listen and Learn (Introduction):** Teachers introduce the standard and key academic language. Students learn the important questions to ask or steps to follow as they apply the standard to text.

- **Practice Together (Modeled Instruction):** Teachers think aloud as they model applying the standard to select trade book pages. Then they model how to apply the standard in the related Student Book activities.

- **Practice Together (Guided Practice):** Teachers ask a series of targeted questions that help students apply the standard to another text selection. Students discuss the Student Book activities together before recording their answers independently.

- **Practice by Myself (Independent Practice):** Teachers read aloud a third text selection as well as the Student Book activities. Students work independently to apply the standard, and then conclude by discussing their work together and reflecting on the skill.

Suggested Daily Pacing

The model below shows how to pace a Focus Lesson over a period of three days. The optional feature gives you the flexibility to make the best choices for your allotted instructional time.

Ready Common Core Focus Lesson

	Day 1 (30 minutes)		Day 2 (30 minutes)		Day 3 (30 minutes)
Teacher Resource Book	Tap Children's Prior Knowledge	Part 1: Introduction	Part 2: Modeled Instruction	Part 3: Guided Practice	Part 4: Independent Practice
Student Book		Listen and Learn	Practice Together	Practice Together	Practice by Myself
Optional Teacher Resource Book Features					Differentiated Instruction

Connecting with the *Ready*® Teacher Toolbox

Designed for use with ***Ready*® Common Core**, the Teacher Toolbox provides a host of multilevel resources teachers can use to differentiate instruction. If you purchased the Teacher Toolbox, you should have received an insert with access codes and information. Please contact Customer Service at (800)-225-0248 if you need this information. Visit *www.teacher-toolbox.com* to get started.

How Do I Use the Teacher Toolbox?

Lessons are conveniently organized to match your print materials, making it easy to find additional resources for teaching the skills and standards associated with each lesson. All of these resources are perfect for use with any interactive whiteboard or other computer projection screen.

Available for Grades K–8

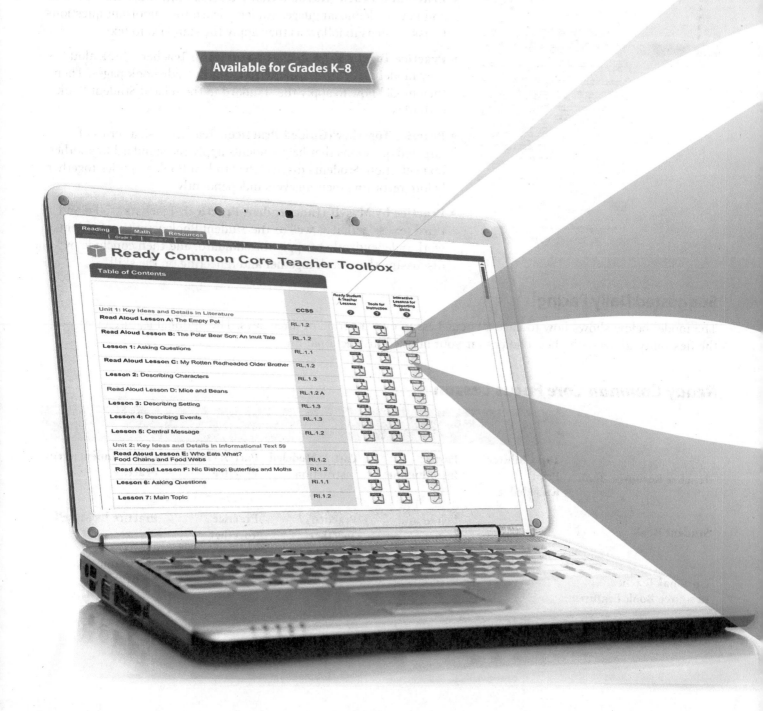

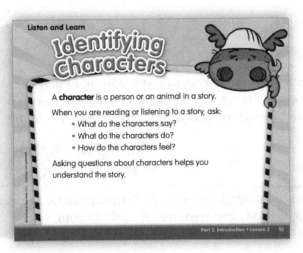

Ready® Lessons

Ready® lessons make it easy for teachers to focus on particular skills, or even reteach skills that students may not have mastered at earlier grade levels. What you get:

- Every lesson in this book is available as an individual PDF file, which you can project for whole-class and small-group use.

- Prerequisite student lesson PDFs—and the accompanying Teacher Resource Book lesson—from prior grades are available to administer as remediation.

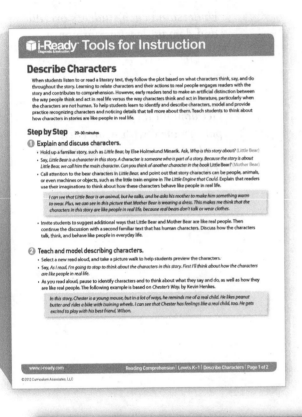

Tools for Instruction

Research-based, best-practice routines and activities for the classroom and small groups provide ways to teach or review standards and prerequisite skills.

Guided Interactive Tutorials

Guided interactive tutorials give teachers another engaging way to provide whole-class or small-group instruction. Lessons follow a consistent structure of explicit instruction and guided practice. Immediate corrective feedback continuously supports students.

A17

Using *i-Ready*® Diagnostic with *Ready*® Common Core

If you have already purchased **i-Ready® Diagnostic**, you can use its robust reporting to monitor students' overall and domain-specific reading proficiency as they move through **Ready® Common Core**. Specifically, use the Diagnostic Results for a Student report and the Instructional Groupings report to identify Next Step skills for student instruction.

Diagnostic Results for a Student

Available for Grades K–12

Each student's Diagnostic Results report gives teachers insight into the performance of that student, with clear next steps for instruction with detailed recommendations and resources in each domain.

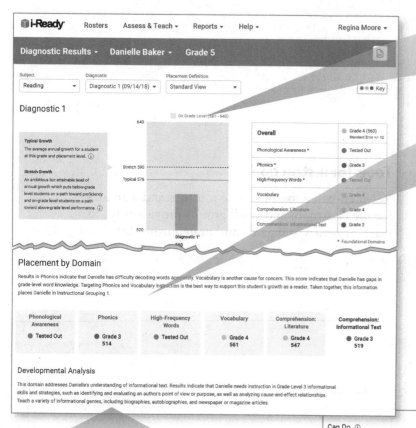

Understand each student's overall and domain level performance.

Get domain level insights into performance with what each student can do and next steps for teacher-led instruction.

*Detailed analysis of student needs provides the same information that a reading specialist would, but with **i-Ready Diagnostic**, it's completely automated.*

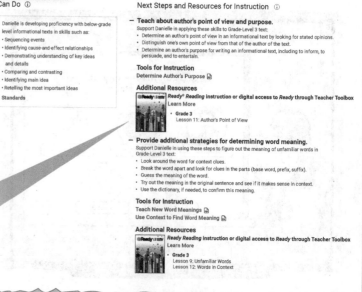

*Recommends specific lessons in **Ready Common Core**.*

A18

Instructional Groupings

The **Instructional Groupings** report shows teachers exactly how to group students so that students who are struggling with the same skills get the most out of small-group instruction. The report also gives effective instructional recommendations and resources for each group profile.

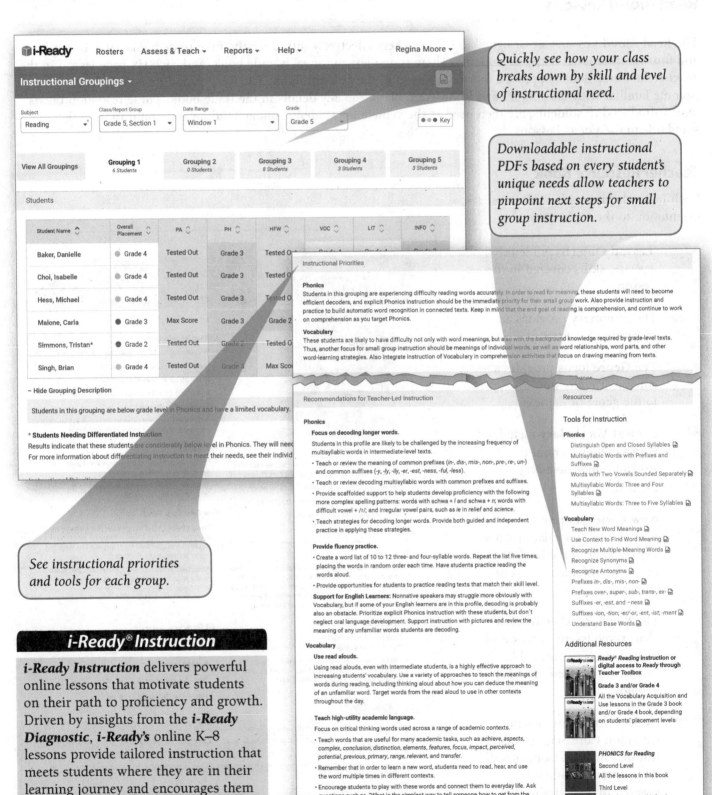

> Quickly see how your class breaks down by skill and level of instructional need.

> Downloadable instructional PDFs based on every student's unique needs allow teachers to pinpoint next steps for small group instruction.

> See instructional priorities and tools for each group.

i-Ready® Instruction

i-Ready Instruction delivers powerful online lessons that motivate students on their path to proficiency and growth. Driven by insights from the **i-Ready Diagnostic**, **i-Ready's** online K–8 lessons provide tailored instruction that meets students where they are in their learning journey and encourages them as they develop new skills. Learn more at i-Ready.com/empower.

Features of *Ready® Common Core*

This section guides teachers to the key features of the Teacher Resource Book and the Student Book. Numbered boxes call out and describe the features. Use this section to familiarize yourself with the overall structure of the *Ready Common Core* Read Aloud Lessons (pages A20–A27) and Focus Lessons (pages A28–A33).

Read Aloud Lessons

The Read Aloud Lessons are designed to help teachers effectively introduce the nine trade books (five literature and four informational texts) to students. There is one lesson for each trade book, and each six-page lesson in the Teacher Resource Book supports a four-page lesson in the Student Book. The Read Aloud Lessons help students become familiar with the content and knowledgeable of the key details in the trade book. These read aloud texts, once introduced to students, are then used as the vehicle for students' understanding and application of the standards in the Focus Lessons.

Teacher Resource Book

Each lesson begins with a full-page orientation to the trade book.

1 **Lesson Objectives** identify specific skills covered in the lesson.

2 The **Summary** provides an overview of the text.

3 The **Genre** focus provides a student-friendly introduction to the genre of the text.

4 **Critical Vocabulary** includes words that are central to students' understanding of the text.

5 **New Concepts** provides background information on a key concept in the book that might be unfamiliar to your students.

6 The ***Ready Teacher Toolbox*** chart provides an overview of related resources available online in the ***Ready Teacher Toolbox***.

7 **CCSS Focus** identifies the Common Core State Standard featured in the lesson, as well as Additional Standards covered in activities in the Teacher Resource Book.

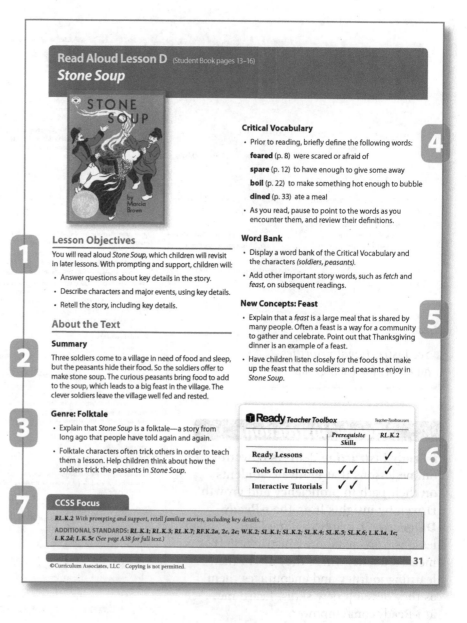

A20

Each of the five Read Aloud Lessons for Literature introduces students to a literature trade book used in the program. These lessons emphasize story elements. In Part 1, students listen as the teacher reads the entire trade book and then they identify the characters in the story.

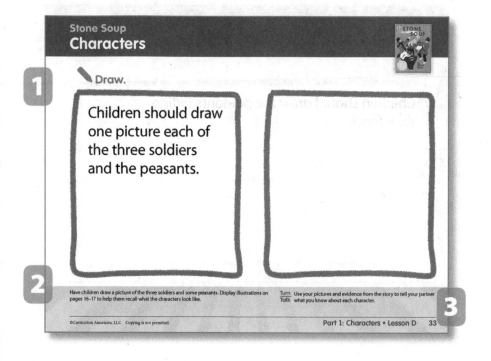

Student Book

1 Students draw characters from the story, reinforcing their understanding of story elements and who the story is about.

2 Teacher directions appear in the shaded area at the bottom of the Student Book page. More detailed instruction appears in the Step by Step section of the Teacher Resource Book.

3 **Turn and Talk** provides students an opportunity to share their pictures and talk about characters in the story.

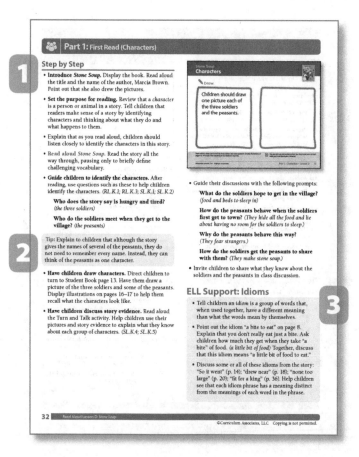

Teacher Resource Book

1 **Step by Step** guides students through each lesson part. Bulleted, bold text highlights the instructional moves in each part of the lesson.

2 Written by experienced teachers, **Tips** provide thoughtful, practical suggestions for deepening students' understanding and appreciation of the text.

3 **ELL Support** provides background on concepts, content, and potentially unfamiliar words to help make text more accessible to English Language Learners.

In Part 2, students listen as the teacher rereads the beginning of the trade book aloud. The teacher then uses prompts provided in the Teacher Resource Book to guide students through answering questions about the key details in this part of the story.

Student Book

1 Students use text evidence to draw a picture about an important story event.

2 **Turn and Talk** employs peer talk and interaction to answer text-related questions using evidence from the story.

> **Teaching Tip:** After students complete their drawings, teachers may wish to have them write or dictate captions for their pictures, using characters' names and describing what characters are doing.

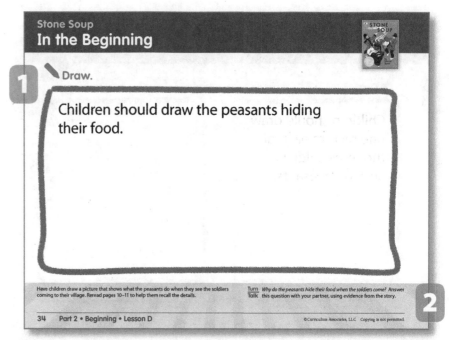

Teacher Resource Book

1 Suggested prompts guide students to identify important story events and extract key ideas from the trade book. Questions build toward a gradual understanding of the text's meaning.

2 **Tier Two Vocabulary** provides practice with key words or phrases from the trade book that are likely to be encountered in other contexts.

3 **Close Reading** engages students in strategies for extracting meaning from the text. Sometimes this activity is a deep dive into text details; other times it's a broader look at the text structure or organization.

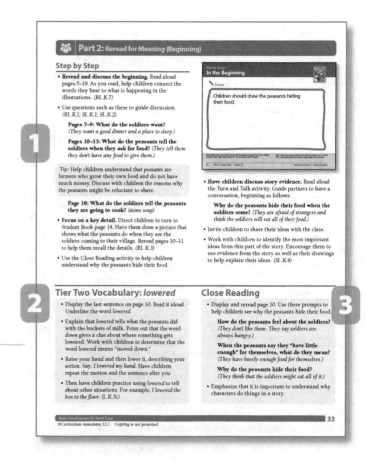

In Part 3, students listen as the teacher rereads the middle of the trade book aloud. Students once again discuss and ask and answer questions about the key details in this part of the story.

Student Book

1 Teacher annotations provide explicit examples to assist in evaluating students' responses to the Student Book activities.

2 In **Turn and Talk**, students gain practice answering questions and sharing their thinking with a partner.

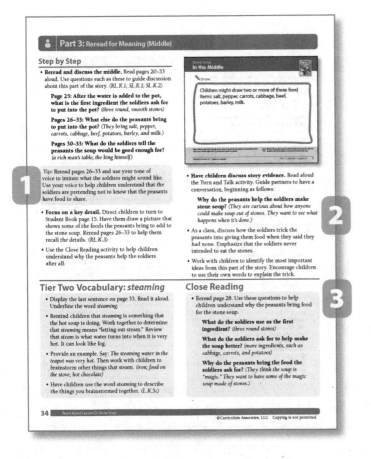

Teacher Resource Book

1 **Tips** give teachers point-of-use suggestions for implementing the skill as well as support in inclusion, vocabulary, text complexity, standard complexity, and background on concepts or content.

2 In **Turn and Talk**, partners have a conversation, using text evidence to describe story events.

3 **Close Reading** is part of the instructional flow. It helps students tackle the more challenging parts of a text, focusing on details such as sentences, words, and pictures.

A23

In Part 4, students listen as the teacher rereads the end of the trade book aloud. The teacher checks literal comprehension as students ask and answer questions about this part of the story. The teacher guides students in a retelling of the text.

Student Book

1 **Turn and Talk** questions identify key insights for students to understand from the text, such as a problem and solution.

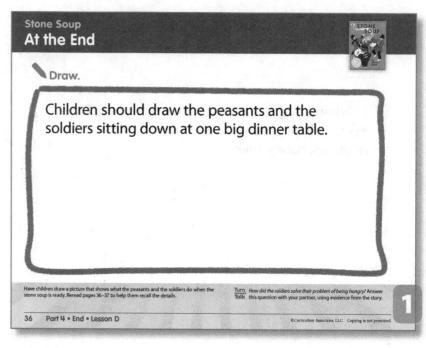

Teacher Resource Book

1 **Retell the Text:** To reinforce the content of the story, all students participate by role-playing a retelling of the beginning, middle, and end of the story.

2 **Integrating Foundational Skills** helps teachers integrate foundational standard instruction by providing specific questions and short activities that apply specific standards. CCSS codes are provided at point of use.

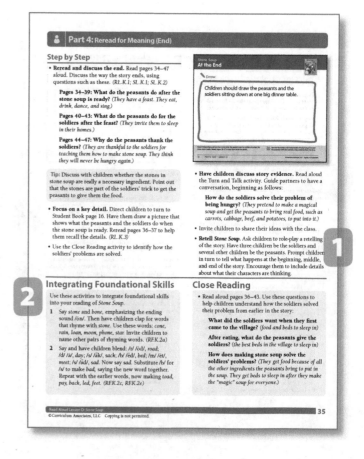

Teacher Resource Book

Additional Activities provide meaningful standards-based Writing, Speaking and Listening, and Language activities. CCSS codes are identified at point of use next to each activity, allowing the teacher to easily integrate standards instruction.

Additional Activities   **RA Lesson D**

Writing Activity

Write an Explanation (W.K.2; L.K.1.a; L.K.2.d)

- Tell children that you will work together to write a recipe for stone soup. Reread pages 20–33 from *Stone Soup*. Ask children to tell what soup ingredients they hear as you read. Write the ingredients on chart paper. (*stones, salt, pepper, carrots, cabbage, beef, potatoes, barley, milk*)

- Next, have children tell the steps for making the soup. Guide them using questions such as these: *What do we do first? Then what do we add? What do we do last?* As children respond, write the steps in order. Call on volunteers to share the pen in order to write letters and simple VC and CVC words that they know.

- After completing the recipe, reread it together with children. Have children draw a picture of the completed soup.

Speaking and Listening Activity

Describe a Feast (SL.K.4; SL.K.6)

- Display the illustrations on pages 36–39, and reread the pages aloud. Review the feast that the soldiers and peasants had when the stone soup was finished.

- Have children take turns describing what the soldiers and peasants ate and drank, where the feast took place, and what they did during and after the feast. Reread as needed to help them recall details from the story.

- Remind children that describing words tell what things look, feel, smell, taste, and sound like. Help them brainstorm some of these words from each category to use as they describe the feast.

Language Activity

Prepositions (L.K.1.e)

- Tell children that *prepositions* are words that tell more about nouns, verbs, or adjectives. Explain that there are many different prepositions, but today you will focus on prepositions that help tell where something is.

- Display and read the following sentence from page 10 of *Stone Soup*: "They pushed sacks of barley under the hay in the lofts." Underline the words *under* and *in*.

- Explain that the word *under* is a preposition. Ask a volunteer to tell or demonstrate what it means to be under something. Help them understand that *under* means having something above.

- Then explain that the word *in* is a preposition. Ask a volunteer to tell or demonstrate what it means to be in something. They may need to define *in* as the opposite of *out*.

- Return to the sentence and discuss with children where the peasants hid the barley.

- Continue to practice with other "where" prepositions in the story, such as *down* (page 10), *over* (page 11), and *through* (page 14).

- Have children use the prepositions in oral sentences about topics of their choice.

Read Aloud Lesson—Informational Text

Each of the four Read Aloud Lessons for Informational Text introduces students to an informational text trade book used in the program. These lessons emphasize main topics and key details in the informational texts. In Part 1, students listen as the teacher reads the entire trade book, and then they identify the main topic of the book. In Part 2, students listen as the teacher rereads a section of the trade book aloud. Students identify and discuss key details in this part of the book.

Student Book

Each lesson includes identification and drawing activities that explore the book and build content knowledge.

1 In Part 1, students identify what the book is mostly about and then draw an important thing they learned from the book.

2 **Turn and Talk** prompts students to have a conversation about the important thing they learned from the book. Students are guided to use their drawings and evidence from the book to support their ideas.

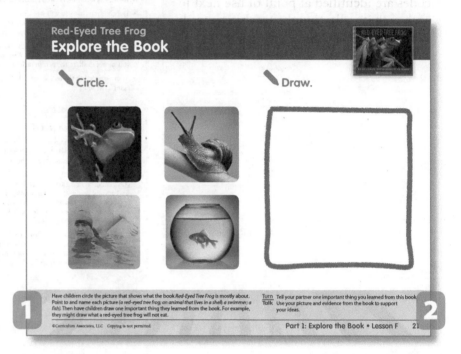

3 In Part 2, students draw a picture of an important detail from this part of the text.

Read Aloud Lesson—Informational Text

In Parts 3 and 4, students listen as the teacher rereads two more sections of the trade book aloud. Students ask and answer questions about the key details in these parts of the text. The teacher then guides students in a review of the important details in the entire book.

In Parts 3 and 4, students continue to focus on recalling details and demonstrating their understanding by drawing a picture of an important detail in each part of the text.

Each **Turn and Talk** provides students an opportunity to talk about each other's thinking as they answer a question using evidence from the book.

Focus Lessons

Each of the eighteen Focus Lessons targets a specific Kindergarten Common Core standard for Literature or Informational Text. Nine trade books, which are introduced to students in the Read Aloud Lessons, are used as the vehicle for students' understanding and application of the standards in the Focus Lessons. The gradual-release instructional design of the Focus Lessons allows students to take increasing responsibility for applying the standard to the Read Aloud text as the lesson progresses.

The Focus Lessons begin with a Tap Children's Prior Knowledge activity in the Teacher Resource Book and end with differentiated instruction suggestions and an explanation of how the kindergarten standard connects to the overarching Anchor Standard. Each six-page lesson in the Teacher Resource Book supports a four-page lesson in the Student Book. Student Book activities vary from lesson to lesson. The structure of the activity on the three Practice pages within an individual lesson is the same, however, so students become familiar with the activity format as they progress through a lesson. This allows students to gradually work toward completing the pages on their own.

Teacher Resource Book

1 **CCSS** identifies the Common Core State Standard featured in the lesson.

2 **Required Read Alouds** list the trade books used in the lesson.

3 **Lesson Objectives** identify specific skills covered in the lesson.

4 **The Learning Progression** helps teachers see the standard in context.

5 **Tap Children's Prior Knowledge** provides a quick activity to activate students' knowledge of prerequisite and related skills, laying the instructional foundation for the featured standard.

6 The **Ready Teacher Toolbox** chart provides an overview of related resources available online in the **Ready Teacher Toolbox**.

7 **Additional CCSS** identifies additional standards covered in the lesson.

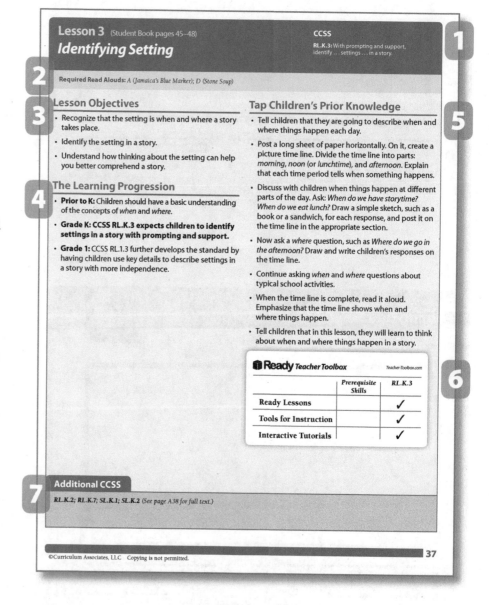

Lesson 3 (Student Book pages 45–48)
Identifying Setting

CCSS
RL.K.3: With prompting and support, identify ... settings ... in a story.

Required Read Alouds: A (Jamaica's Blue Marker); D (Stone Soup)

Lesson Objectives
- Recognize that the setting is when and where a story takes place.
- Identify the setting in a story.
- Understand how thinking about the setting can help you better comprehend a story.

The Learning Progression
- **Prior to K:** Children should have a basic understanding of the concepts of *when* and *where*.
- **Grade K:** CCSS RL.K.3 expects children to identify settings in a story with prompting and support.
- **Grade 1:** CCSS RL.1.3 further develops the standard by having children use key details to describe settings in a story with more independence.

Tap Children's Prior Knowledge
- Tell children that they are going to describe when and where things happen each day.
- Post a long sheet of paper horizontally. On it, create a picture time line. Divide the time line into parts: *morning, noon* (or *lunchtime*), and *afternoon*. Explain that each time period tells when something happens.
- Discuss with children when things happen at different parts of the day. Ask: *When do we have storytime? When do we eat lunch?* Draw a simple sketch, such as a book or a sandwich, for each response, and post it on the time line in the appropriate section.
- Now ask a *where* question, such as *Where do we go in the afternoon?* Draw and write children's responses on the time line.
- Continue asking *when* and *where* questions about typical school activities.
- When the time line is complete, read it aloud. Emphasize that the time line shows when and where things happen.
- Tell children that in this lesson, they will learn to think about when and where things happen in a story.

Ready *Teacher Toolbox* — Teacher-Toolbox.com

	Prerequisite Skills	RL.K.3
Ready Lessons		✓
Tools for Instruction		✓
Interactive Tutorials		✓

Additional CCSS
RL.K.2; RL.K.7; SL.K.1; SL.K.2 (See page A38 for full text.)

©Curriculum Associates, LLC   Copying is not permitted.

37

A28

The Listen and Learn page introduces the standard to the students. This page explains the standard in student-friendly language, defines important academic vocabulary, and lists questions and strategies good readers use when applying the targeted standard to text. Students listen and follow along in their Student Books as the teacher reads the page aloud.

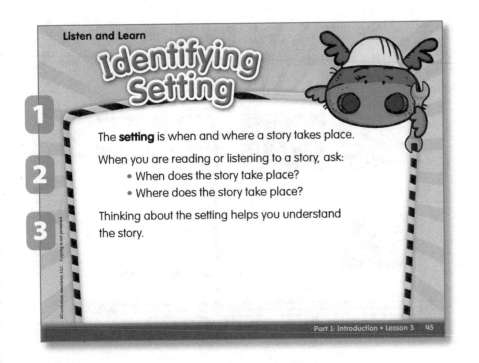

Student Book

1 Each Listen and Learn page introduces the standard with child-friendly explanations of academic vocabulary.

2 Bulleted text provides strategies proficient readers use to access text.

3 The conclusion provides a rationale for why and how good readers use the concept developed in the lesson.

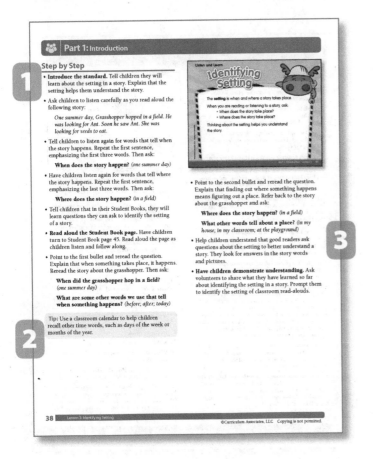

Teacher Resource Book

1 The teacher walks students through the Listen and Learn page. Students are guided to ask questions related to the standard.

2 A point-of-use **Tip** may provide teachers with instructional strategies in developing academic vocabulary.

3 Students reflect on what they have learned and then apply the standard to familiar texts.

In Part 2, students listen as the teacher reads aloud a short passage from a designated trade book. The teacher uses think-aloud support to model how to apply the standard to the text. The teacher then models completing the Student Book page. Students practice applying the standard and then complete the Student Book page, using the teacher's modeling as their guide.

Student Book

1 The cover of the trade book used for this part of the lesson appears in the right top corner.

2 Students apply the standard to a specific part of the story. For example, they identify where and when the story takes place in the Student Book.

3 Teacher directions appear in the shaded area at the bottom of the Student Book page. More detailed instruction appears in the corresponding page in the Teacher Resource Book (see below).

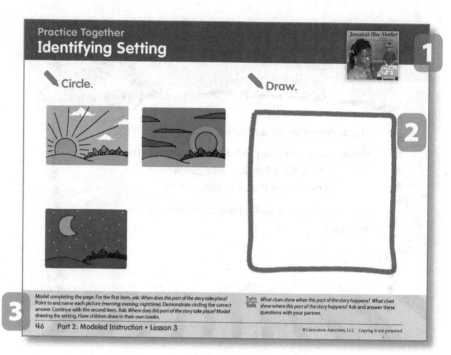

Teacher Resource Book

1 The teacher uses a think-aloud to model how to apply the standard to the text.

2 Point-of-use **Tips** address student needs by anticipating confusion and providing guidance.

3 **Close Reading** activities engage students in a strategy that helps them extract meaning from the text for a specific purpose.

4 The teacher models a **Turn and Talk** with a student partner, showing how to find textual evidence to support answers. **Turn and Talk** instruction is scaffolded through the lesson.

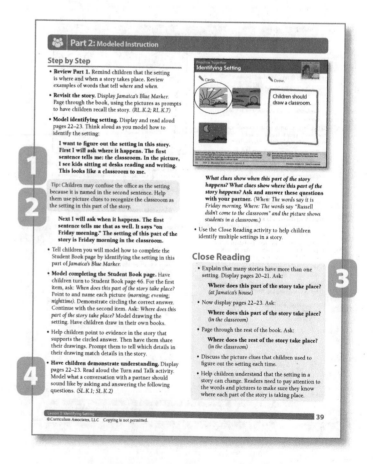

A30

In Part 3, students listen as the teacher reads aloud a selection from a second designated trade book. As part of the gradual-release instructional design, the teacher uses prompts provided in the Teacher Resource Book to guide students through applying the standard to the text selection.

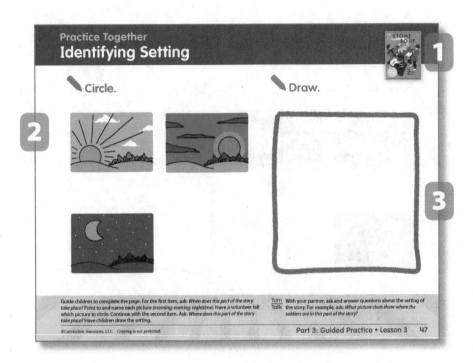

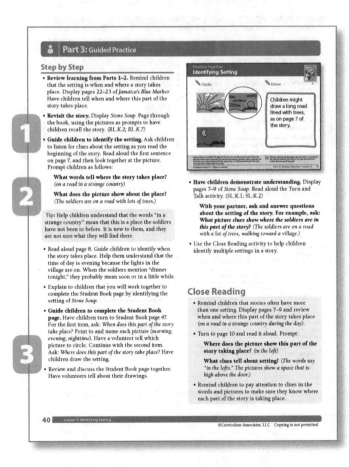

Student Book

1 A selection from a second read aloud text is used in Part 3 of the lesson. The cover of the trade book used for this part of the lesson appears in the top-right corner of the Practice Together page.

2 The activity format is continued throughout the lesson. The predictable page structure supports student mastery of the standard.

3 Activities such as matching, drawing, labeling, and identifying information occur throughout the Student Book.

Teacher Resource Book

1 The teacher revisits the second trade book and then reads aloud the targeted section of the story for this part of the lesson.

2 The teacher transitions from modeling to using questions to guide students in applying the standard to the text. The teacher then guides students to answer questions in the Student Book. Together, they review and discuss their responses.

3 The teacher guides students to answer the **Turn and Talk** question, and then they review and discuss their responses.

In Part 4, students listen as the teacher reads aloud a different passage from the trade book used in Part 3. As the final step of the gradual-release model, students independently apply the standard. After the teacher reads the answer choices aloud, students complete the Student Book page independently. Students then discuss their work together, reflecting on their learning.

Student Book

1 As the final step of the gradual-release model, students are now prepared to work independently to answer text-dependent questions and demonstrate their understanding of the standard.

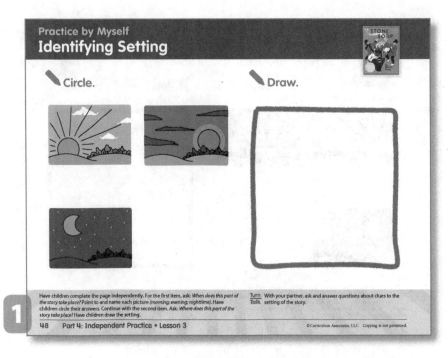

Teacher Resource Book

1 Students apply the standard to a different passage from the second trade book.

2 The lesson closes with students reflecting on their learning to reinforce the standard. They discuss what questions they learned to ask about the standard.

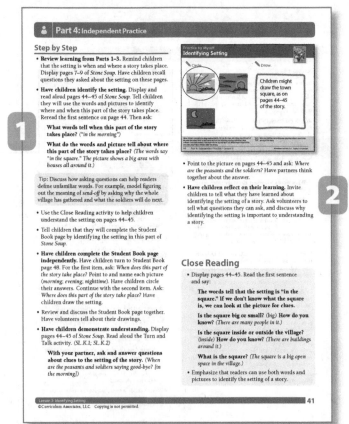

Teacher Resource Book

1 **Assessment and Remediation** provides activities that support students who have difficulty understanding the concepts of the standard. The standard is broken down into its essential elements, and activities address each potential difficulty.

2 The activities are concrete, interactive, and hands-on, taking a different approach to the standard in different ways.

3 The goal of **Connect to the Anchor Standard** is to show teachers how to anticipate the way students will use the standard with more complex texts as they move up through the grades. The activities, using the same trade books as in the lesson, are a bit more challenging, showing how the standard becomes gradually more complex.

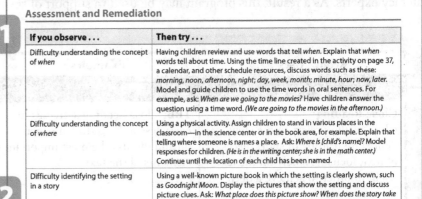

Differentiated Instruction

Assessment and Remediation

1

If you observe . . .	Then try . . .
Difficulty understanding the concept of *when*	Having children review and use words that tell *when*. Explain that *when* words tell about time. Using the time line created in the activity on page 37, a calendar, and other schedule resources, discuss words such as these: *morning, noon, afternoon, night; day, week, month; minute, hour; now, later.* Model and guide children to use the time words in oral sentences. For example, ask: *When are we going to the movies?* Have children answer the question using a time word. *(We are going to the movies in the afternoon.)*
Difficulty understanding the concept of *where*	Using a physical activity. Assign children to stand in various places in the classroom—in the science center or in the book area, for example. Explain that telling where someone is names a place. Ask: *Where is [child's name]?* Model responses for children. *(He is in the writing center; she is in the math center.)* Continue until the location of each child has been named.
Difficulty identifying the setting in a story	Using a well-known picture book in which the setting is clearly shown, such as *Goodnight Moon.* Display the pictures that show the setting and discuss picture clues. Ask: *What place does this picture show? When does the story take place?* If children need additional support, ask either/or questions: *Is this a bedroom or a classroom? Is it daytime or nighttime?*

2

Connect to the Anchor Standard

3

R3: *Analyze how and why individuals, events, and ideas develop and interact over the course of a text.*

Throughout the grades, Standard 3 progresses from having students simply recognize when and where a story takes place to having them describe the setting in more depth based on key details. Students will learn to compare and contrast two or more settings and explore how settings impact the development of a story. Students might consider questions such as these: *What details about the setting help me better understand characters and events? Why does an author use more than one setting in a story? If the setting were different, how might the story change?* Use the following activities to help children begin this transition.

• Point out that most of *Jamaica's Blue Marker* takes place at school, but some scenes happen at Jamaica's home. Read aloud page 14 and pages 20–21. Have children consider why the author changes the setting from school to Jamaica's home on these pages. Discuss the scene where Jamaica's family explains how Russell might be feeling about moving and how their perspective changes Jamaica's feelings about Russell. *(SL.K.1)*

• Read aloud pages 8–11 of *Stone Soup* and recall the setting—a village of peasants. Review that peasants are farmers who grow their own food. Have children consider how the story might have changed if the setting were different. Ask: *What might have happened if the soldiers had arrived at a king's castle?* Guide them to understand that a king might have given the soldiers food and a place to stay. Then the soldiers would not have had to play the trick of making stone soup.

42　Lesson 3: Identifying Setting

Supporting Research

Overview

Ready® Common Core is founded on research from a variety of federal initiatives, national literacy organizations, and literacy experts. As a result, this program may be used in support of several instructional models.

Ready® Uses . . .	Examples	Research Says . . .
Instructional Strategies		
Close Reading Close reading refers to the slow, deliberate reading of short pieces of text, focusing solely on the text itself, in order to achieve a deep understanding.	**TRB:** Close Reading activities in every lesson help students focus on and discuss the most important elements of the text.	"Close reading and gathering knowledge from specific texts should be at the heart of classroom activities and not be consigned to the margins when completing assignments." (Coleman & Pimentel, Revised Publishers' Criteria, 2012, p. 8)
Multiple Readings Through reading a text more than once, students are able to access different levels of its meaning.	**TRB:** Read Aloud Lessons allow teachers to read the trade books in their entirety and then reread to review key ideas. Focus Lessons require students to revisit each trade book multiple times in order to apply particular Common Core skills.	"Students should be asked to glean the information they need from multiple readings of a text, each with a specific purpose. In particular, aligned curriculum should explicitly direct . . . teachers to return to these portions in read-alouds." (Coleman & Pimentel, Revised Publishers' Criteria, 2012, p. 8)
Text-Dependent Questions Questions that are text-dependent can be answered only by information contained in the text itself, not personal opinion or background knowledge.	**SB:** Questions in each *Ready* lesson are text-dependent. Students are required to support answers with evidence from the text.	"Materials that accompany texts should ask students to think about what they have read or heard and then ask them to draw evidence from the text in support of their ideas about the reading." (Coleman & Pimentel, Revised Publishers' Criteria, 2012, p. 7)
Citing Textual Evidence Students become actively engaged as they provide evidence directly from the text to support their inferences.	**SB:** Questions in the *Ready* lessons specifically require students to cite evidence from the text to support their answers.	"Students cite specific evidence when offering an oral or written interpretation of a text. They use relevant evidence when supporting their own points in writing and speaking . . ." (Common Core State Standards, 2010, p. 7)
Building Content Knowledge Texts that are of high quality and substance allow students to build content knowledge as they develop and strengthen their reading skills.	**SB:** Students deepen their content knowledge by drawing pictures based on newly learned concepts. **TRB:** Read Aloud Informational Text Lessons relate to grade-appropriate science and social studies content and feature a close review of new concepts and vocabulary, as well as scaffolding for students to practice applying text-based academic language in discussion and Student Book activities.	"Students establish a base of knowledge across a wide range of subject matter by engaging with works of quality and substance." (Common Core State Standards, 2012, p. 7)

©Curriculum Associates, LLC   Copying is not permitted.

Ready® Uses . . .	Examples	Research Says . . .
Instructional Strategies (continued)		
Direct Instruction Scripted lesson plans include explicit step-by-step instruction of reading and learning strategies and lesson objectives.	**TRB:** Parts 1–4 of each lesson provide teachers with scaffolded step-by-step, explicit instructions to help students meet each lesson objective.	"The research demonstrates that the types of questions, the detailed step-by-step breakdowns, and the extensive practice with a range of examples . . . will significantly benefit students' comprehension." (Gersten & Carnine, 1986, p. 72)
Scaffolded Instruction Scaffolded instruction is the gradual withdrawal of support through modeled, guided, and independent instruction.	**SB:** Activities are structured consistently from Parts 2–4 so that students can gain confidence working independently in Part 4 after practicing with the teacher in Parts 2–3. **TRB:** The gradual-release model provides appropriate support that is gradually withdrawn as students gain mastery of the standard.	"Scaffolded instruction optimizes student learning by providing a supportive environment while facilitating student independence." (Larkin, 2002)
Prior Knowledge Prior knowledge activities activate knowledge from previous experiences.	**TRB:** Tap Children's Prior Knowledge at the beginning of each Focus Lesson engages students in a discussion to review known concepts that are related to the new skill.	"Research clearly emphasizes that for learning to occur, new information must be integrated with what the learner already knows." (Rumelhart, 1980)
An Integrated Model of Literacy The processes of communication (reading, writing, listening, and speaking) are closely connected, a fact which should be reflected in literacy instruction.	**TRB:** Read Aloud Lessons give teachers opportunities to integrate Foundational Reading standards into text selections. Furthermore, Additional Activities in these lessons allow students to apply text knowledge to the areas of Writing, Speaking & Listening, and Language.	"While the Standards delineate specific expectations in reading, writing, speaking, listening, and language, each standard need not be a separate focus for instruction. Often, several standards can be addressed by a single, rich task." (Common Core State Standards, 2010, p. 5)
Instructional Features		
Complex Text A major emphasis of the Common Core State Standards is for students to encounter appropriately complex texts at each grade level in order to develop the skills and conceptual knowledge they need for success in school and life.	**TRB:** All read aloud texts in *Ready* were carefully selected based on the Common Core requirements for complexity and guided by the text exemplars listed in Appendix B of the Standards.	"To grow, our students must read lots, and more specifically, they must read lots of 'complex' texts—texts that offer them new language, new knowledge, and new modes of thought." (Adams, 2009, p. 182)

Ready® Uses . . .	Examples	Research Says . . .
Instructional Features (continued)		
Balance of Informational and Literary Text The Common Core State Standards align with the requirements of the National Assessment of Educational Progress (NAEP) in calling for a greater emphasis on informational text.	**SB:** Six units alternate Literary and Informational text. Genres include realistic fiction, folktale, poetry, fantasy, reference, science, and biography. **TRB:** The Read Aloud Lesson opener introduces the characteristics of each genre.	"Most of the required reading in college and workforce training programs is informational in structure and challenging in content . . . . the Standards follow NAEP's lead in balancing the reading of literature with the reading of informational texts. . . ." (Common Core State Standards, 2010, pp. 4–5. See also National Assessment Governing Board, 2008)
ELL Support Some teaching strategies that have been proven to be effective for English learners include scaffolded instruction, use of graphic organizers, and modeling of language by teachers and peers.	**SB:** Features such as Turn and Talk partner discussions support English learners throughout the lesson. **TRB:** In Read Aloud Lessons, ELL Support boxes provide linguistic instruction pertinent to the unique content in each particular trade book.	Researchers state that one of the best practices for teaching ELL students is to model standard pronunciation and grammar. (Mohr & Mohr, 2007)
General Academic Vocabulary (Tier Two) General academic, or Tier Two, words are words a reader encounters in rich, complex texts of all types.	**TRB:** Tier Two Vocabulary boxes in Read Aloud Lessons support the teacher in helping students use text-based strategies to figure out the meanings of challenging words.	"Tier Two words are frequently encountered in complex written texts and are particularly powerful because of their wide applicability to many sorts of reading. Teachers thus need to be alert to the presence of Tier Two words and determine which ones need careful attention." (Common Core State Standards, Appendix A, 2010, p. 33. The three-tier model of vocabulary is based on the work of Beck, McKeown, & Kucan, 2002, 2008)

References

Adams, M. J. (2009). The challenge of advanced texts: The interdependence of reading and learning. In Hiebert, E. H. (ed.), *Reading more, reading better: Are American students reading enough of the right stuff?* (pp. 183–189). New York, NY: Guilford.

Beck, I. L., McKeown, M. G., & Kucan, L. (2002). *Bringing words to life: Robust vocabulary instruction.* New York, NY: Guilford.

Beck, I. L., McKeown, M. G., & Kucan, L. (2008). *Creating robust vocabulary: Frequently asked questions and extended examples.* New York, NY: Guilford.

Boyles, N. (2012/2013). Closing in on close reading. *Educational Leadership*, 70(4), 36–41.

Coleman, D., & Pimentel, S. (2012). *Revised Publishers' Criteria for the Common Core State Standards in English Language Arts and Literacy, Grades K–2.* Accessed at: *http://www.corestandards.org/resources.*

Fisher, D., Frey, N., & Lapp, D. (2012). *Text complexity: Raising rigor in reading.* Washington, DC: International Reading Association.

Gersten, R., & Carnine, D. (1986). Direct instruction in reading comprehension. *Educational Leadership*, 43(7), 70–79.

Hess, K. K., Carlock, D., Jones, B., & Walkup, J. R. (2009). *What exactly do "fewer, clearer, and higher standards" really look like in the classroom? Using a cognitive rigor matrix to analyze curriculum, plan lessons, and implement assessments.* Accessed at: *http://www.nciea.org/cgi-bin/pubspage.cgi?sortby=pub_date.*

Larkin, M. (2002). *Using scaffolded instruction to optimize learning.* ERIC Digest ED474301 2002-12-00. Retrieved from *www.eric.ed.gov.*

Mohr, K., & Mohr, E. (2007). *Extending English language learners' classroom interactions using the response protocol.* Accessed at: *http://www.readingrockets.org/article/26871.*

National Assessment Governing Board. (2008). *Reading framework for the 2009 National Assessment of Educational Progress.* Washington, D.C.: U.S. Government Printing Office.

National Governors Association Center for Best Practices and Council of Chief State School Officers. (2010). *Common Core State Standards for English Language Arts and Literacy in History/Social Studies, Science, and Technical Subjects.* Accessed at: *http://www.corestandards.org/the-standards.*

———. *English Language Arts Appendix A.* Accessed at: *http://www.corestandards.org/the-standards.*

Partnership for Assessment of Readiness for College and Careers. (2011). *PARCC model content frameworks: English language arts/literacy grades 3–11.* Accessed at: *http://www.parcconline.org/parcc-model-content-frameworks.*

Pashler, H., Bain, P., Bottge, B., Graesser, A., Koedinger, K., McDaniel, M., & Metcalfe, J. (2007). *Organizing instruction and study to improve student learning* (NCER 2007–2004). Washington, D.C.: National Center for Education Research, Institute of Education Sciences, U.S. Department of Education. Retrieved from *http://ncer.ed.gov.*

Rumelhart, D. E. (1980). Schemata: the building blocks of cognition. In Spiro, R. J., Bruce, B. C., & Brewer Erlbaum, W. F. (eds.), *Theoretical issues in reading comprehension* (pp. 33–58).

Smarter Balanced Assessment Consortium. (2012). *General Item Specifications.* Accessed at: *http://www.smarterbalanced.org/wordpress/wp-content/uploads/2012/05/TaskItemSpecifications/ItemSpecifications/GeneralItemSpecifications.pdf.*

Correlation Charts

Common Core State Standards Coverage by *Ready*®

The chart below correlates each Common Core State Standard to each **Ready® Common Core** lesson that offers comprehensive instruction on that standard. Use this chart to determine which lessons your students should complete based on their mastery of each standard.

Common Core State Standards for Kindergarten—Reading Standards	Ready Common Core Student Lesson(s)	Additional Coverage in Teacher Resource Book Lesson(s)
Reading Standards for Literature		
Key Ideas and Details		
RL.K.1 With prompting and support, ask and answer questions about key details in a text.	1	A, B, C, D, E
RL.K.2 With prompting and support, retell stories, including key details.	A, B, C, D, E, 5	1, 2, 3, 4, 9, 10, 11, 14, 15
RL.K.3 With prompting and support, describe characters, settings, and major events in a story.	2, 3, 4	A, B, C, D, E
Craft and Structure		
RL.K.4 Ask and answer questions about unknown words in a text.	9, 10	—
RL.K.5 Recognize common types of texts (e.g., storybooks, poems).	11	—
RL.K.6 With prompting and support, name the author and illustrator of a story and define the role of each in telling the story.	12	—
Integration of Knowledge and Ideas		
RL.K.7 With prompting and support, describe the relationship between illustrations and the story in which they appear (e.g., what moment in a story an illustration depicts).	14	A, B, C, D, E, 1, 2, 3, 4, 9, 10, 11, 15
RL.K.8 (Not applicable to literature)	N/A	N/A
RL.K.9 With prompting and support, compare and contrast the adventures and experiences of characters in familiar stories.	15	—
Range of Reading and Level of Text Complexity		
RL.K.10 Actively engage in group reading activities with purpose and understanding.	All Lessons	
Reading Standards for Informational Text		
Key Ideas and Details		
RI.K.1 With prompting and support, ask and answer questions about key details in a text.	6	F, G, H, I, 7
RI.K.2 With prompting and support, identify the main topic and retell key details of a text.	F, G, H, I, 7	6, 8, 12, 13, 16, 17, 18
RI.K.3 With prompting and support, describe the connection between two individuals, events, ideas, or pieces of information in a text.	8	F, G, H, I
Craft and Structure		
RI.K.4 With prompting and support, ask and answer questions about unknown words in a text.	12	—
RI.K.5 Identify the front cover, back cover, and title page of a book.	13	—
RI.K.6 Name the author and illustrator of a text and define the role of each in presenting the ideas or information in a text.	13	—
RI.K.7 With prompting and support, describe the relationship between illustrations and the text in which they appear (e.g., what person, place, thing, or idea in the text an illustration depicts).	16	F, G, H, I, 6, 7, 8, 12, 13, 17, 18

Common Core State Standards © 2010. National Governors Association Center for Best Practices and Council of Chief State School Officers. All rights reserved.

A38

Common Core State Standards for Kindergarten—Reading Standards	Ready Common Core Student Lesson(s)	Additional Coverage in Teacher Resource Book Lesson(s)
Reading Standards for Informational Text (continued)		
Integration of Knowledge and Ideas		
RI.K.8 With prompting and support, identify the reasons an author gives to support points in a text.	17	—
RI.K.9 With prompting and support, identify basic similarities in and differences between two texts on the same topic (e.g., in illustrations, descriptions, or procedures).	18	—
Range of Reading and Level of Text Complexity		
RI.K.10 Actively engage in group reading activities with purpose and understanding.	All Lessons	

Additional Coverage of Common Core ELA Standards, Kindergarten	Ready Common Core Teacher Resource Book Lesson(s)
Reading Standards for Foundational Skills	
Print Concepts	
RF.K.1a Follow words from left to right, top to bottom, and page by page.	A, C
RF.K.1b Recognize that spoken words are represented in written languages by specific sequences of letters.	B, E
RF.K.1c Understand that words are separated by spaces in print.	A, C
RF.K.1d Recognize and name all upper- and lowercase letters of the alphabet.	B, E, G
Phonological Awareness	
RF.K.2a Recognize and produce rhyming words.	A, D
RF.K.2b Count, pronounce, blend, and segment syllables in spoken words.	B
RF.K.2c Blend and segment onsets and rimes of single-syllable spoken words.	D, E, I
RF.K.2d Isolate and pronounce the initial, medial vowel, and final sounds (phonemes) in three-phoneme (consonant-vowel-consonant, or CVC) words. (This does not include CVCs ending with /l/, /r/, or /x/.)	F, G, H
RF.K.2e Add or substitute individual sounds (phonemes) in simple, one-syllable words to make new words.	D, E, F, G, H
Phonics and Word Recognition	
RF.K.3a Demonstrate basic knowledge of one-to-one letter-sound correspondences by producing the primary sound or many of the most frequent sounds for each consonant.	F, I
RF.K.3b Associate the long and short sounds with the common spellings (graphemes) for the five major vowels.	H, I
RF.K.3c Read common high-frequency words by sight (e.g., *the, of, to, you, she, my, is, are, do, does*).	C, E, G
RF.K.3d Distinguish between similarly spelled words by identifying the sounds of the letters that differ.	F, H, I
Writing Standards	
Text Types and Purposes	
W.K.1 Use a combination of drawing, dictating, and writing to compose opinion pieces in which they tell a reader the topic or the name of the book they are writing about and state an opinion or preference about the topic or book (e.g., *My favorite book is...*).	A, C, H
W.K.2 Use a combination of drawing, dictating, and writing to compose informative/explanatory texts in which they name what they are writing about and supply some information about the topic.	D, F, I
W.K.3 Use a combination of drawing, dictating, and writing to narrate a single event or several loosely linked events, tell about the events in the order in which they occurred, and provide a reaction to what happened.	B, E, G

Speaking and Listening Standards

Comprehension and Collaboration

SL.K.1	Participate in collaborative conversations with diverse partners aboutkindergarten topics and texts with peers and adults in small and larger groups.	A, B, C, D, E, F, G, H, I, 1 ,2, 3, 4, 5, 6, 7, 8, 9, 10, 11, 12, 13, 14, 15, 16, 17, 18
SL.K.2	Confirm understanding of a text read aloud or information presented orally or through other media by asking and answering questions about key details and requesting clarification if something is not understood.	A, B, C, D, E, F, G, H, I, 1 ,2, 3, 4, 5, 6, 7, 8, 9, 10, 11, 12, 13, 14, 15, 16, 17, 18
SL.K.3	Ask and answer questions in order to seek help, get information, or clarify something that is not understood.	B, I

Presentation of Knowledge and Ideas

SL.K.4	Describe familiar people, places, things, and events and, with prompting and support, provide additional detail.	A, B, C, D, E, F, G, H, I
SL.K.5	Add drawings or other visual displays to descriptions as desired to provide additional detail.	A, B, C, D, E, F, G, H, I
SL.K.6	Speak audibly and express thoughts, feelings, and ideas clearly.	D, E, F, G, H

Language Standards

Conventions of Standard English

L.K.1a	Print many upper- and lowercase letters.	B, D, E, F, G, H
L.K.1b	Use frequently occurring nouns and verbs.	C, E
L.K.1c	Form regular plural nouns orally by adding /s/ or /es/ (e.g., *dog, dogs; wish, wishes*).	I
L.K.1d	Understand and use question words (interrogatives) (e.g., *who, what, where, when, why, how*).	B
L.K.1e	Use the most frequently occurring prepositions (e.g., *to, from, in, out, on, off, for, of, by, with*).	D
L.K.1f	Produce and expand complete sentences in shared language activities.	G, H, I
L.K.2a	Capitalize the first word in a sentence and the pronoun I.	A, C
L.K.2b	Recognize and name end punctuation.	F, G, H
L.K.2c	Write a letter or letters for most consonant and short-vowel sounds (phonemes).	E, F, G, H
L.K.2d	Spell simple words phonetically, drawing on knowledge of sound-letter relationships.	D, E

Vocabulary Acquisition and Use

L.K.4a	Identify new meanings for familiar words and apply them accurately (e.g., knowing *duck* is a bird and learning the verb to *duck*).	G
L.K.4b	Use the most frequently occurring inflections and affixes (e.g., *-ed, -s, re-, un-, pre-, -ful, -less*) as a clue to the meaning of an unknown word.	B, I
L.K.5a	Sort common objects into categories (e.g., shapes, foods) to gain a sense of the concepts the categories represent.	H
L.K.5b	Demonstrate understanding of frequently occurring verbs and adjectives by relating them to their opposites (antonyms).	H
L.K.5c	Identify real-life connections between words and their use (e.g., note places at school that are colorful).	A, B, C, D, E, F, G, H, I
L.K.5d	Distinguish shades of meaning among verbs describing the same general action (e.g., *walk, march, strut, prance*) by acting out the meanings.	A

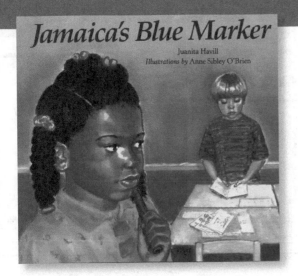

Lesson Objectives

You will read aloud *Jamaica's Blue Marker,* which children will revisit in later lessons. With prompting and support, children will:

- Answer questions about key details in the story.

- Describe characters and major events, using key details.

- Retell the story, including key details.

About the Text

Summary

Jamaica is angry because Russell borrows her blue marker and scribbles on her drawing. She learns that Russell is moving to a new town, but she is still too upset to make him a going-away card. Then she sees how sad he is, so she gives him her blue marker to use at his new school.

Genre: Realistic Fiction

- *Jamaica's Blue Marker* is realistic fiction—a kind of story that tells about characters and events that are like people and events in real life.

- Use the cover illustration to point out that the characters look like children seen in real life.

Critical Vocabulary

- Prior to reading, briefly define the following words:

  reason (p. 14) a thought, feeling, action, or event that explains why something else happens

  bother (p. 17) to make someone angry or uncomfortable

  moving (p. 17) going away to live in a new place

  upset (p. 21) feeling sad, angry, or worried

- As you read, pause to point to the words as you encounter them, and review their definitions.

Word Bank

- Display a word bank of the Critical Vocabulary and the characters' names (*Jamaica; Russell; Mrs. Wirth; Jamaica's mom and dad; Jamaica's brother, Ossie*).

- Add other important story words, such as *scribbled* and *going-away party* on subsequent readings.

New Concepts: Sympathy

- Explain that *sympathy* means thinking about and understanding another person's feelings.

- Talk about times you have felt sympathy, such as a time you felt sad for someone who was ill or upset. Have children listen for times Jamaica feels sympathy for Russell.

Ready *Teacher Toolbox*   Teacher-Toolbox.com

	Prerequisite Skills	RL.K.2
Ready Lessons		✓
Tools for Instruction	✓ ✓	✓
Interactive Tutorials	✓ ✓	

CCSS Focus

RL.K.2: *With prompting and support, retell familiar stories, including key details.*

ADDITIONAL STANDARDS: RL.K.1; RL.K.3; RL.K.7; RF.K.1.a, c; RF.K.2.a; W.K.1; SL.K.1; SL.K.2; SL.K.4; SL.K.5; L.K.2.a; L.K.5.c; L.K.5.d *(See page A38 for full text.)*

Step by Step

- **Introduce *Jamaica's Blue Marker*.** Display the book. Read aloud the title and the name of the author, Juanita Havill. Then read aloud the name of the illustrator, Anne Sibley O'Brien, and explain that she drew the pictures.

- **Set the purpose for reading.** Tell children that readers make sense of a story by finding out who the story is about and thinking about what happens to them. Explain that the people or animals in a story are called *characters*.

- Explain that as you read aloud, children should listen closely to identify the characters in this story.

- **Read aloud *Jamaica's Blue Marker*.** Read the story all the way through, pausing only to briefly define challenging vocabulary. Then think aloud:

  I want to figure out who the characters are. When I reread and look at the pictures, I notice that the story is about people. The story tells a lot about what Jamaica does and feels. I think Jamaica is one of the characters.

- **Guide children to identify the characters.** After reading, brainstorm all of the characters in the story with children. Record their responses on chart paper. Use questions such as these to identify the characters. (RL.K.1; RL.K.3; SL.K.1; SL.K.2)

  Who is the story mostly about?
  (*Jamaica and Russell*)

  Who are some of the other characters?
  (*Mrs. Wirth, Jamaica's mother, father, and brother*)

  Tip: If children need extra support identifying the characters, display the pictures and have children name the characters in them. Point out that Jamaica and Russell appear in many of the pictures.

- **Have children draw characters.** Direct children to turn to Student Book page 1. Have them draw a picture of Jamaica and Russell. Display illustrations on pages 5–7, 19, and 25 to help them recall what each character looks like.

- **Have children discuss story evidence.** Read aloud the Turn and Talk activity. Have children use their pictures and story evidence to explain what they know about each character. (SL.K.4; SL.K.5)

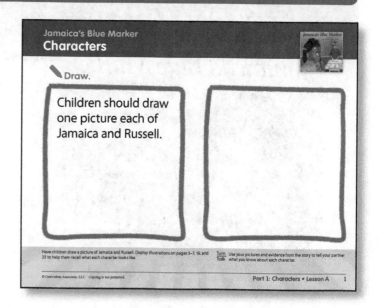

- Guide their discussions with the following prompts:

  What does Russell do after Jamaica lets him borrow her blue marker? (*He scribbles on Jamaica's picture.*)

  What does Jamaica give Russell at his going-away party? (*her blue marker*)

- Invite children to share what they know about Jamaica and Russell, as well as any other characters from the story, in class discussion.

ELL Support: Plural Nouns

- Explain that some words tell about more than one person, place, or thing. Use an example, such as pointing to and naming one pencil and then several pencils.

- Point out that in English, the letter *s* is often added to the end of a naming word to make it tell about more than one.

- Point out the word *eyes* on page 5. Explain that the letter *s* at the end of the word lets children know that it means more than one eye.

- Browse through the book, pointing out plural nouns such as *markers, leaves, circles,* and *squiggles.* Have children point out the letter *s* at the end of each word and say both the singular and plural forms of the word with you.

Step by Step

- **Reread and discuss the beginning.** Read aloud pages 5–15. Use questions such as these to guide discussion. (*RL.K.1; RL.K.7; SL.K.1; SL.K.2*)

    Page 6: What does Mrs. Wirth ask Jamaica to do? (*share her markers with Russell*)

    Pages 6–9: What are Jamaica and Russell doing? (*drawing pictures with Jamaica's markers*)

    Pages 9–11: What does Russell do with Jamaica's blue marker? (*He draws squiggles on his paper and then scribbles on Jamaica's picture.*)

    Pages 12–15: How does Jamaica feel about what Russell does? (*She is angry and upset.*)

Tip: Point out that looking at the characters' faces in the illustrations can give readers evidence about how the characters feel.

- **Focus on a key detail.** Direct children to turn to Student Book page 2. Have them draw a picture to show how Jamaica feels after Russell scribbles on her drawing. Reread pages 10–12 to help them recall the details. (*RL.K.3*)

- Use the Close Reading activity to help children understand why Jamaica is angry and calls Russell "mean."

- **Have children discuss story evidence.** Read aloud the Turn and Talk activity. Guide partners to have a conversation, beginning as follows:

    How do you know that Jamaica feels angry? (*She shouts. She looks upset in the illustration. She tells Mrs. Wirth that Russell "wrecked" her picture.*)

- Invite children to share their ideas with the class.

- Work with children to identify the most important ideas from this part of the story. Encourage them to use evidence from the story as well as their drawings to help explain their ideas. (*SL.K.4*)

Tier Two Vocabulary: *peeked*

- Display the fifth sentence on page 8. Read it aloud. Underline the word *peeked*.

- Help children understand that Jamaica looks at Russell's paper. Ask: *Does Jamaica look at Russell's paper for a long time or a short time?*

- Together, determine that the word *peeked* means "gave a quick look." Have children demonstrate peeking at something.

- Provide an example, such as *I peeked behind the door to see if Tom was hiding there.*

- Have children complete this sentence frame: *I peeked at _____.* (*L.K.5.c*)

Close Reading

- Help children understand why Jamaica is angry and calls Russell "mean." Display and read aloud pages 14–15. Prompt:

    How does Jamaica tell her father about her picture? (*She shows him the ruined picture. She says she couldn't make another one as good.*)

    What does Jamaica do when she looks at her picture? (*She tries not to cry.*)

    What does Jamaica call Russell? Why? (*a "mean brat"; she is upset that he ruined her picture*)

- Discuss how Jamaica feels and why she expresses her feelings by calling Russell a name.

Step by Step

- **Reread and discuss the middle.** Read pages 16–25 aloud. Use questions such as these to guide discussion about this part of the story. (*RL.K.1; SL.K.1; SL.K.2*)

  Pages 16–17: What does Mrs. Wirth ask the class to do for Russell? Why? (*She asks them to make cards. Russell is moving away.*)

  Pages 18–23: How do Jamaica's feelings about Russell change? (*She is still angry and won't make a card. Then she starts to feel sad for him because he has to move.*)

  Pages 24–25: What happens before Jamaica can make a good-bye card for Russell? (*Mrs. Wirth asks Jamaica to collect all the cards.*)

Tip: Point out that twice it seems that Jamaica might make a card for Russell, but Mrs. Wirth asks her to collect all the cards before she finishes. The stack of cards does not include one from Jamaica.

- Use the Close Reading activity to help children understand why Jamaica changes her mind and decides she wants to make a card for Russell.

- **Focus on a key detail.** Direct children to turn to Student Book page 3. Have them draw a picture that shows how Jamaica feels when she thinks about moving. Reread pages 20–21 to help them recall the details. (*RL.K.3*)

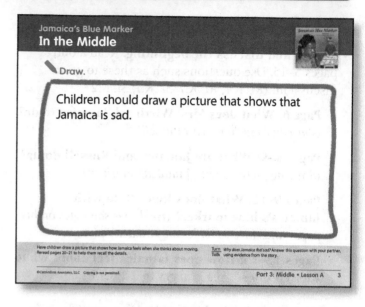

- **Have children discuss story evidence.** Read aloud the Turn and Talk activity. Guide partners to have a conversation, beginning as follows:

  Why does Jamaica feel sad? (*She wouldn't want to leave the places she loves.*)

- As a class, discuss how Jamaica's feelings about Russell change in this part of the story and why. Emphasize that Jamaica begins to understand how Russell might feel about moving. (*SL.K.4*)

- Work together to identify the most important ideas from this part of the story. Encourage children to use their own words to describe Jamaica's feelings about moving.

Tier Two Vocabulary: *stack*

- Display the paragraph on page 25. Read it aloud. Underline the word *stack*.

- Ask children what they think the group of cards that Jamaica puts in Russell's desk looks like. Work together to decide that the word *stack* means "a pile, often arranged neatly."

- Act out putting things in a stack, such as piling up books. Use *stack* to describe the pile.

- Provide a new example, such as, *I put the plates in a stack.*

- Have children name some things they might put in a stack, such as loose papers. (*L.K.5.c*)

Close Reading

- Reread pages 20–22. Use these questions to help children understand why Jamaica changes her mind and decides she wants to make a card for Russell. Prompt:

  What does Jamaica say about moving? (*She tells her family that she wouldn't like to move.*)

  What evidence tells you that Jamaica starts to think about how Russell feels? (*She gets sad when she thinks about how it would feel to move. She realizes that next week he will be gone.*)

  Why does Jamaica decide she wants to make a card for Russell? (*She understands that he must be sad to move and feels less angry with him.*)

Step by Step

- **Reread and discuss the end.** Display and read aloud pages 26–32. Discuss the way the story ends, using questions such as these. (RL.K.1; SL.K.1; SL.K.2)

 Pages 26–27: What does Jamaica do because she didn't make a card for Russell? (*She gives him her blue marker.*)

 Pages 28–29: How does Jamaica feel about Russell at the end of the story? (*She likes him and wishes that he wasn't moving.*)

 Tip: Help children understand that Russell's feelings have changed as well. At the beginning of the story, he scribbled on Jamaica's drawing. Now he tells her that she draws "the best pictures in the class."

 Pages 30–31: What does Russell do when Jamaica waves good-bye to him? (*He holds up the blue marker Jamaica gave him and waves it.*)

- Use the Close Reading activity to help children identify evidence that shows why Jamaica gives Russell her blue marker.

- **Focus on a key detail.** Direct children to turn to Student Book page 4. Have them draw a picture that shows what Jamaica does at the end of the story. Reread page 26 to help them recall the details. (RL.K.3)

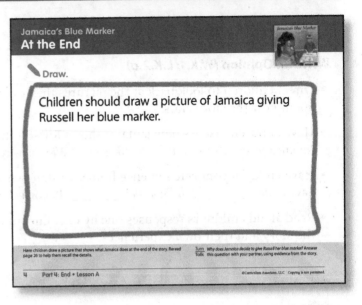

- **Have children discuss story evidence.** Read aloud the Turn and Talk activity. Guide partners to have a conversation, beginning as follows:

 Why does Jamaica decide to give Russell her blue marker? (*She feels badly that she didn't make him a card. She says she'll miss him.*)

- Invite children to share ideas with the class.

- **Retell *Jamaica's Blue Marker*.** Give each of three small groups one part of the story to retell. Page through the book, asking each group in turn to tell what happens at the beginning, middle, and end of the story. Reread parts of the story as needed.

Integrating Foundational Skills

Use these activities to integrate foundational skills into your reading of *Jamaica's Blue Marker*.

1 Read aloud pages 25–26, tracking print. Point out reading top to bottom, left to right, and page to page, asking children to help you. Point to words one by one, explaining the space between words. Have children frame words. (RF.K.1.a; RF.K.1.c)

2 Explain that rhyming words sound alike. Say *blue* and *shoe*, emphasizing the like ending sound. Have children raise their hands if a word you say rhymes with *blue*. Use these words: *do, two, boat, flew, man, grew*. Call on volunteers to name other words that rhyme with *blue*. (RF.K.2.a)

Close Reading

- Help children look for evidence to explain why Jamaica gives Russell her blue marker. Display and read aloud pages 28–32. Then prompt:

 What does Jamaica learn about Russell's feelings? (*that he wants to stay in their class*)

 What does Jamaica say that helps you know that she likes Russell? (*that she wishes he wasn't moving and that she will miss him*)

 What do the words "as if he'd won a prize" tell you about Russell and the blue marker? (*that the blue marker is important to him; it is the marker Russell chose when they were drawing, so Jamaica knows he likes it*)

Writing Activity

Write an Opinion (W.K.1; L.K.2.a)

- Direct children to look back at the pictures they drew on page 4 of their Student Books. Ask them to think about how the story ends.

- Have children discuss how Jamaica shows Russell that she likes him. Ask: *Do you think this is a good way for Jamaica to show Russell that she likes him? Why or why not?*

- Have children complete sentence frames to state whether or not they like what Jamaica did. Say: *I like _____. I did not like _____.* Record their responses on chart paper.

- Read aloud children's responses one by one. Encourage children to explain their opinions, using details from the story and their own experiences.

Speaking and Listening Activity

Talk About Apologizing (SL.K.1; SL.K.4)

- Help children recall how Jamaica acted after Russell scribbled on her drawing.

- Discuss the importance of apologizing.

- Talk about what might have happened if Russell had apologized to Jamaica. Would the rest of the story have been different?

- Assign story characters to children.

- Invite them to act out some of the situations that the class discussed. Begin with the scene of Jamaica sharing her blue marker with Russell.

- Encourage children to use dialogue to tell what the characters are doing and how they are feeling.

- Remind children to take turns speaking and to listen respectfully.

Language Activity

Shades of Meaning (L.K.5.d)

- Explain to children that some words have similar meanings, such as the following words from the story: *peeked* (page 8), *looked* (page 14), and *noticed* (page 30).

- Discuss how the words are the same and different. Include other similar and perhaps more familiar words, such as *watched, viewed, glanced,* and *stared* in the discussion.

- Call on volunteers to act out each word. Guide them to see how each word tells something a little different about ways of looking.

- Point out that writers use specific words to tell readers exactly what they mean. Use each word above in a sentence to demonstrate its particular meaning, guiding children to act out each example.

- Invite children to come up with their own example sentences for each word and have them act each one out.

Lesson Objectives

You will read aloud *The Art Lesson,* which children will revisit in later lessons. With prompting and support, children will:

- Answer questions about key details in the story.
- Describe characters and major events, using key details.
- Retell the story, including key details.

About the Text

Summary

Tommy wants to be an artist when he grows up. But in first grade, he is supposed to copy what the art teacher does, and Tommy knows that real artists don't copy. So Tommy and his teacher find a way to make both of them happy. In the end, Tommy grows up to be an artist.

Genre: Realistic Fiction

- Explain to children that realistic fiction, like *The Art Lesson,* tells about characters and events that could exist or happen in real life.
- Show several pictures from *The Art Lesson* and ask children if the places seem real or make-believe.

Critical Vocabulary

- Prior to reading, briefly define the following words:

  artist (p. 3) a person who is good at making art

  copy (p. 6) to do something exactly like someone else

  practice (p. 6) to do something over and over to get better at it

  lessons (p. 15) times when you learn something

- As you read, pause to point to the words as you encounter them, and review their definitions.

Word Bank

- Display a word bank of the Critical Vocabulary and the characters' names *(Tommy, Miss Bird, Miss Landers, Mrs. Bowers, etc.).*
- Add other important story words, such as *real* and *crayons,* on subsequent readings.

New Concepts: Being an Artist

- Explain that an artist is a person who creates art, such as drawings, paintings, music, or sculptures.
- Talk about different artists children are familiar with. Show examples of different kinds of art and ask children to talk about which they like best. Have them look for the art that Tommy creates in *The Art Lesson.*

Ready *Teacher Toolbox*   Teacher-Toolbox.com

	Prerequisite Skills	RL.K.2
Ready Lessons		✓
Tools for Instruction	✓ ✓	✓
Interactive Tutorials	✓ ✓	

CCSS Focus

RL.K.2: *With prompting and support, retell familiar stories, including key details.*

ADDITIONAL STANDARDS: RL.K.1; RL.K.3; RL.K.7; RF.K.1.b, d; RF.K.2.b; W.K.3; SL.K.1; SL.K.2; SL.K.3; SL.K.4; SL.K.5; L.K.1.a, d; L.K.4.b; L.K.5.c *(See page A38 for full text.)*

Step by Step

- **Introduce *The Art Lesson.*** Display the book. Read aloud the title and the name of the author, Tomie (pronounced "Tommy") dePaola. Point out that he also drew the pictures.

- **Set the purpose for reading.** Remind children that a *character* is a person or animal in a story. Tell children that readers make sense of a story by identifying characters and thinking about what they do and what happens to them.

- Explain that as you read aloud, children should listen closely to identify the characters in this story.

- **Read aloud *The Art Lesson.*** Read the story all the way through, pausing only to briefly define challenging vocabulary.

- **Guide children to identify the characters.** After reading, use questions such as these to identify the characters. *(RL.K.1; RL.K.3; SL.K.1; SL.K.2)*

    What characters do we read about in the story? *(Tommy, his friends, his cousins, his mom and dad, Miss Bird, Miss Landers, Mrs. Bowers)*

    Who is the story mostly about? *(Tommy)*

    Who are Tommy's teachers? *(Miss Bird is his kindergarten teacher. Miss Landers is his first-grade teacher. Mrs. Bowers is his art teacher.)*

    Who tells Tommy to copy pictures of Pilgrims? *(Mrs. Bowers)*

> **Tip:** Make sure that children understand that the picture on page 32 shows Tommy as a grown-up, drawing pictures as an artist.

- **Have children draw characters.** Direct children to turn to Student Book page 5. Have them draw a picture of Tommy and Mrs. Bowers. Display illustrations on pages 3 and 26 to help them recall what each character looks like.

- **Have children discuss story evidence.** Read aloud the Turn and Talk activity. Have children use their pictures and story evidence to explain what they know about each character. *(SL.K.4; SL.K.5)*

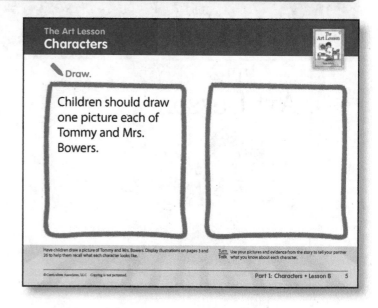

- Guide their discussions with the following prompts:

    What does Tommy like to do best? *(draw pictures)*

    Why doesn't Tommy want to copy the Pilgrim and turkey picture? *(He thinks that real artists don't copy.)*

    Why does Mrs. Bowers want Tommy to draw what everyone else draws? *(to be fair to the class)*

    What does Tommy get to do after he draws the Pilgrims and turkey? *(He gets to draw his own picture with his own crayons without copying.)*

- Invite children to share what they know about Tommy and Mrs. Bowers, as well as any other characters, in class discussion.

ELL Support: Proper Nouns

- Explain that nouns are words that name people, places, and things. Tell children that some nouns name a specific person, place, or thing.

- Point to and read aloud the name *Tommy* (page 3). Tell children that *Tommy* names one boy. Explain that names like *Tommy* begin with a capital letter.

- Point to and read aloud more names in the book. Have children point to each name's capital letter.

- Explain that the names of days are also nouns, and they begin with capital letters. Point to and read the word *Monday* on page 12. Point out the capital *M*. Then write the names of other days on the board. Have volunteers underline the capital letters.

Step by Step

- **Reread and discuss the beginning.** Read aloud pages 3–14, pausing to identify the characters in the illustrations and connect them to their actions.

- Use questions such as these to guide discussion. (RL.K.1; SL.K.1; SL.K.2)

   Pages 3–5: What does Tommy like to do? (draw)

   Pages 6–7: Why does Tommy practice drawing and not copying? (His cousins tell him not to copy and to keep practicing.)

   Pages 8–11: How do you know that Tommy's family likes his drawings? (They hang them up.)

   Pages 12–14: Where do Tommy's parents ask him to stop drawing? (on his sheets and on the walls of the new house)

- **Focus on a key detail.** Direct children to turn to Student Book page 6. Have them draw a picture that shows what Tommy likes to do. Reread pages 3–5 to help them recall the details. (RL.K.3)

> **Tip:** Point out the things that Tommy's friends like to do best (page 4), emphasizing that their interests are different from Tommy's. As needed, define the words *collected* and *cartwheels*.

- Use the Close Reading activity to help children understand why Tommy practices drawing and never copies.

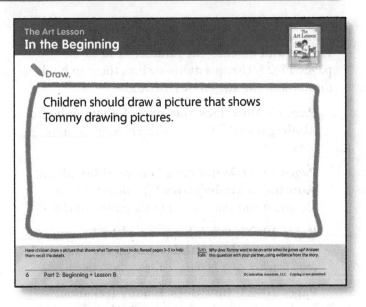

- **Have children discuss story evidence.** Read aloud the Turn and Talk activity. Guide partners to have a conversation, beginning as follows:

   Why does Tommy want to be an artist when he grows up? (Drawing is his favorite thing to do.)

- Invite children to share their ideas with the class.

- Work with children to identify the most important ideas from this part of the story. Encourage them to use evidence from the story as well as their drawings to help explain their ideas. (SL.K.4)

Tier Two Vocabulary: *favorite*

- Display the last sentence on page 3. Read it aloud. Underline the word *favorite*.

- Ask what Tommy likes to do best. Help children understand that Tommy likes drawing more than any other thing.

- Work with children to determine that the word *favorite* means "the one you like the best."

- Provide an example of one of your personal favorites. Say: *My favorite color is purple. I like purple better than any other color.*

- Have children tell about their favorite color: *My favorite color is _____.* (L.K.5.c)

Close Reading

- Help children understand why Tommy practices drawing and never copies. Display page 6. Read it aloud. Then prompt:

   What evidence shows that Tommy's cousins know about art and being artists? (The words say they are in art school learning to be real artists. The picture shows them painting.) (RL.K.7)

   What do Tommy's cousins tell him about becoming an artist? (to not copy and to practice, practice, practice)

   Why does Tommy listen to his cousins? (They are grown up. They are learning to be artists. He wants to be an artist when he grows up, too.)

Step by Step

- **Reread and discuss the middle.** Read aloud pages 15–23. Use questions such as these to guide discussion. (RL.K.1; SL.K.1; SL.K.2)

    Page 15: How does Tommy feel about going to kindergarten? (*He can't wait. He wants to have art lessons.*)

    Pages 16–17: What does Tommy think about painting in kindergarten? (*He doesn't like it. He says it isn't fun. He thinks the paint is awful.*)

    Pages 20–23: What happens when Tommy wants to use his birthday crayons in first grade? (*His teacher says he has to use school crayons.*)

    Pages 20–23: How does Tommy feel about having to use school crayons? (*He feels upset.*)

Tip: Use voice inflection to emphasize how Tommy feels about using school crayons and getting only one piece of paper. Modify your voice when reading the words in all capital letters to reflect Tommy's disbelief.

- Use the Close Reading activity to discuss Tommy's feelings about his new crayons.

- **Focus on a key detail.** Direct children to turn to Student Book page 7. Have them draw a picture that shows how Tommy feels when Miss Landers tells him that he can't use his new crayons. Reread pages 22–23 to help children recall the details. (RL.K.3)

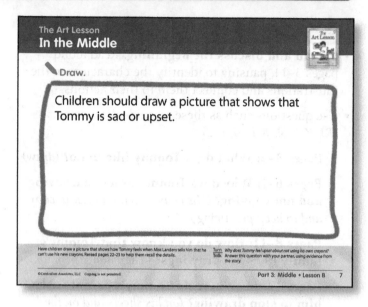

The Art Lesson
In the Middle

Draw.

Children should draw a picture that shows that Tommy is sad or upset.

Have children draw a picture that shows how Tommy feels when Miss Landers tells him that he can't use his new crayons. Reread pages 22–23 to help them recall the details.

Turn Talk · Why does Tommy feel upset about not using his own crayons? Answer this question with your partner, using evidence from the story.

©Curriculum Associates, LLC Copying is not permitted. Part 3: Middle · Lesson B 7

- **Have children discuss story evidence.** Read aloud the Turn and Talk activity. Guide partners to have a conversation, beginning as follows:

    Why does Tommy feel upset about not using his own crayons? (*He feels that he can't practice being an artist using only school crayons.*)

- As a class, discuss Tommy's hopes for how art lessons in school might be. Emphasize that the reality is different from how he wishes it to be. (SL.K.4)

- Work together to identify the most important ideas from this part of the story. Encourage children to use their own words to describe Tommy's experiences of painting in kindergarten and using crayons in first grade.

Tier Two Vocabulary: *stick*

- Display the last sentence on page 16. Read it aloud. Underline the word *stick*.

- Help children understand that Tommy's paint did not go on the paper the way he wanted it to. Ask: *Did the paint attach to the paper or fall off?*

- Work together to decide that the word *stick* means "to stay on."

- Provide a personal example. Say: *I use glue to help glitter stick to paper.*

- Have children talk about things that stick, using this sentence starter:

    _____ *makes things stick to paper.* (L.K.5.c)

Close Reading

- Help children understand Tommy's feelings about his new crayons. Read aloud pages 22–23. Prompt:

    Why can't Tommy use his new crayons at school? (*Everyone must use school crayons.*)

    What picture evidence shows how Tommy feels about not using his crayons? (*He looks sad and disappointed in the pictures.*) (RL.K.7)

    What story evidence tells why his birthday crayons are important to Tommy? (*He wonders how he can practice being an artist without them.*)

- Help children understand that Tommy's wishes and the school's rules are different.

Step by Step

- **Reread and discuss the end.** Read aloud pages 24–32. Discuss the way the story ends, using questions such as these. (RL.K.1; RL.K.7; SL.K.1; SL.K.2)

  Page 24: What does Tommy bring to school on the morning of the art lesson? (*his own crayons*)

  Page 26: What does Mrs. Bowers ask the class to do? (*copy her drawing of Pilgrims and a turkey*)

  Page 27: Why does Tommy think it is not a real art lesson? (*He thinks that real artists don't copy.*)

  Pages 28–29: What does Mrs. Bowers say when Tommy says he doesn't want to copy? (*She tells him he can draw another picture after he copies the first one. She says it's only fair to the rest of the class.*)

  Pages 30–32: What do we find out about Tommy by the end of the story? (*that he finally becomes a real artist when he grows up*)

  Tip: Use pages 30–32 to help children understand that readers often need to use evidence in the words and pictures together. Point out that the illustrations show what "he did" as a child and what "he still does" as a grown-up.

- **Focus on a key detail.** Have children turn to Student Book page 8. Have them draw a picture that shows what Tommy draws to be fair to the class. Reread pages 28–30 to help them recall the details. (RL.K.3)

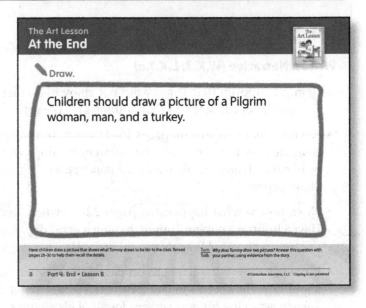

The Art Lesson
At the End

✏ Draw.

Children should draw a picture of a Pilgrim woman, man, and a turkey.

- **Have children discuss story evidence.** Read aloud the Turn and Talk activity and review pages 30–31. Guide partners to have a conversation, beginning as follows:

  Why does Tommy draw two pictures? (*He agrees to copy the first picture with the rest of the class so he can draw his own picture, too.*)

- Invite children to share their ideas with the class.

- Use the Close Reading activity to help children understand that Tommy does become a real artist.

- **Retell *The Art Lesson*.** Guide a retelling of the story, paging through the book and calling on children to tell what happens at the beginning, middle, and end. Reread parts of the story as needed.

Integrating Foundational Skills

Use these activities to integrate foundational skills into your reading of *The Art Lesson*.

1 Read aloud page 24, tracking the print. Explain that each word you say is on the page. Explain that words are made up of letters. Point to and have children name the letters in *Tommy*, noting the capital *T*. Call on children to name other capital and lowercase letters. (RF.K.1.b; RF.K.1.d)

2 Say *Tommy* and clap for each syllable. Repeat with several characters' names, clapping and counting syllables together. Then say *Tom-my* in two syllables; have children blend the syllables. Repeat with several characters' names. (RF.K.2.b)

Close Reading

- Help children understand that Tommy grows up and does become a real artist. Display and read aloud pages 29–32. Then prompt:

  What does Tommy say he will try to do? (*follow Mrs. Bowers's idea to draw the Pilgrims and turkey first, then draw his own picture after*)

  What do the pictures on pages 30–31 show? (*p. 30: Tommy's copied drawing of the Pilgrims and turkey; p. 31: Tommy's own picture*) (RL.K.7)

  What does the picture on page 32 show? How do you know this? (*It shows Tommy as a grown-up and a real artist. His drawings are there, and the words say that he still does draw.*)

Writing Activity

Write a Narrative *(W.K.3; L.K.1.a)*

- Remind children that Tommy did not enjoy his art lessons very much. Explain that together you will rewrite the middle of the story so that Tommy gets the art lessons he had been hoping for.

- Review what happens on pages 16–17 when Tommy paints his picture in kindergarten. Ask children to imagine how this day would be different if things were going well for Tommy. Prompt: *What would the paint be like that Tommy used? Would the paper be any different? How so?* Take notes of children's responses on chart paper.

- Next, review what happens on pages 22–23 when Tommy's first-grade class practices using their crayons. Have children imagine Tommy having a good day. Ask: *Which crayons would Tommy get to use—school crayons or his own crayons? Why do you think so? How many pieces of paper would Tommy get?*

- Finally, review what happens on pages 26–27 when Mrs. Bowers teaches her art lesson. Have children think about how the art lesson could be better. Ask: *Would Tommy have to copy the Thanksgiving picture? Would Tommy get to use his new crayons for all of his pictures?*

- Tell children they will now write a class story about how Tommy enjoyed his art lessons. Call on children to describe the events in order, using the terms *first, next,* and *last.* Encourage them to include the details they just discussed. Children may also want to draw pictures to accompany the story.

Speaking and Listening Activity

Talk About Favorite Things *(SL.K.3; SL.K.5; L.K.1.d)*

- Assign partners the role of Tommy or one of his friends. Have partners work together to discuss the favorite things that their characters like to do.

- Encourage them to ask each other questions about the things they like to do, and to use story details as well as new details in their answers.

- As needed, explain to children that questions often begin with one of the following words: *who, what, where, when, why,* or *how.*

- Have children draw pictures of their characters doing their favorite thing. Encourage children to include details from their discussions.

- Invite pairs of children to present their drawings to the class.

Language Activity

Prefix *un-* *(L.K.4.b)*

- Display and read aloud pages 13–14 of *The Art Lesson.* Point to the words *finished* and *unfinished.*

- Write the word *finished* on the board. Ask children what it means. *(done; complete)*

- Beneath *finished,* write the word *unfinished.* Point out that the letters *un* have been added at the beginning of *finished* to make *unfinished.*

- Explain that the letters *un* at the beginning of this word mean "not." Work together to decide that the word *unfinished* means "not finished."

- Write the following word pair for children: *safe/ unsafe.* Discuss each word's meaning and how the letters *un* change a word's meaning.

- Continue with some or all of the following word pairs: *real/unreal, opened/unopened, fair/unfair, wanted/unwanted; kind/unkind; zipped/unzipped.*

Lesson 1 (Student Book pages 37–40)

Asking Questions

CCSS

RL.K.1: With prompting and support, ask and answer questions about key details in a text.

Required Read Alouds: A (*Jamaica's Blue Marker*); B (*The Art Lesson*)

Lesson Objectives

- Recognize question words.
- Understand that questions begin with question words.
- Ask questions about words and pictures to identify key details in stories.
- Understand why asking and answering questions aids comprehension.

The Learning Progression

- **Prior to K:** Children should have a basic understanding of the concepts of questions and answers. They should also be able to demonstrate knowledge of some details in a familiar story, such as naming one or more characters or events.

- **Grade K: CCSS RL.K.1 expects children to ask and answer questions about key details in a story with prompting and support.**

- **Grade 1:** CCSS RL.1.1 advances the standard by having children ask and answer questions about key details in a story more independently.

Tap Children's Prior Knowledge

- Tell children that a *question* is something they can ask to find out information. Display your lunch bag. Tell children they can ask questions to find out more about the bag and what is inside of it.

- Model asking questions about the bag, such as the following: *What color is the bag? What is in the bag?*

- Remove items from the bag, one at a time. Ask questions about the details of each item: *What is in this sandwich? What type of bread is this? Who made the sandwich? How did she make it? When did she make it?*

- Quickly provide answers to each of the questions, and then help children ask their own questions about the bag and its contents. Prompt them as needed, reminding them that they are trying to find out new information about the bag and each item in it.

- Guide children to understand that in order to find out more about something, they ask questions and then look for the answers.

- Tell children that in this lesson, they will learn how to ask questions about details in a story. Explain that answering the questions will help them understand what happens in the story.

Ready *Teacher Toolbox*   Teacher-Toolbox.com

	Prerequisite Skills	RL.K.1
Ready Lessons		✓
Tools for Instruction		✓
Interactive Tutorials		

Additional CCSS

RL.K.2; RL.K.7; SL.K.1; SL.K.2; SL.K.4 (See page A38 for full text.)

Part 1: Introduction

Step by Step

- **Introduce the standard.** Tell children they will learn how to ask and answer questions about stories. Explain that asking questions and finding the answers helps readers better understand the details in a story.

- Ask children to listen carefully as you read aloud the following story:

  On Monday, Ben went to the park to play. First, he played on a swing. Then he went fast down a slide. Monday was a fun day for Ben!

- Model asking a question about the story. Think aloud:

  I will ask questions about this story to make sure I understand the important details. My first question is *Where did Ben go?* I will read again. (Reread first sentence.) **I see that Ben went to the park. That tells me an important detail.**

Tip: Remind children that *details* are pieces of information. Review the details of the lunch bag from the activity on page 13. Emphasize that asking and answering questions about the bag and its contents helped children notice many details.

- Continue asking questions about the story:

  I will ask another question: *What did Ben do at the park?* I will read again to find the answer. (Reread first two sentences.) **First he played on a swing.** (Reread last two sentences.) **Then he went down a slide. This tells me what Ben did at the park.**

- Review that asking questions helped you find out information about Ben's trip to the park.

- Tell children that in their Student Books, they will learn questions they can ask about details in a story.

- **Read aloud the Student Book page.** Have children turn to Student Book page 37. Read aloud the page as children listen and follow along.

- Point to and reread each question word. Have children repeat each word after you. Point to the word *Where*, and invite a volunteer to tell the *where* question you asked about the story. Repeat with the word *What*.

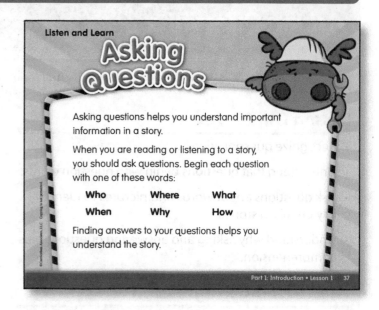

- Reread the story. Use the remaining question words on the Student Book page to ask additional questions about the story. Guide children to answer the questions using details from the story.

  Who is in the story? (*Ben*)

  When did Ben go to the park? (*on Monday*)

  How did Ben go down the slide? (*He went fast.*)

  Why did Ben go to the park? (*to play*)

- Help children understand that good readers ask questions about a story to better understand important details. They look for answers in the story words and pictures.

- **Have children demonstrate understanding.** Have volunteers share what they have learned so far about asking and answering questions about story details. Encourage them to give examples of questions they can ask, using familiar classroom read-alouds.

Part 2: Modeled Instruction

Step by Step

- **Review Part 1.** Remind children that they can ask questions to find out details, or important information, in a story. Review the question words they can use: *who, where, what, when, why, how.*

- **Revisit the story.** Display *The Art Lesson.* Page through the book, using the pictures as prompts to have children recall the story. *(RL.K.2; RL.K.7)*

- **Model asking questions.** Explain that you are going to model asking and answering questions about the story. Display and read aloud pages 3–5. Think aloud:

  There are lots of details here. I will ask questions to make sure I understand them. First I will ask: *What do Tommy's friends like to do?* The words say that Jack collected turtles. (Point) This must be Jack in the picture, holding a turtle. Next the words say Herbie makes cities in his sandbox. (Point) This must be Herbie because I see sand castles.

- Reread the last sentence. Have children tell what Jeannie likes to do. Invite a volunteer to identify her in the pictures.

- Continue thinking aloud:

  The words tell us that drawing was Tommy's favorite thing to do, but what else can we find out? I will ask: *What does Tommy use to draw?* Since the words don't tell me, I will look for the answer in the picture. He is holding a red crayon and lying next to a box of crayons. That is what Tommy uses to draw.

- Tell children you will model how to complete the Student Book page by asking and answering questions about this part of *The Art Lesson.*

- **Model completing the Student Book page.** Have children turn to page 38. For the first item, ask: *What does Jack collect?* Point to and name each picture (*sand castles; turtles; drawings*). Demonstrate circling the correct answer. Continue with the second item. Ask: *What does Tommy use to draw?* (*crayons; paint; markers*)

Tip: As you model circling the correct answer for the first item, think aloud about why the sand castles and drawings are not correct, referring to evidence you remember from the words and pictures. For the second item, prompt children to do the same.

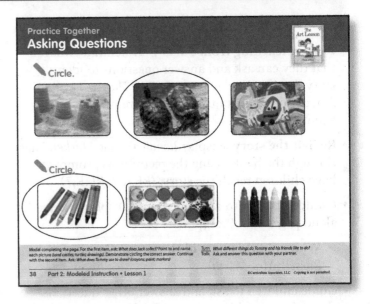

- **Have children demonstrate understanding.** Display pages 3–5. Read aloud the Turn and Talk activity. Model what a conversation with a partner should sound like by asking and answering the question below. *(SL.K.1; SL.K.2)*

  ***What different things do Tommy and his friends like to do?* Ask and answer this question with your partner.** (*draw; collect turtles; make cities of sand; do cartwheels and headstands*)

- For additional support, point to each picture on page 4 and ask: *Who is this friend? What is he or she doing?* Have partners think together about the answer.

- Use the Close Reading activity to provide additional practice with asking and answering questions.

Close Reading

- Tell children that readers ask and answer questions to learn more about characters.

- Display and reread page 5. Prompt:

  What does Tommy draw? Look at the picture. What do you notice about Tommy's drawings here and the pictures on this page (point to page 4)**?** (*They look the same.*)

  So what do you think Tommy likes to draw? (*his friends doing their favorite things*)

- Discuss how asking and answering this question helps readers learn more about Tommy.

Part 3: Guided Practice

Step by Step

- **Review learning from Parts 1–2.** Remind children that they can ask and answer questions to identify story details. Display pages 3–5 of *The Art Lesson*. Ask children what questions they remember asking about these pages.

- **Revisit the story.** Display *Jamaica's Blue Marker*. Page through the book, using the pictures as prompts to have children recall the story. (RL.K.2; RL.K.7)

- **Guide children to ask questions.** Display and read aloud pages 6–7. Prompt:

    Who is in this part of the story? (*Jamaica; Russell; Mrs. Wirth*)

- Guide children to ask and answer other questions about the story, beginning with *where, what,* and *why.* Use the following questions for support as needed.

    Where are Jamaica and Russell? (*in a classroom*)

    What is Jamaica drawing? (*a tree*)

    What does Mrs. Wirth ask Jamaica to share? (*her markers*)

    Why does Russell need to share Jamaica's markers? (*because he doesn't have any markers*)

    Tip: The words do not specify where the story takes place, so guide children to make an educated decision. Point to the chalkboard and student table and ask where these are normally found. Then help children reason that Mrs. Wirth is Jamaica's teacher.

- Tell children you will work together to complete the Student Book page by asking and answering questions about this part of *Jamaica's Blue Marker*.

- **Guide children to complete the Student Book page.** Have children turn to page 39. For the first item, ask: *Where are Jamaica and Russell?* Point to and name each picture (*at the playground; in the classroom; at home*). Have a volunteer tell which picture to circle. Continue with the second item. Ask: *What does Jamaica share?* (*markers; construction paper; chalk*)

- Discuss the answers to the Student Book page. Help children point to evidence in the story that supports the correct answers.

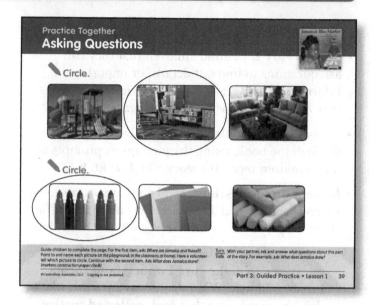

Practice Together
Asking Questions

Circle.

Circle.

Guide children to complete the page. For the first item, ask: *Where are Jamaica and Russell?* Point to and name each picture (*at the playground; in the classroom; at home*). Have a volunteer tell which picture to circle. Continue with the second item. Ask: *What does Jamaica share?* (*markers; construction paper; chalk*)

Turn and Talk: With your partner, ask and answer *what* questions about this part of the story. For example, ask: *What does Jamaica draw?*

©Curriculum Associates, LLC   Copying is not permitted.   Part 3: Guided Practice • Lesson 1   39

- Use the Close Reading activity to help children understand that answers cannot always be found directly in the words.

- **Have children demonstrate understanding.** Display pages 6–7 of *Jamaica's Blue Marker*. Read aloud the Turn and Talk activity. (SL.K.1; SL.K.2)

    With your partner, ask and answer *what* questions about this part of the story. For example, ask: *What does Jamaica draw?* (*a tree*)

- Invite partners to share their *what* questions with the class.

Close Reading

- Tell children that the answers to some questions cannot be found right in the words. Display and reread pages 6–7. Then think aloud:

    ***How does Jamaica feel about sharing?* The words do not say how she feels, but they do say that she didn't want to share her markers. How do you feel when you have to share but you don't want to?** (*unhappy*)

    Look at the picture. How does Jamaica's face look? (*unhappy*)

- Decide together that Jamaica feels unhappy about sharing. Emphasize that even though the words did not say "Jamaica feels unhappy," you used word and picture clues to answer the question.

Step by Step

- **Review learning from Parts 1–3.** Remind children that they can ask and answer questions to find key details in a story. Display pages 6–7 of *Jamaica's Blue Marker*. Have children recall questions they asked about these pages.

- **Have children ask and answer questions.** Display pages 8–9 of *Jamaica's Blue Marker*, and read them aloud. Tell children they will practice asking and answering questions about this part of the story. Review the question words on Student Book page 37.

- Have children ask questions beginning with the various question words. Use the following questions for support as needed.

  Who sits down next to Jamaica? (*Russell*)

  What does Russell use to draw? (*a blue marker*)

  How does Russell get the blue marker? (*He grabs it from Jamaica's markers.*)

  What does Russell draw? (*blue squiggly circles*)

> **Tip:** Discuss how picture clues can sometimes help readers figure out the meaning of an unfamiliar word. Point to and read the word *squiggly*. Have children look at the picture and tell what *squiggly* means.

- Tell children they will complete the Student Book page by asking and answering questions about this part of *Jamaica's Blue Marker*.

- **Have children complete the Student Book page independently.** Have children turn to page 40. For the first item, ask: *What does Russell draw?* Point to and name each picture (*a tree; a piece of cake; squiggly circles*). Have children circle their answers. Continue with the second item. Ask: *What does Russell use to draw?* (*paint; a blue marker; modeling clay*)

- Discuss the answers to the Student Book page. Help children point to evidence in the story that supports the correct answers.

- Use the Close Reading activity to show children how they can use story clues to answer questions.

- **Have children demonstrate understanding.** Display pages 8–9 of *Jamaica's Blue Marker*. Read aloud the Turn and Talk activity. (*SL.K.1; SL.K.2*)

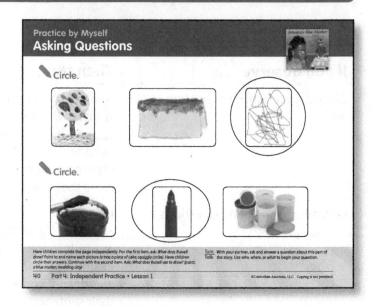

- **With your partner, ask and answer a question about this part of the story. Use *who*, *where*, or *what* to begin your question.** (*Who uses a brown marker? [Jamaica]*)

- **Have children reflect on their learning.** Invite children to tell why readers ask and answer questions about stories. Emphasize that asking and answering questions helps readers notice and remember important details.

- Have children name words they can use to ask questions about a story.

Close Reading

- Remind children that readers often need to use clues to answer questions about a story. Display and reread pages 8–9. Ask: *How is Russell feeling?*

- Guide children to find evidence about Russell's feelings in the words and pictures. Prompt:

  Does Russell ask Jamaica which marker he can use? (*No. He just takes one.*)

  How does Russell's face look? (*unhappy*)

  If someone behaves this way, how do you think they feel? (*upset; angry*)

  Do you think Russell is feeling this way? (*yes*)

- Explain that if the words do not answer a question, readers can often figure out the answer by thinking about what the characters say and do.

Assessment and Remediation

If you observe . . .	Then try . . .
Difficulty recognizing question words	Asking children which of two words is a question word. For example, ask: *Which of these is a question word:* where *or* best? Continue with word pairs such as these: *soon/what, day/how, who/clock, why/paint, green/when.* Once children can easily identify question words, have them ask questions about classroom objects or a familiar story. Prompt them to tell what question word they used.
Difficulty formulating questions	Having children say what they are thinking about, using the phrase "I wonder . . ." and then turning their sentence into a question. Model an example: *I wonder where David is today. Where is David today?* Model an example for each question word. Then have children say their own "I wonder . . ." sentences, and guide them to formulate questions based on their sentences.
Difficulty answering questions about details	Displaying an everyday object such as a banana. Ask questions such as these: *What is this? Where can you get this? How do you eat it? Why is this a good snack?* Continue with additional objects as needed to provide sufficient practice for children.

Connect to the Anchor Standard

R1: Read closely to determine what the text says explicitly and to make logical inferences from it; cite specific textual evidence when writing or speaking to support conclusions drawn from the text.

Throughout the grades, Standard 1 focuses students' attention on key details in stories. Early readers learn to ask simple questions and find answers located directly in the text and pictures. In later grades, readers are expected to answer both literal and inferential questions, basing their thinking on clues, details, and examples from the books they read. Students might ask questions such as these: *Why is it important to notice the details in a story? Are the answers to questions here on the page or do I need to make an inference? What clues in the story help me answer this question?* Use the following activities to help children begin this transition.

- Read aloud pages 8–9 of *The Art Lesson.* Then ask: *How do Tommy's mom and dad feel about his pictures?* Discuss with children what clues they can use to answer the question. Reread the words on each page. Then display the pictures. Ask: *What are Tommy's mom and dad doing? (hanging up his pictures)* Discuss reasons why they might do this, and allow children to use their own experiences for support. Decide together that Tommy's mom and dad feel proud of his pictures. (*SL.K.1; SL.K.2; SL.K.4*)

- Read aloud pages 5–6 of *Jamaica's Blue Marker.* Ask: *What kind of student is Jamaica?* Help children look for clues, such as the way Jamaica follows the teacher's instructions and how she feels annoyed that Russell never has what he needs. Invite children to answer the question and use their experiences to defend their answers.

Lesson Objectives

You will read aloud *Chrysanthemum*, which children will revisit in later lessons. With prompting and support, children will:

- Answer questions about key details in the story.
- Describe characters and major events, using key details.
- Retell the story, including key details.

About the Text

Summary

Chrysanthemum is a happy little mouse who thinks her name is perfect, until she starts going to school. There, other children don't think her name is so perfect. With the support of her parents and a teacher, Chrysanthemum learns to love her name again.

Genre: Fantasy

- *Chrysanthemum* is a fantasy, or a story that cannot happen in real life. Explain that in some fantasies, animals might act like real people.
- Use the cover illustration to point out that Chrysanthemum is a girl mouse character.

Critical Vocabulary

- Prior to reading, briefly define the following words:

  perfect (p. 3) the best; without negative characteristics

  scarcely (p. 10) barely; not quite; almost

  wilted (p. 10) to shrivel or shrink

  dreadful (p. 10) awful; miserable

- As you read, pause to point to the words as you encounter them, and review their definitions.

Word Bank

- Display a word bank of the Critical Vocabulary and the characters' names (*Chrysanthemum, Victoria, Mrs. Chud, Mrs. Twinkle, etc.*).
- Add other important story words, such as *miserably* and *wonder*, on subsequent readings.

New Concepts: Flowers

- Remind children that Chrysanthemum is named after a flower, and that many parts of the story talk about flowers.
- Talk about how flowers grow, how they bloom, and how they can shrink and wilt. Ask children what flowers need to grow (*water, sun, soil*), and what happens when flowers don't get what they need. Tell children to listen for ways Chrysanthemum is compared to a flower.

■ Ready *Teacher Toolbox*

Teacher-Toolbox.com

	Prerequisite Skills	RL.K.2
Ready Lessons		✓
Tools for Instruction	✓ ✓	✓
Interactive Tutorials	✓ ✓	

CCSS Focus

RL.K.2 *With prompting and support, retell familiar stories, including key details.*

ADDITIONAL STANDARDS: **RL.K.1; RL.K.3; RL.K.7; RF.K.1.a, c; RF.K.3.c; W.K.1; SL.K.1; SL.K.2; SL.K.4; SL.K.5; L.K.1.b; L.K.2.a; L.K.5.c** *(See page A38 for full text.)*

Step by Step

- **Introduce *Chrysanthemum*.** Display the book. Read aloud the title and the name of the author, Kevin Henkes. Point out that he is also the illustrator.

- **Set the purpose for reading.** Remind children that *characters* are the people or animals in a story. Tell children that readers make sense of a story by identifying the characters and thinking about what they do and what happens to them.

- Explain that as you read aloud, children should listen closely to identify the characters in this story.

- **Read aloud *Chrysanthemum*.** Read the story all the way through, pausing only to briefly define challenging vocabulary.

- **Guide children to identify the characters.** After reading, use questions such as these to help children identify the characters. (*RL.K.1; RL.K.3; SL.K.1; SL.K.2*)

  What characters did we read about in the story? (*Chrysanthemum, Chrysanthemum's mother and father, Mrs. Chud, Victoria, Jo, Rita, and Mrs. Twinkle*)

  Which character has a special name? (*Chrysanthemum*)

  Which other character has a special name? (*Mrs. Twinkle*)

  Which characters make Chrysanthemum feel bad about her name? (*Victoria, Jo, and Rita*)

- **Have children draw characters.** Direct children to turn to Student Book page 9. Have them draw a picture of Chrysanthemum and Victoria. Display illustrations on pages 8, 11, and 19 to help them recall what each character looks like.

> **Tip:** Display the book cover and reread the title. Point out that book titles often tell who one or more of the characters are. Explain that Chrysanthemum is the main character in this story.

- **Have children discuss story evidence.** Read aloud the Turn and Talk activity. Help children use their pictures and story evidence to explain what they know about each character. (*SL.K.4; SL.K.5*)

- Guide their discussions with the following prompts:

  How does Chrysanthemum feel about her name at the beginning of the story? (*She thinks it's perfect.*)

  Why does Victoria think Chrysanthemum's name is strange? (*She says it has too many letters. She thinks it is odd that the name is a flower.*)

  How does Mrs. Twinkle help Chrysanthemum feel better about her name? (*She explains that she is also named after a flower.*)

- Invite children to share what they know about Chrysanthemum and Victoria, as well as any other characters, in class discussion.

ELL Support: Opposite Words

- Explain the concept of opposites using simple examples such as *hot/cold, up/down, on/off.*

- Point to the words *perfect* and *dreadful* on page 10.

- Explain that these two words are *opposite words* and are important to understanding the different ways Chrysanthemum feels about her name.

- To demonstrate the difference between the two words, pantomime a *perfect* emotion, like feeling proud or happy. Then pantomime a *dreadful* emotion, like feeling sad or upset.

- Ask children to point to and say the words *perfect* and *dreadful.* Together, discuss what each of the words mean.

Step by Step

- **Reread and discuss the beginning.** Read aloud pages 3–8, pausing to point out how the pictures show Chrysanthemum growing from a baby to a child.

- Use questions such as these to guide discussion. (*RL.K.1; SL.K.1; SL.K.2*)

  Pages 3–4: What is the perfect name that the parents give their new baby? (*Chrysanthemum*)

  Pages 5–7: What does Chrysanthemum love the most? (*her name*)

  Page 8: What does Chrysanthemum say as she runs all the way to school on her first day? How does she feel? (*She says "Hooray!" She feels excited.*)

- Use the Close Reading activity to help children make connections between words and pictures.

- **Focus on a key detail.** Direct children to turn to Student Book page 10. Have them draw a picture that shows how Chrysanthemum feels about her name at the beginning of the story. Reread pages 5–7 to help them recall the details. (*RL.K.3*)

> **Tip:** To emphasize how Chrysanthemum feels about her name, do a choral reading of pages 6 and 7, having children join in with the phrases "She loved the way it sounded" and "She loved the way it looked" as well as the repetition of the name Chrysanthemum.

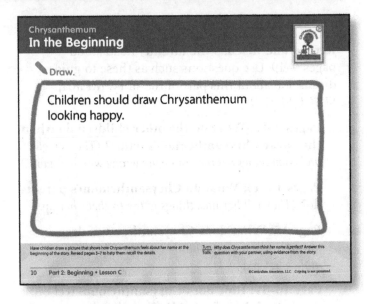

Chrysanthemum
In the Beginning

✎ Draw.

Children should draw Chrysanthemum looking happy.

Have children draw a picture that shows how Chrysanthemum feels about her name at the beginning of the story. Reread pages 5–7 to help them recall the details.

Turn Talk *Why does Chrysanthemum think her name is perfect?* Answer this question with your partner, using evidence from the story.

10   Part 2: Beginning • Lesson C   ©Curriculum Associates, LLC Copying is not permitted.

- **Have children discuss story evidence.** Read aloud the Turn and Talk activity. Guide partners to have a conversation, beginning as follows:

  Why does Chrysanthemum think her name is perfect? (*She loves the way it sounds and how it looks.*)

- Invite children to share their ideas with the class.

- Work with children to identify the most important ideas from this part of the story. Encourage them to use evidence from the story as well as their drawings to help explain their ideas. (*SL.K.4*)

Tier Two Vocabulary: *appreciate*

- Display the last sentence on page 5. Read it aloud. Underline the word *appreciate*.

- Ask how Chrysanthemum feels about her name.

- Work with children to determine that the word *appreciate* means "to be thankful for something or someone."

- Provide an example of something you appreciate. Say: *I appreciate all the children in this class!*

- Then have volunteers talk about things they appreciate. Provide this sentence frame:
  I appreciate _____.

- Discuss the examples children present. (*L.K.5.c*)

Close Reading

- Remind children that good readers make connections between words and pictures. Display page 5 and read the text aloud. Tell children to look closely at all the pictures. Then prompt:

  What do the words say about how Chrysanthemum feels? (*Chrysanthemum loves her name.*)

  How do the pictures help you understand how Chrysanthemum feels? (*She looks happy in all the pictures. She also says "I love my name!" in the last picture.*) (*RL.K.7*)

- Explain that together, the words and pictures show how Chrysanthemum feels about her name.

Step by Step

- **Reread and discuss the middle.** Read aloud pages 9–19. Use questions such as these to guide discussion about this part of the story. (RL.K.1; SL.K.1; SL.K.2)

  Pages 9–12: What do the other children do when they hear Chrysanthemum's name? (*They giggle and point things out they think are wrong with her name.*)

  Pages 13–14: What do Chrysanthemum's parents do? (*They tell her nice things to try to cheer her up.*)

  Page 15: What does Chrysanthemum dream about? (*She dreams that her name is Jane, which makes her happy.*)

  Page 16–19: How does Chrysanthemum feel on the second day of school? (*She still feels sad.*)

- Use the Close Reading activity to help children think about why Chrysanthemum's feelings about her name have changed in this part of the story.

- **Focus on a key detail.** Direct children to turn to Student Book page 11. Have them draw a picture that shows what happens when Chrysanthemum goes to school. Reread pages 9–10 to help them recall the details. (RL.K.3)

Tip: If children are struggling with what to draw, have them close their eyes and visualize as you reread page 10. Prompt them to draw what they imagine.

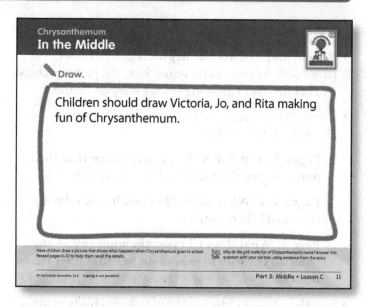

Chrysanthemum
In the Middle

Draw.

Children should draw Victoria, Jo, and Rita making fun of Chrysanthemum.

Have children draw a picture that shows what happens when Chrysanthemum goes to school. Reread pages 9–10 to help them recall the details. | **Turn Talk** Why do the girls make fun of Chrysanthemum's name? Answer this question with your partner, using evidence from the story.

©Curriculum Associates, LLC Copying is not permitted. Part 3: Middle • Lesson C 11

- **Have children discuss story evidence.** Read aloud the Turn and Talk activity. Guide partners to have a conversation, beginning as follows:

  Why do the girls make fun of Chrysanthemum's name? (*They can't believe she is named after a flower. They think her name is too long.*)

- As a class, discuss how Chrysanthemum is teased. Emphasize how her feelings about her name have changed from the beginning of the story. (SL.K.4)

- Work together to identify the most important ideas from this part of the story. Encourage children to describe in their own words what it means when the text says Chrysanthemum "wilted."

Tier Two Vocabulary: *precious*

- Display the fifth paragraph on page 13. Read it aloud. Underline the word *precious*.

- Discuss how Chrysanthemum's parents say that her name is precious. They think her name is beautiful and special. Together with children, determine that *precious* means "beautiful or special."

- Provide an example of something that is precious. Say: *This book is precious to me because it is the first book I ever read as a child.*

- Then have children take turns using the word by naming something or someone that is precious to them.

Close Reading

- Help children understand why Chrysanthemum's feelings about her name have changed in this part of the story. Reread pages 10–11. Then prompt:

  What evidence tells you that the other children are teasing Chrysanthemum? (*The other girls make fun of her name, and Victoria continues to say what's wrong with her name.*)

  What evidence tells you that Chrysanthemum feels sad? (*The words says that she thinks her name is not perfect and is "absolutely dreadful." The picture on page 10 shows her looking very sad.*)

- Point out that the teasing hurts Chrysanthemum's feelings and changes how she feels about her name.

Step by Step

- **Reread and discuss the end.** Read aloud pages 20–32. Discuss the way the story ends, using questions such as these. (*RL.K.1; SL.K.1; SL.K.2*)

  Pages 22–23: Why does Chrysanthemum wear an outfit with seven pockets? (*so she can load the pockets with good-luck charms*)

  Pages 27–28: What does Mrs. Twinkle do to stop the girls from teasing Chrysanthemum? (*She tells the girls that her first name is long, too. She says she was named after a flower. She says she wants to name her first baby girl Chrysanthemum.*)

  Page 29: How does Chrysanthemum feel after Mrs. Twinkle tells about her name? (*She feels very happy.*)

  Page 30–32: How do the girls' feelings about Chrysanthemum's name change at the end of the story? (*They feel jealous of Chrysanthemum's name. They want flower names, too.*)

- **Focus on a key detail.** Direct children to turn to Student Book page 12. Have them draw a picture that shows who helps Chrysanthemum feel happy about her name again. Reread pages 27–29 to help them recall the details. (*RL.K.3*)

- Use the Close Reading activity to help children identify evidence about how Chrysanthemum feels about her name at the end of the story.

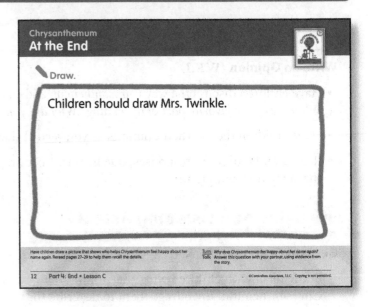

- **Have children discuss story evidence.** Read aloud the Turn and Talk activity. Guide partners to have a conversation, beginning as follows:

  Why does Chrysanthemum feel happy about her name again? (*A favorite teacher, Mrs. Twinkle, likes her name. The girls have stopped teasing her and want flower names for themselves.*)

- Invite children to share ideas with the class.

- **Retell *Chrysanthemum*.** Guide a round-robin retelling. Children can use their Student Books as they take turns naming important ideas. Reread parts of the story as needed.

Integrating Foundational Skills

Use these activities to integrate foundational skills into your reading of *Chrysanthemum*.

1. Display page 20. Reread it. Have children identify the spaces that separate the printed words on the page. Then display pages 21–22, asking children to follow the words from left to right, top to bottom, and page by page, including the words in the pictures. (*RF.K.1.a; RF.K.1.c*)

2. Display page 24. Reread it. Point to examples of common high-frequency words and have children read them by sight. (*the, to, her, was, were, they, an, of, a*) Repeat with page 25. (*the, in, for, was, as, the, a*) (*RF.K.3.c*)

Close Reading

- Explain that active readers draw conclusions from details in a story. Have children look for evidence that shows how Chrysanthemum's feelings about her name have changed again by the end of the story.

- Display pages 30–31. Read the text aloud. Then prompt children:

  What evidence shows that the girls will no longer tease Chrysanthemum? (*They all choose flowers for their names.*)

  What evidence shows that Chrysanthemum is happy about her name again? (*The words say that she knows her name is perfect. The picture shows her skipping happily.*)

Writing Activity

Write an Opinion (W.K.1)

- Have children discuss the way *Chrysanthemum* ends. Ask: *Did you like the way this story ends? Why or why not? What was your favorite part of the ending? Why did you like that part best?*

- Have children dictate their opinions as you record their responses on chart paper.

- Read aloud children's responses, one by one. Encourage children to explain their opinions, using details from the story text and pictures.

Speaking and Listening Activity

Get into Character (SL.K.4)

- Brainstorm with children what they know about Chrysanthemum. Encourage them to describe the way she thinks, feels, and acts. Then do the same with Victoria. Write children's ideas in two columns on chart paper.

- Have children work in pairs to act out a conversation between Chrysanthemum and Victoria. One child will pretend to be Chrysanthemum, and the other child will pretend to be Victoria.

- Encourage children to use what they know from the conversation that takes place in the story, but also to add in observations that aren't written. For instance, Chrysanthemum might say, "I don't know why Victoria is being mean to me. I don't like it. It hurts my feelings."

- Invite volunteers to share their reenactments with the class.

Language Activity

Common and Proper Nouns (L.K.1.b; L.K.2.a)

- Remind children that a *noun* is a word that names a person, place, or thing. Explain that there are different kinds of nouns—common nouns and proper nouns.

- Turn to pages 18–19 of *Chrysanthemum* and point out the picture of students napping and the word *students*. Explain that the word *students* is a common noun because it names a general group of people. It could refer to many types of students.

- Then point out the words *Chrysanthemum* and *Victoria*. Explain that these are examples of proper nouns. A proper noun names a specific person, place, or thing. A proper noun begins with a capital letter no matter where it is in a sentence. Names are examples of proper nouns.

- Using examples from the story, work with children to pair proper nouns with their common nouns. (*Mrs. Twinkle/teacher; Delphinium/flower*)

Identifying Characters

CCSS

RL.K.3: With prompting and support, identify characters . . . in a story.

Required Read Alouds: *B (The Art Lesson); C (Chrysanthemum)*

Lesson Objectives

- Recognize that characters are the people or animals that a story is about.

- Identify the characters in a story.

- Use word and picture evidence to tell more about characters in a story.

- Understand that asking questions about characters can help readers better understand a story.

The Learning Progression

- **Prior to K:** Children should have a basic understanding of who is in a story as well as who says and does things. Children should also be able to ask and answer *who* questions about stories.

- **Grade K: CCSS RL.K.3 expects children to identify characters in a story with prompting and support.**

- **Grade 1:** CCSS RL.1.3 further develops the standard by having children not only identify characters but also use details from the story to describe them.

Tap Children's Prior Knowledge

- Gather a few storybooks you have read with children. If possible, choose books that have clear illustrations of the characters. Display the cover of one book and quickly recall the story together.

- Tell children you are going to ask a *who* question about this story. Remind them that they answer a *who* question with a name.

- Ask: *Who is in this story?* For additional support, point to each character in the illustration and ask: *Who is this?*

- Repeat this process with books that span a variety of character types, including humans, animals, and anthropomorphic objects like Thomas the Tank Engine. Also include books that have many characters and books that have only a few characters.

- After reviewing several books, help children see that when they answer the question *Who is in the story?*, they are naming the characters in the story.

- Tell children that in this lesson, they will name the characters in a story and learn to ask questions about them. Answering the questions will help them understand more about the characters.

Ready Teacher Toolbox

Teacher-Toolbox.com

	Prerequisite Skills	**RL.K.3**
Ready Lessons		✓
Tools for Instruction	✓	✓
Interactive Tutorials		✓

Additional CCSS

RL.K.2; RL.K.7; SL.K.1; SL.K.2 (See page A38 for full text.)

Step by Step

- **Introduce the standard.** Tell children they will name the characters in a story and learn some questions they can ask to find out more about them. Explain that learning more about the characters helps readers better understand a story.

- Ask children to listen carefully as you read aloud the following story:

  Emily was so excited to see the lions at the zoo. She pulled her friend Carlos by the hand. "Come on, let's hurry to the front so we can see!" she said. But Carlos stood still. "I think I will stay here," he said. He didn't want to tell Emily that he was scared.

- Remind children that a *character* is a person in a story. Ask: *Who is in this story? (Emily; Carlos)* Then say:

  When we read a story, the first thing we notice is the characters, or who is in the story. We know this story is about Emily and Carlos. Next, we ask questions to learn more about the characters. We think about what the characters say, what they do, and how they feel.

  Tip: Briefly review with children words they can use to describe the way someone feels. Make a list of children's suggestions to use throughout the lesson.

- Tell children to listen closely for details about Emily as you reread the story. Then ask:

  What does Emily say to Carlos? *("Come on, let's hurry to the front so we can see!")*

  What does Emily do? *(She pulls on Carlos' hand.)*

  How does Emily feel? *(excited)*

- Explain that asking these questions about Emily helps you learn important details about her.

- Tell children that in their Student Books, they will learn questions they can ask to find out more about characters in a story.

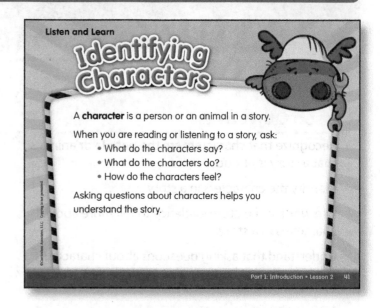

Listen and Learn

Identifying Characters

A **character** is a person or an animal in a story.

When you are reading or listening to a story, ask:
- What do the characters say?
- What do the characters do?
- How do the characters feel?

Asking questions about characters helps you understand the story.

Part 1: Introduction • Lesson 2   41

- **Read aloud the Student Book page.** Have children turn to Student Book page 41. Read aloud the page as children listen and follow along.

- Point to the first bullet, and briefly review what Emily says. Invite children to repeat what Emily does and how she feels as you reread the remaining questions.

- Tell children they will practice answering the same questions about Carlos. Have them listen closely as you reread the story. Then ask:

  What does Carlos say to Emily? *("I think I will stay here.")*

  What does Carlos do? *(He stands still.)*

  How does Carlos feel? *(scared)*

- Invite children to tell about the characters in their own words. Discuss how knowing what the characters say and do and how they feel can help readers understand what is happening in the story.

- **Have children demonstrate understanding.** Ask volunteers to share what they have learned so far about identifying story characters and asking questions to learn more about them. Encourage children to tell about characters they know from familiar classroom read-alouds.

Step by Step

- **Review Part 1.** Remind children that a *character* is a person or animal in a story. Review the questions they can ask to learn more about characters.

- **Revisit the story.** Display *The Art Lesson.* Page through the book, using the pictures as prompts to have children recall the story. *(RL.K.2; RL.K.7)*

- **Model identifying characters.** Explain that you will model identifying and finding out more about the characters in a story. Display and read aloud page 3. Then think aloud:

  First I ask *Who is in this story?* **The words tell me that it is Tommy. He must be the boy here in this picture. Now I will try to learn more about him from the details in the story.**

  What does the character say? **Tommy doesn't say anything here, so I'll move on.** ***What does the character do?*** **I see in the picture that Tommy is drawing. The words say "He drew pictures everywhere he went." This goes along with the detail that he wants to be an artist. I can tell that drawing is important to Tommy.**

- Reread the last sentence, and ask:

  How does Tommy feel about drawing? *(happy; it is his favorite thing to do)*

- Explain that authors do not always explicitly say how a character feels. Sometimes readers must interpret this based on the details in the story. Point to Tommy's smile and the words "It was his favorite thing to do" as evidence that shows how he feels about drawing.

- Use the Close Reading activity to look for additional clues about the character's feelings.

- Tell children you will model how to complete the Student Book page by identifying and learning more about the character in this part of *The Art Lesson.*

- **Model completing the Student Book page.** Have children turn to Student Book page 42. For the first item, ask: *Who is this story mostly about?* Point to and name each picture *(a girl; a boy; a baby).* Demonstrate circling the correct answer. Continue with the second item. Ask: *What does Tommy want to be when he grows up? (a baker; an artist; a baseball player)*

Tip: Clarify for children that the images in the top row are not the exact characters from the story. Prior to circling the correct answer, model asking yourself *Is Tommy a girl, a boy, or a baby?*

- **Have children demonstrate understanding.** Display page 3. Read aloud the Turn and Talk activity. Model what a conversation with a partner should sound like by asking and answering the following question. *(SL.K.1; SL.K.2)*

  What does Tommy do to show he wants to be an artist? Ask and answer this question with your partner. *(He draws everywhere. He calls drawing his favorite thing to do. He puts his pictures up for sale.)*

Close Reading

- Remind children to use picture clues to find out how a character feels. Display page 3, and have children look closely at the illustration. Ask:

  Why does the picture of the juggler have a 5¢ note above it? *(The picture is for sale.)*

  Tommy thinks his drawings are good enough for someone to buy. What word might tell how he feels about his drawings? *(proud)*

  What is all over the sidewalk? *(drawings)*

  Do the drawings on the sidewalk tell us that Tommy is proud of his drawings, too? *(yes)* **Explain why.** *(He wants everyone to see them.)*

Step by Step

- **Review learning from Parts 1–2.** Remind children that they can ask questions about what a character says, does, and feels to learn about the character. Display page 3 of *The Art Lesson.* Ask children to review what Tommy does and how he feels about drawing.

- **Revisit the story.** Display *Chrysanthemum.* Page through the book, using the pictures as prompts to have children recall the story. *(RL.K.2; RL.K.7)*

- **Guide children to identify characters.** Tell children to listen for a character's name as you read. Display and read aloud pages 5–7, including the text in the illustrations. Ask:

    Who is in this story? *(Chrysanthemum)*

    Look at the pictures. Is Chrysanthemum a person? *(No. She is a mouse.)*

- Review that in many stories, animals or other non-human things can act just like people. Readers use their imaginations to pretend the characters are people.

- Remind children that they can ask and answer questions to learn more about characters. Have them listen as you read again for what Chrysanthemum does and how she feels.

    What does Chrysanthemum do? *(grows up; listens to her name; says her name; writes her name)*

    How does Chrysanthemum feel about her name? *(She loves it.)*

- Explain to children that you will work together to complete the Student Book page by identifying and learning more about the character in *Chrysanthemum.*

- **Guide children to complete the Student Book page.** Have children turn to Student Book page 43. For the first item, ask: *Who is the character in this story?* Point to and name each picture *(a mouse; an elephant; a penguin).* Have a volunteer tell which picture to circle. Continue with the second item. Ask: *How does Chrysanthemum feel about her name in this part of the story? (sad; surprised; happy)*

- Discuss the answers to the Student Book page. Help children point to evidence in the story that supports the correct answers.

- Use the Close Reading activity to provide additional practice in identifying a character's feelings.

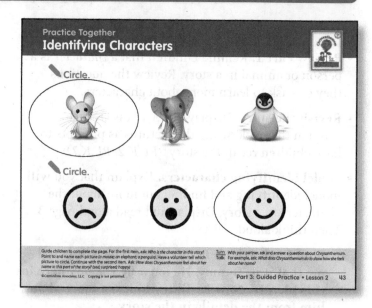

- **Have children demonstrate understanding.** Display pages 5–7 of *Chrysanthemum.* Read aloud the Turn and Talk activity. *(SL.K.1; SL.K.2)*

    With your partner, ask and answer a question about Chrysanthemum. For example, ask: *What does Chrysanthemum do to show how she feels about her name?* *(She whispers her name to herself. She draws hearts when she writes her name.)*

- Invite partners to share their questions with the class. Discuss the answers and help children find evidence in the story to support them.

Close Reading

- Guide children to use picture clues to find out how a character feels. Display page 7 and focus on the first picture. Ask:

    What face is Chrysanthemum making in the top picture? *(She is smiling.)*

    What is Chrysanthemum doing with her hands in the second picture? *(holding her heart)*

    What is drawn around Chrysanthemum's name in the bottom picture? *(hearts)*

- Discuss with children what they do to show they love something. Compare their answers with what Chrysanthemum is doing in the pictures.

Step by Step

- **Review learning from Parts 1–3.** Remind children that identifying characters and asking questions about them can help readers understand a story. Ask children to tell what they have already learned about *Chrysanthemum* from the beginning of the story.

- **Have children identify characters.** Display pages 18–19 of *Chrysanthemum*. Tell children to listen as you read to find out who is in this part of the story. (*Victoria; Mrs. Chud; Chrysanthemum*)

- Reread page 18 and display the picture. Ask:

  What is Chrysanthemum named after? (*a flower*)

  (Point to the picture.) **What is Chrysanthemum doing?** (*frowning and covering her ears*)

  Why is she doing this? (*Victoria is teasing her.*)

- Reread page 19 and display the illustration. Ask:

  How does Chrysanthemum feel about her name now? (*She feels sad.*)

> **Tip:** Model figuring out the meaning of *miserably* by rereading the text and looking at how unhappy Chrysanthemum looks in the picture. Help children define it in their own words and use it independently.

- Use the Close Reading activity to help children notice when a character's feelings change.

- Tell children that they will complete the Student Book page independently by identifying details about the character in this part of *Chrysanthemum*.

- **Have children complete the Student Book page independently.** Have children turn to page 44. For the first item, ask: *What is Chrysanthemum named after?* Point to and name each picture (*a dress; a flower; sneakers*). Have children circle their answers. Continue with the second item. Ask: *How does Chrysanthemum feel about her name in this part of the story?* (*happy; sad; surprised*)

- Discuss the answers to the Student Book page. Help children point to evidence in the story that supports the correct answers.

- **Have children demonstrate understanding.** Display pages 18–19 of *Chrysanthemum*. Read aloud the Turn and Talk activity. (*SL.K.1; SL.K.2*)

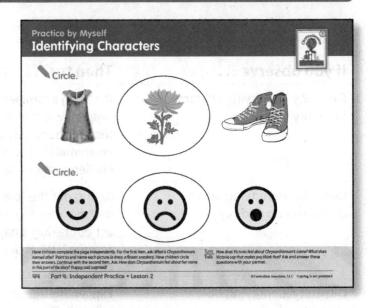

How does Victoria feel about Chrysanthemum's name? What does Victoria say that makes you think that? Ask and answer these questions with your partner. (*Victoria cannot believe Chrysanthemum's name. She says it is a flower that lives in a garden with worms and dirty things.*)

- Invite children to share their ideas with the class. Help them find evidence in the story to support their answers.

- **Have children reflect on their learning.** Invite children to tell what a *character* is and name the questions they can ask to learn more about them. Discuss how readers can use words and picture clues to learn what characters say, do, and feel.

Close Reading

- Tell children that characters can change the way they feel throughout a story. Reread page 19. Ask:

  What face is Chrysanthemum making? (*She is frowning.*)

  What clues in the words tell us how Chrysanthemum feels? (*the words "thought Chrysanthemum miserably"*)

  Why is Chrysanthemum sad now when she was happy before? (*Victoria keeps teasing her and making her feel bad about her name.*)

- Emphasize that it is important to notice when characters' feelings change in a story.

Assessment and Remediation

If you observe . . .	Then try . . .
Difficulty identifying characters in a story	Retelling a familiar story with just one character, such as *The Fox and the Grapes*. Ask: *Who is the character in the story?* Before children respond, remind them that the answer to a *who* question is the name of a person or an animal that acts like a person. As children become more comfortable, challenge them with stories that have multiple characters.
Difficulty identifying what characters do and say	Acting out the role of a familiar story character, such as Hare in *The Tortoise and the Hare*. Say: *I can beat you in a race, Tortoise.* Jog a few laps, and then act out taking a nap. Ask: *What does Hare say? ("I can beat you in a race, Tortoise.") What does Hare do? (runs and takes a nap)* Repeat for the character of Tortoise.
Difficulty identifying how characters feel	Explaining that sometimes authors show how characters feel instead of telling it. Demonstrate various feelings through facial expressions and body language. For example, put on a big smile and jump up and down. Say: *This is awesome!* Ask children to tell how you feel. *(happy; excited)* Repeat with other feelings, such as *sad, mad, scared,* and *worried*. Have children join in pantomiming and identifying each other's feelings. Then help children practice identifying a character's feelings by looking at words and actions.

Connect to the Anchor Standard

R3: *Analyze how and why individuals, events, and ideas develop and interact over the course of a text.*

Throughout the grades, Standard 3 explores the concept of characters as central to a story's framework. As they progress through the grades, students will be required to go beyond simply identifying characters' actions and emotions to analyzing their motivations and the impact of their actions on story events. As students examine characters individually and in relation to other characters, they may ask questions such as these: *How do the characters react to challenges and obstacles? How do the characters' actions move the story in a particular direction? How would the story have changed if the characters had acted differently? How do the characters interact with each other? What effect does this have on the story?* Use the following activities to help children begin this transition.

- Read aloud pages 7–11 of *The Art Lesson*. Ask: *How does Tommy's family feel about his love of drawing? What makes you think that?* Then have children imagine that Tommy's family tells him to put away his crayons and stop drawing. Discuss how the story might have had a different ending if that had happened. *(SL.K.1; SL.K.2)*

- Read aloud page 17 of *Chrysanthemum*. Ask children to tell what Chrysanthemum's classmates think of her name. Talk about how that makes her feel. Then read aloud page 30. Discuss how the classmates' attitude toward Chrysanthemum's name has changed and the reason why. Talk about how this change affects the way Chrysanthemum feels at the end of the story.

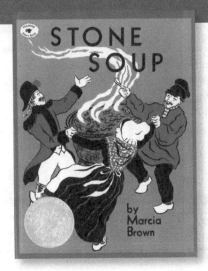

STONE SOUP

by Marcia Brown

Lesson Objectives

You will read aloud *Stone Soup,* which children will revisit in later lessons. With prompting and support, children will:

• Answer questions about key details in the story.

• Describe characters and major events, using key details.

• Retell the story, including key details.

About the Text

Summary

Three soldiers come to a village in need of food and sleep, but the peasants hide their food. So the soldiers offer to make stone soup. The curious peasants bring food to add to the soup, which leads to a big feast in the village. The clever soldiers leave the village well fed and rested.

Genre: Folktale

• Explain that *Stone Soup* is a folktale—a story from long ago that people have told again and again.

• Folktale characters often trick others in order to teach them a lesson. Help children think about how the soldiers trick the peasants in *Stone Soup.*

Critical Vocabulary

• Prior to reading, briefly define the following words:

feared (p. 8) were scared or afraid of

spare (p. 12) to have enough to give some away

boil (p. 22) to make something hot enough to bubble

dined (p. 33) ate a meal

• As you read, pause to point to the words as you encounter them, and review their definitions.

Word Bank

• Display a word bank of the Critical Vocabulary and the characters *(soldiers, peasants).*

• Add other important story words, such as *fetch* and *feast,* on subsequent readings.

New Concepts: Feast

• Explain that a *feast* is a large meal that is shared by many people. Often a feast is a way for a community to gather and celebrate. Point out that Thanksgiving dinner is an example of a feast.

• Have children listen closely for the foods that make up the feast that the soldiers and peasants enjoy in *Stone Soup.*

Ready *Teacher Toolbox* Teacher-Toolbox.com

	Prerequisite Skills	RL.K.2
Ready Lessons		✓
Tools for Instruction	✓ ✓	✓
Interactive Tutorials	✓ ✓	

CCSS Focus

RL.K.2 *With prompting and support, retell familiar stories, including key details.*

ADDITIONAL STANDARDS: RL.K.1; RL.K.3; RL.K.7; RF.K.2a, 2c, 2e; W.K.2; SL.K.1; SL.K.2; SL.K.4; SL.K.5; SL.K.6; L.K.1a, 1e; L.K.2d; L.K.5c *(See page A38 for full text.)*

Step by Step

- **Introduce Stone Soup.** Display the book. Read aloud the title and the name of the author, Marcia Brown. Point out that she also drew the pictures.

- **Set the purpose for reading.** Review that a *character* is a person or animal in a story. Tell children that readers make sense of a story by identifying characters and thinking about what they do and what happens to them.

- Explain that as you read aloud, children should listen closely to identify the characters in this story.

- **Read aloud Stone Soup.** Read the story all the way through, pausing only to briefly define challenging vocabulary.

- **Guide children to identify the characters.** After reading, use questions such as these to help children identify the characters. *(RL.K.1; RL.K.3; SL.K.1; SL.K.2)*

  Who does the story say is hungry and tired? *(the three soldiers)*

  Who do the soldiers meet when they get to the village? *(the peasants)*

  > **Tip:** Explain to children that although the story gives the names of several of the peasants, they do not need to remember every name. Instead, they can think of the peasants as one character.

- **Have children draw characters.** Direct children to turn to Student Book page 13. Have them draw a picture of the three soldiers and some of the peasants. Display illustrations on pages 16–17 to help them recall what the characters look like.

- **Have children discuss story evidence.** Read aloud the Turn and Talk activity. Help children use their pictures and story evidence to explain what they know about each group of characters. *(SL.K.4; SL.K.5)*

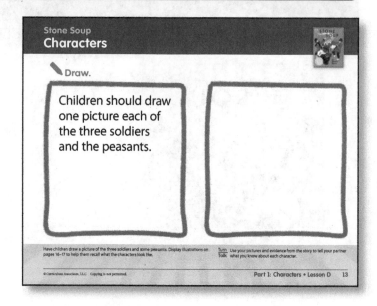

- Guide their discussions with the following prompts:

  What do the soldiers hope to get in the village? *(food and beds to sleep in)*

  How do the peasants behave when the soldiers first get to town? *(They hide all the food and lie about having no room for the soldiers to sleep.)*

  Why do the peasants behave this way? *(They fear strangers.)*

  How do the soldiers get the peasants to share with them? *(They make stone soup.)*

- Invite children to share what they know about the soldiers and the peasants in class discussion.

ELL Support: Idioms

- Tell children an *idiom* is a group of words that, when used together, have a different meaning than what the words mean by themselves.

- Point out the idiom "a bite to eat" on page 8. Explain that you don't really eat just a bite. Ask children how much they get when they take "a bite" of food. *(a little bit of food)* Together, discuss that this idiom means "a little bit of food to eat."

- Discuss some or all of these idioms from the story: "So it went" (p. 14); "drew near" (p. 18); "none too large" (p. 20); "fit for a king" (p. 36). Help children see that each idiom phrase has a meaning distinct from the meanings of each word in the phrase.

Step by Step

- **Reread and discuss the beginning.** Read aloud pages 7–19. As you read, help children connect the words they hear to what is happening in the illustrations. *(RL.K.7)*

- Use questions such as these to guide discussion. *(RL.K.1; SL.K.1; SL.K.2)*

    Pages 7–9: What do the soldiers want?
    (They want a good dinner and a place to sleep.)

    Pages 10–15: What do the peasants tell the soldiers when they ask for food? *(They tell them they don't have any food to give them.)*

    Tip: Help children understand that *peasants* are farmers who grow their own food and do not have much money. Discuss with children the reasons why the peasants might be reluctant to share.

    Page 18: What do the soldiers tell the peasants they are going to cook? *(stone soup)*

- **Focus on a key detail.** Direct children to turn to Student Book page 14. Have them draw a picture that shows what the peasants do when they see the soldiers coming to their village. Reread pages 10–11 to help them recall the details. *(RL.K.3)*

- Use the Close Reading activity to help children understand why the peasants hide their food.

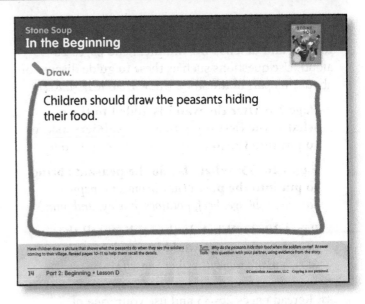

Stone Soup
In the Beginning

✎ Draw.

Children should draw the peasants hiding their food.

Have children draw a picture that shows what the peasants do when they see the soldiers coming to their village. Reread pages 10–11 to help them recall the details. | **Turn Talk** *Why do the peasants hide their food when the soldiers come?* Answer this question with your partner, using evidence from the story.

14 Part 2: Beginning • Lesson D ©Curriculum Associates, LLC Copying is not permitted.

- **Have children discuss story evidence.** Read aloud the Turn and Talk activity. Guide partners to have a conversation, beginning as follows:

    Why do the peasants hide their food when the soldiers come? *(They are afraid of strangers and think the soldiers will eat all of their food.)*

- Invite children to share their ideas with the class.

- Work with children to identify the most important ideas from this part of the story. Encourage them to use evidence from the story as well as their drawings to help explain their ideas. *(SL.K.4)*

Tier Two Vocabulary: *lowered*

- Display the last sentence on page 10. Read it aloud. Underline the word *lowered*.

- Explain that *lowered* tells what the peasants did with the buckets of milk. Point out that the word *down* gives a clue about where something gets lowered. Work with children to determine that the word *lowered* means "moved down."

- Raise your hand and then lower it, describing your action. Say: *I lowered my hand.* Have children repeat the motion and the sentence after you.

- Then have children practice using *lowered* to tell about other situations. For example, *I lowered the box to the floor.* *(L.K.5c)*

Close Reading

- Display and reread page 10. Use these prompts to help children see why the peasants hide their food.

    How do the peasants feel about the soldiers? *(They don't like them. They say soldiers are always hungry.)*

    When the peasants say they "have little enough" for themselves, what do they mean? *(They have barely enough food for themselves.)*

    Why do the peasants hide their food? *(They think that the soldiers might eat all of it.)*

- Emphasize that it is important to understand why characters do things in a story.

Step by Step

- **Reread and discuss the middle.** Read pages 20–33 aloud. Use questions such as these to guide discussion about this part of the story. *(RL.K.1; SL.K.1; SL.K.2)*

  Page 25: After the water is added to the pot, what is the first ingredient the soldiers ask for to put into the pot? *(three round, smooth stones)*

  Pages 26–33: What else do the peasants bring to put into the pot? *(They bring salt, pepper, carrots, cabbage, beef, potatoes, barley, and milk.)*

  Pages 30–33: What do the soldiers tell the peasants the soup would be good enough for? *(a rich man's table; the king himself)*

  Tip: Reread pages 26–33 and use your tone of voice to imitate what the soldiers might sound like. Use your voice to help children understand that the soldiers are pretending not to know that the peasants have food to share.

- **Focus on a key detail.** Direct children to turn to Student Book page 15. Have them draw a picture that shows some of the foods the peasants bring to add to the stone soup. Reread pages 26–33 to help them recall the details. *(RL.K.3)*

- Use the Close Reading activity to help children understand why the peasants help the soldiers after all.

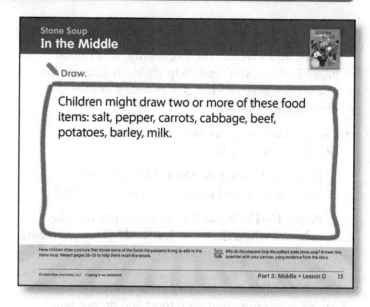

Stone Soup
In the Middle

Draw.

Children might draw two or more of these food items: salt, pepper, carrots, cabbage, beef, potatoes, barley, milk.

Have children draw a picture that shows some of the foods the peasants bring to add to the stone soup. Reread pages 26–33 to help them recall the details.

Turn Talk *Why do the peasants help the soldiers make stone soup?* Answer this question with your partner, using evidence from the story.

©Curriculum Associates, LLC Copying is not permitted. Part 3: Middle • Lesson D 15

- **Have children discuss story evidence.** Read aloud the Turn and Talk activity. Guide partners to have a conversation, beginning as follows:

  Why do the peasants help the soldiers make stone soup? *(They are curious about how anyone could make soup out of stones. They want to see what happens when it's done.)*

- As a class, discuss how the soldiers trick the peasants into giving them food when they said they had none. Emphasize that the soldiers never intended to eat the stones.

- Work with children to identify the most important ideas from this part of the story. Encourage children to use their own words to explain the trick.

Tier Two Vocabulary: *steaming*

- Display the last sentence on page 33. Read it aloud. Underline the word *steaming*.

- Remind children that *steaming* is something that the hot soup is doing. Work together to determine that *steaming* means "letting out steam." Review that *steam* is what water turns into when it is very hot. It can look like fog.

- Provide an example. Say: *The steaming water in the teapot was very hot.* Then work with children to brainstorm other things that steam. *(iron; food on the stove; hot chocolate)*

- Have children use the word *steaming* to describe the things you brainstormed together. *(L.K.5c)*

Close Reading

- Reread page 28. Use these questions to help children understand why the peasants bring food for the stone soup.

  What do the soldiers use as the first ingredient? *(three round stones)*

  What do the soldiers ask for to help make the soup better? *(more ingredients, such as cabbage, carrots, and potatoes)*

  Why do the peasants bring the food the soldiers ask for? *(They think the soup is "magic." They want to have some of the magic soup made of stones.)*

Step by Step

- **Reread and discuss the end.** Read pages 34–47 aloud. Discuss the way the story ends, using questions such as these. (*RL.K.1; SL.K.1; SL.K.2*)

    Pages 34–39: What do the peasants do after the stone soup is ready? (*They have a feast. They eat, drink, dance, and sing.*)

    Pages 40–43: What do the peasants do for the soldiers after the feast? (*They invite them to sleep in their homes.*)

    Pages 44–47: Why do the peasants thank the soldiers? (*They are thankful to the soldiers for teaching them how to make stone soup. They think they will never be hungry again.*)

> **Tip:** Discuss with children whether the stones in stone soup are really a necessary ingredient. Point out that the stones are part of the soldiers' trick to get the peasants to give them the food.

- **Focus on a key detail.** Direct children to turn to Student Book page 16. Have them draw a picture that shows what the peasants and the soldiers do when the stone soup is ready. Reread pages 36–37 to help them recall the details. (*RL.K.3*)

- Use the Close Reading activity to identify how the soldiers' problems are solved.

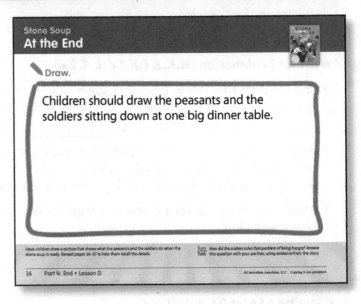

Stone Soup
At the End

Draw.

Children should draw the peasants and the soldiers sitting down at one big dinner table.

Have children draw a picture that shows what the peasants and the soldiers do when the stone soup is ready. Reread pages 36–37 to help them recall the details.

Turn Talk *How did the soldiers solve their problem of being hungry? Answer this question with your partner, using evidence from the story.*

16   Part 4: End • Lesson D   ©Curriculum Associates, LLC Copying is not permitted.

- **Have children discuss story evidence.** Read aloud the Turn and Talk activity. Guide partners to have a conversation, beginning as follows:

    How do the soldiers solve their problem of being hungry? (*They pretend to make a magical soup and get the peasants to bring real food, such as carrots, cabbage, beef, and potatoes, to put into it.*)

- Invite children to share their ideas with the class.

- **Retell *Stone Soup*.** Ask children to role-play a retelling of the story. Have three children be the soldiers and several other children be the peasants. Prompt children in turn to tell what happens at the beginning, middle, and end of the story. Encourage them to include details about what their characters are thinking.

Integrating Foundational Skills

Use these activities to integrate foundational skills into your reading of *Stone Soup*.

1   Say *stone* and *bone*, emphasizing the ending sound /ōn/. Then have children clap for words that rhyme with *stone*. Use these words: *cone, rain, loan, moon, phone, star.* Invite children to name other pairs of rhyming words. (*RF.K.2a*)

2   Say and have children blend: /r/ /ōd/, *road*; /d/ /ā/, *day*; /s/ /ăk/, *sack*; /b/ /ěd/, *bed*; /m/ /ēt/, *meet*; /s/ /ăd/, *sad*. Now say *sad*. Substitute /b/ for /s/ to make *bad*, saying the new word together. Repeat with the earlier words, now making *toad, pay, back, led, feet.* (*RF.K.2c, RF.K.2e*)

Close Reading

- Read aloud pages 36–43. Use these questions to help children understand how the soldiers solved their problem from earlier in the story:

    What did the soldiers want when they first came to the village? (*food and beds to sleep in*)

    After eating, what do the peasants give the soldiers? (*the best beds in the village to sleep in*)

    How does making stone soup solve the soldiers' problems? (*They get food because of all the other ingredients the peasants bring to put in the soup. They get beds to sleep in after they make the "magic" soup for everyone.*)

Writing Activity

Write an Explanation (W.K.2; L.K.1.a; L.K.2.d)

- Tell children that you will work together to write a recipe for stone soup. Reread pages 20–33 from *Stone Soup*. Ask children to tell what soup ingredients they hear as you read. Write the ingredients on chart paper. (*stones, salt, pepper, carrots, cabbage, beef, potatoes, barley, milk*)

- Next, have children tell the steps for making the soup. Guide them using questions such as these: *What do we do first? Then what do we add? What do we do last?* As children respond, write the steps in order. Call on volunteers to share the pen in order to write letters and simple VC and CVC words that they know.

- After completing the recipe, reread it together with children. Have children draw a picture of the completed soup.

Speaking and Listening Activity

Describe a Feast (SL.K.4; SL.K.6)

- Display the illustrations on pages 36–39, and reread the pages aloud. Review the feast that the soldiers and peasants had when the stone soup was finished.

- Have children take turns describing what the soldiers and peasants ate and drank, where the feast took place, and what they did during and after the feast. Reread as needed to help them recall details from the story.

- Remind children that describing words tell what things look, feel, smell, taste, and sound like. Help them brainstorm some of these words from each category to use as they describe the feast.

Language Activity

Prepositions (L.K.1.e)

- Tell children that *prepositions* are words that tell more about nouns, verbs, or adjectives. Explain that there are many different prepositions, but today you will focus on prepositions that help tell where something is.

- Display and read the following sentence from page 10 of *Stone Soup*: "They pushed sacks of barley under the hay in the lofts." Underline the words *under* and *in*.

- Explain that the word *under* is a preposition. Ask a volunteer to tell or demonstrate what it means to be under something. Help them understand that *under* means having something above.

- Then explain that the word *in* is a preposition. Ask a volunteer to tell or demonstrate what it means to be in something. They may need to define *in* as the opposite of *out*.

- Return to the sentence and discuss with children where the peasants hid the barley.

- Continue to practice with other "where" prepositions in the story, such as *down* (page 10), *over* (page 11), and *through* (page 14).

- Have children use the prepositions in oral sentences about topics of their choice.

Identifying Setting

CCSS

RL.K.3: With prompting and support, identify . . . settings . . . in a story.

Required Read Alouds: A *(Jamaica's Blue Marker)*; D *(Stone Soup)*

Lesson Objectives

- Recognize that the setting is when and where a story takes place.

- Identify the setting in a story.

- Understand how thinking about the setting can help you better comprehend a story.

The Learning Progression

- **Prior to K:** Children should have a basic understanding of the concepts of *when* and *where*.

- **Grade K: CCSS RL.K.3 expects children to identify settings in a story with prompting and support.**

- **Grade 1:** CCSS RL.1.3 further develops the standard by having children use key details to describe settings in a story with more independence.

Tap Children's Prior Knowledge

- Tell children that they are going to describe when and where things happen each day.

- Post a long sheet of paper horizontally. On it, create a picture time line. Divide the time line into parts: *morning, noon* (or *lunchtime*), and *afternoon*. Explain that each time period tells when something happens.

- Discuss with children when things happen at different parts of the day. Ask: *When do we have storytime? When do we eat lunch?* Draw a simple sketch, such as a book or a sandwich, for each response, and post it on the time line in the appropriate section.

- Now ask a *where* question, such as *Where do we go in the afternoon?* Draw and write children's responses on the time line.

- Continue asking *when* and *where* questions about typical school activities.

- When the time line is complete, read it aloud. Emphasize that the time line shows when and where things happen.

- Tell children that in this lesson, they will learn to think about when and where things happen in a story.

Ready *Teacher Toolbox*   Teacher-Toolbox.com

	Prerequisite Skills	RL.K.3
Ready Lessons		✓
Tools for Instruction		✓
Interactive Tutorials		✓

Additional CCSS

RL.K.2; RL.K.7; SL.K.1; SL.K.2 *(See page A38 for full text.)*

Step by Step

- **Introduce the standard.** Tell children they will learn about the setting in a story. Explain that the setting helps them understand the story.

- Ask children to listen carefully as you read aloud the following story:

   One summer day, Grasshopper hopped in a field. He was looking for Ant. Soon he saw Ant. She was looking for seeds to eat.

- Tell children to listen again for words that tell when the story happens. Repeat the first sentence, emphasizing the first three words. Then ask:

   When does the story happen? *(one summer day)*

- Have children listen again for words that tell where the story happens. Repeat the first sentence, emphasizing the last three words. Then ask:

   Where does the story happen? *(in a field)*

- Tell children that in their Student Books, they will learn questions they can ask to identify the setting of a story.

- **Read aloud the Student Book page.** Have children turn to Student Book page 45. Read aloud the page as children listen and follow along.

- Point to the first bullet and reread the question. Explain that when something takes place, it happens. Reread the story about the grasshopper. Then ask:

   When did the grasshopper hop in a field? *(one summer day)*

   What are some other words we use that tell when something happens? *(before; after; today)*

> **Tip:** Use a classroom calendar to help children recall other time words, such as days of the week or months of the year.

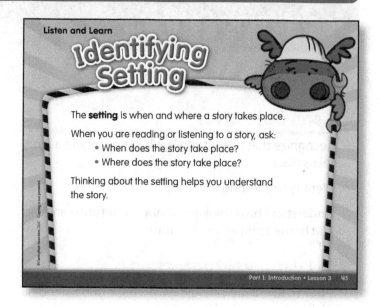

Listen and Learn

Identifying Setting

The **setting** is when and where a story takes place.

When you are reading or listening to a story, ask:
- When does the story take place?
- Where does the story take place?

Thinking about the setting helps you understand the story.

Part 1: Introduction • Lesson 3   45

- Point to the second bullet and reread the question. Explain that finding out where something happens means figuring out a place. Refer back to the story about the grasshopper and ask:

   Where does the story happen? *(in a field)*

   What other words tell about a place? *(in my house; in my classroom; at the playground)*

- Help children understand that good readers ask questions about the setting to better understand a story. They look for answers in the story words and pictures.

- **Have children demonstrate understanding.** Ask volunteers to share what they have learned so far about identifying the setting in a story. Prompt them to identify the setting of classroom read-alouds.

Part 2: Modeled Instruction

Step by Step

- **Review Part 1.** Remind children that the setting is where and when a story takes place. Review examples of words that tell *where* and *when*.

- **Revisit the story.** Display *Jamaica's Blue Marker*. Page through the book, using the pictures as prompts to have children recall the story. (RL.K.2; RL.K.7)

- **Model identifying setting.** Display and read aloud pages 22–23. Think aloud as you model how to identify the setting:

   I want to figure out the setting in this story. First I will ask where it happens. The first sentence tells me: the classroom. In the picture, I see kids sitting at desks reading and writing. This looks like a classroom to me.

   Tip: Children may confuse the office as the setting because it is named in the second sentence. Help them use picture clues to recognize the classroom as the setting in this part of the story.

   Next I will ask when it happens. The first sentence tells me that as well. It says "on Friday morning." The setting of this part of the story is Friday morning in the classroom.

- Tell children you will model how to complete the Student Book page by identifying the setting in this part of *Jamaica's Blue Marker*.

- **Model completing the Student Book page.** Have children turn to Student Book page 46. For the first item, ask: *When does this part of the story take place?* Point to and name each picture (*morning; evening; nighttime*). Demonstrate circling the correct answer. Continue with the second item. Ask: *Where does this part of the story take place?* Model drawing the setting. Have children draw in their own books.

- Help children point to evidence in the story that supports the circled answer. Then have them share their drawings. Prompt them to tell which details in their drawing match details in the story.

- **Have children demonstrate understanding.** Display pages 22–23. Read aloud the Turn and Talk activity. Model what a conversation with a partner should sound like by asking and answering the following questions. (SL.K.1; SL.K.2)

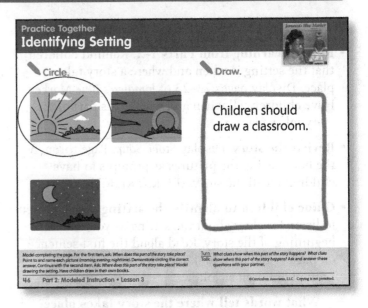

What clues show when this part of the story happens? What clues show where this part of the story happens? Ask and answer these questions with your partner. (When: The words say it is Friday morning. Where: The words say "Russell didn't come to the classroom" and the picture shows students in a classroom.)

- Use the Close Reading activity to help children identify multiple settings in a story.

Close Reading

- Explain that many stories have more than one setting. Display pages 20–21. Ask:

   Where does this part of the story take place? (at Jamaica's house)

- Now display pages 22–23. Ask:

   Where does this part of the story take place? (in the classroom)

- Page through the rest of the book. Ask:

   Where does the rest of the story take place? (in the classroom)

- Discuss the picture clues that children used to figure out the setting each time.

- Help children understand that the setting in a story can change. Readers need to pay attention to the words and pictures to make sure they know where each part of the story is taking place.

Step by Step

- **Review learning from Parts 1–2.** Remind children that the setting is when and where a story takes place. Display pages 22–23 of *Jamaica's Blue Marker*. Have children tell when and where this part of the story takes place.

- **Revisit the story.** Display *Stone Soup*. Page through the book, using the pictures as prompts to have children recall the story. (RL.K.2; RL.K.7)

- **Guide children to identify the setting.** Ask children to listen for clues about the setting as you read the beginning of the story. Read aloud the first sentence on page 7, and then look together at the picture. Prompt children as follows:

    What words tell where the story takes place?
    (*on a road in a strange country*)

    What does the picture show about the place?
    (*The soldiers are on a road with lots of trees.*)

> **Tip:** Help children understand that the words "in a strange country" mean that this is a place the soldiers have not been to before. It is new to them, and they are not sure what they will find there.

- Read aloud page 8. Guide children to identify when the story takes place. Help them understand that the time of day is evening because the lights in the village are on. When the soldiers mention "dinner tonight," they probably mean soon or in a little while.

- Explain to children that you will work together to complete the Student Book page by identifying the setting of *Stone Soup*.

- **Guide children to complete the Student Book page.** Have children turn to Student Book page 47. For the first item, ask: *When does this part of the story take place?* Point to and name each picture (*morning; evening; nighttime*). Have a volunteer tell which picture to circle. Continue with the second item. Ask: *Where does this part of the story take place?* Have children draw the setting.

- Review and discuss the Student Book page together. Have volunteers tell about their drawings.

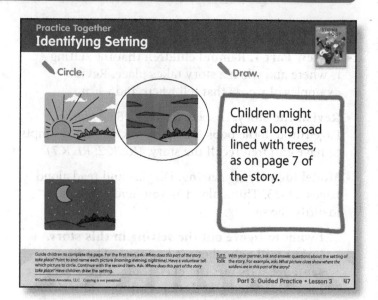

- **Have children demonstrate understanding.** Display pages 7–9 of *Stone Soup*. Read aloud the Turn and Talk activity. (SL.K.1; SL.K.2)

    With your partner, ask and answer questions about the setting of the story. For example, ask: *What picture clues show where the soldiers are in this part of the story?* (*The soldiers are on a road with a lot of trees, walking toward a village.*)

- Use the Close Reading activity to help children identify multiple settings in a story.

Close Reading

- Remind children that stories often have more than one setting. Display pages 7–9 and review when and where this part of the story takes place (*on a road in a strange country during the day*).

- Turn to page 10 and read it aloud. Prompt:

    Where does the picture show this part of the story taking place? (*in the loft*)

    What clues tell about setting? (*The words say "in the lofts." The pictures show a space that is high above the door.*)

- Remind children to pay attention to clues in the words and pictures to make sure they know where each part of the story is taking place.

Step by Step

- **Review learning from Parts 1–3.** Remind children that the setting is when and where a story takes place. Display pages 7–9 of *Stone Soup*. Have children recall questions they asked about the setting on these pages.

- **Have children identify the setting.** Display and read aloud pages 44–45 of *Stone Soup*. Tell children they will use the words and pictures to identify where and when this part of the story takes place. Reread the first sentence on page 44. Then ask:

    What words tell when this part of the story takes place? (*"in the morning"*)

    What do the words and picture tell about where this part of the story takes place? (*The words say "in the square." The picture shows a big area with houses all around it.*)

> **Tip:** Discuss how asking questions can help readers define unfamiliar words. For example, model figuring out the meaning of *send-off* by asking why the whole village has gathered and what the soldiers will do next.

- Use the Close Reading activity to help children understand the setting on pages 44–45.

- Tell children that they will complete the Student Book page by identifying the setting in this part of *Stone Soup*.

- **Have children complete the Student Book page independently.** Have children turn to Student Book page 48. For the first item, ask: *When does this part of the story take place?* Point to and name each picture (*morning; evening; nighttime*). Have children circle their answers. Continue with the second item. Ask: *Where does this part of the story take place?* Have children draw the setting.

- Review and discuss the Student Book page together. Have volunteers tell about their drawings.

- **Have children demonstrate understanding.** Display pages 44–45 of *Stone Soup*. Read aloud the Turn and Talk activity. (*SL.K.1; SL.K.2*)

    With your partner, ask and answer questions about clues to the setting of the story. (*When are the peasants and soldiers saying good-bye? [in the morning]*)

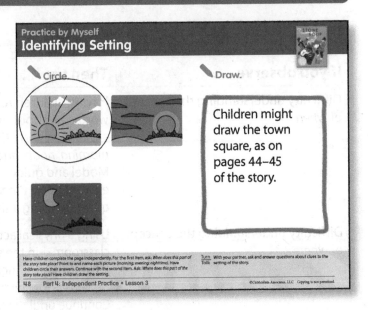

Practice by Myself
Identifying Setting

Circle.

Draw.

Children might draw the town square, as on pages 44–45 of the story.

Have children complete the page independently. For the first item, ask: *When does this part of the story take place?* Point to and name each picture (*morning; evening; nighttime*). Have children circle their answers. Continue with the second item. Ask: *Where does this part of the story take place?* Have children draw the setting.

Turn and Talk With your partner, ask and answer questions about clues to the setting of the story.

48 Part 4: Independent Practice • Lesson 3   ©Curriculum Associates, LLC   Copying is not permitted.

- Point to the picture on pages 44–45 and ask: *Where are the peasants and the soldiers?* Have partners think together about the answer.

- **Have children reflect on their learning.** Invite children to tell what they have learned about identifying the setting of a story. Ask volunteers to tell what questions they can ask, and discuss why identifying the setting is important to understanding a story.

Close Reading

- Display pages 44–45. Read the first sentence and say:

    The words tell that the setting is "in the square." If we don't know what the square is, we can look at the picture for clues.

    Is the square big or small? (*big*) **How do you know?** (*There are many people in it.*)

    Is the square inside or outside the village? (*inside*) **How do you know?** (*There are buildings around it.*)

    What is the square? (*The square is a big open space in the village.*)

- Emphasize that readers can use both words and pictures to identify the setting of a story.

Assessment and Remediation

If you observe . . .	Then try . . .
Difficulty understanding the concept of *when*	Having children review and use words that tell *when*. Explain that *when* words tell about time. Using the time line created in the activity on page 37, a calendar, and other schedule resources, discuss words such as these: *morning, noon, afternoon, night; day, week, month; minute, hour; now, later.* Model and guide children to use the time words in oral sentences. For example, ask: *When are we going to the movies?* Have children answer the question using a time word. *(We are going to the movies in the afternoon.)*
Difficulty understanding the concept of *where*	Using a physical activity. Assign children to stand in various places in the classroom—in the science center or in the book area, for example. Explain that telling where someone is names a place. Ask: *Where is [child's name]?* Model responses for children. *(He is in the writing center; she is in the math center.)* Continue until the location of each child has been named.
Difficulty identifying the setting in a story	Using a well-known picture book in which the setting is clearly shown, such as *Goodnight Moon.* Display the pictures that show the setting and discuss picture clues. Ask: *What place does this picture show? When does the story take place?* If children need additional support, ask either/or questions: *Is this a bedroom or a classroom? Is it daytime or nighttime?*

Connect to the Anchor Standard

R3: *Analyze how and why individuals, events, and ideas develop and interact over the course of a text.*

Throughout the grades, Standard 3 progresses from having students simply recognize when and where a story takes place to having them describe the setting in more depth based on key details. Students will learn to compare and contrast two or more settings and explore how settings impact the development of a story. Students might consider questions such as these: *What details about the setting help me better understand characters and events? Why does an author use more than one setting in a story? If the setting were different, how might the story change?* Use the following activities to help children begin this transition.

- Point out that most of *Jamaica's Blue Marker* takes place at school, but some scenes happen at Jamaica's home. Read aloud page 14 and pages 20–21. Have children consider why the author changes the setting from school to Jamaica's home on these pages. Discuss the scene where Jamaica's family explains how Russell might be feeling about moving and how their perspective changes Jamaica's feelings about Russell. *(SL.K.1)*

- Read aloud pages 8–11 of *Stone Soup* and recall the setting—a village of peasants. Review that peasants are farmers who grow their own food. Have children consider how the story might have changed if the setting were different. Ask: *What might have happened if the soldiers had arrived at a king's castle?* Guide them to understand that a king might have given the soldiers food and a place to stay. Then the soldiers would not have had to play the trick of making stone soup.

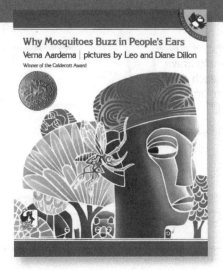

Lesson Objectives

You will read aloud *Why Mosquitoes Buzz in People's Ears*, which children will revisit in later lessons. With prompting and support, children will:

- Answer questions about key details in the story.
- Describe characters and major events, using key details.
- Retell the story, including key details.

About the Text

Summary

A mosquito's lie sets off a chain of events that ends with the death of an owlet. Sad Mother Owl refuses to wake the sun, and the animals meet to find out who is at fault. To this day, the mosquito feels guilty and whines in people's ears about it.

Genre: Folktale

- Why *Mosquitoes Buzz in People's Ears* is a folktale—a story from long ago that people tell again and again.
- Tell children that some folktales explain why something happens. Have them listen closely to this folktale to find out why mosquitoes buzz in people's ears.

Critical Vocabulary

- Prior to reading, briefly define the following words:

  alarm (p. 10) way of getting others to pay attention

  warn (p. 11) to tell others about danger

  council (p. 14) a group that works together to solve a problem

  fault (p. 17) blame for doing something wrong

- As you read, pause to point to the words as you encounter them, and review their definitions.

Word Bank

- Display a word bank of the Critical Vocabulary and the characters' names (*mosquito, Mother Owl, King Lion,* etc.).
- Add other important story words, such as *yam, deaf,* and *mischief,* on subsequent readings.

New Concepts: Mosquitoes

- Ask children if they have ever gotten an itchy bug bite. Explain that the bite probably came from a type of insect called a *mosquito* when they were playing outside.
- Explain that most people think mosquitoes that buzz around them are pests. Have children listen for details in the story about how a mosquito bothers others.

▮ **Ready** *Teacher Toolbox*   *Teacher-Toolbox.com*

	Prerequisite Skills	RL.K.2
Ready Lessons		✓
Tools for Instruction	✓ ✓	✓
Interactive Tutorials	✓ ✓	

CCSS Focus

RL.K.2 *With prompting and support, retell familiar stories, including key details.*

ADDITIONAL STANDARDS: RL.K.1; RL.K.3; RL.K.7; RF.K.1.b, d; RF.K.2.c, e; RF.K.3.c; W.K.3; SL.K.1; SL.K.2; SL.K.4; SL.K.5; SL.K.6; L.K.1.a, b; L.K.2.c, d; L.K.5.c *(See page A38 for full text.)*

Step by Step

- **Introduce Why Mosquitoes Buzz in People's Ears.** Display the book. Read aloud the title and the name of the author, Verna Aardema. Then read the names of the illustrators, Leo and Diane Dillon, and explain that they drew the pictures.

- **Set the purpose for reading.** Review that a *character* is a person or animal in a story. Tell children that readers make sense of a story by identifying the characters and thinking about what they do and what happens to them.

- Explain that as you read aloud, children should listen closely to identify the characters in this story.

- **Read aloud Why Mosquitoes Buzz in People's Ears.** Read the story all the way through, pausing only to briefly define challenging vocabulary and unfamiliar animals, such as the iguana or the python.

Tip: Explain that the nonwords, such as *mek, mek, mek, mek,* on page 7, tell the sounds the animals are making. These sounds help readers imagine what is happening. Invite children to make the sounds with you as you encounter the words.

- **Guide children to identify the characters.** After reading, use questions such as these to help children identify the characters. (*RL.K.1; RL.K.3; SL.K.1; SL.K.2*)

  What animals did we read about in the story?
  (*a mosquito, an iguana, a python, a rabbit, a crow, a monkey, some owls, a lion, an antelope*)

  Which animal started all the trouble?
  (*the mosquito*)

  What did the mosquito do?
  (*She told the iguana a lie.*)

  Which animal was supposed to wake up the sun? (*Mother Owl*)

- **Have children draw characters.** Direct children to turn to Student Book page 17. Have them draw a picture of the mosquito and Mother Owl. Display the illustrations on pages 6, 12, and 27 to help them recall what each character looks like.

- **Have children discuss story evidence.** Read aloud the Turn and Talk activity. Help children use their pictures and story evidence to explain what they know about each character. (*SL.K.4; SL.K.5*)

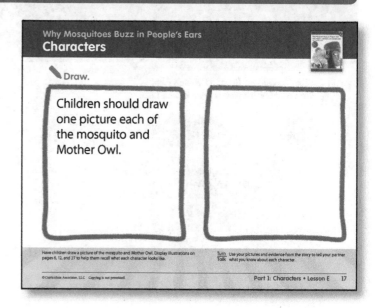

- Guide their discussions with the following prompts:

  Why does Mother Owl feel sad?
  (*One of her babies is dead.*)

  Why does the mosquito buzz in people's ears?
  (*She is asking if everyone is still angry at her.*)

- Invite children to share what they know about the mosquito and Mother Owl, as well as any other animals from the story, in class discussion.

ELL Support: Verbs

- Tell children that some words, called *verbs,* tell about things we do. Explain that verbs help readers understand what is happening in a story.

- Turn to page 9 and read the first sentence aloud. Write it on the board and underline the words *grumbling* and *pass.* Explain that the words tell what the iguana is doing.

- Say: *I am grumbling.* Use your voice to demonstrate the growling noise. Invite children to repeat the sentence using the same tone of voice.

- Continue with *pass,* using your body to show the word's meaning. Invite children to take turns practicing the word and the motion. Then repeat with other verbs throughout the story.

Step by Step

- **Reread and discuss the beginning.** Read aloud and display pages 6–13, pausing to identify the animals in the illustrations and connect them to their actions.

- Use questions such as these to guide discussion. (*RL.K.1; SL.K.1; SL.K.2*)

  Pages 6–7: Why does the iguana put sticks in his ears? (*He doesn't want to hear the mosquito's silly stories anymore.*)

  Pages 10–11: What does the monkey do by accident? (*kills an owlet*)

  Pages 12–13: What important thing does Mother Owl usually do? (*She hoots and wakes up the sun so the night will end.*)

  Tip: Children beginning to learn cause and effect may need additional support in understanding how the chain of events is connected. Isolate each event on pages 6–13 and ask: *Why did this happen?*

- **Focus on a key detail.** Direct children to turn to Student Book page 18. Have them draw a picture that shows what Mother Owl usually does to end the night and bring the morning. Reread pages 12–13 to help children recall the details. (*RL.K.3*)

- Use the Close Reading activity to help children look for evidence in words and pictures.

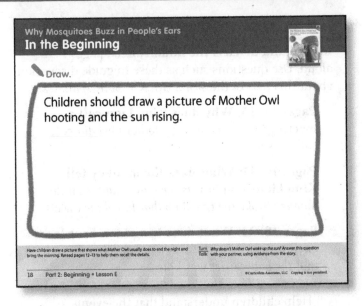

- **Have children discuss story evidence.** Read aloud the Turn and Talk activity. Guide partners to have a conversation, beginning as follows:

  Why doesn't Mother Owl wake up the sun? (*She is too sad because her baby owlet has died.*)

- Invite children to share their ideas with the class.

- Work with children to identify the most important ideas from this part of the story. Encourage them to use evidence from the story as well as their drawings to help explain their ideas. (*SL.K.4*)

Tier Two Vocabulary: *searching*

- Display the first two sentences on page 13. Read them aloud. Underline the word *searching*.

- Ask what Mother Owl was doing for her babies. Help children see that she was trying to find food.

- Then have children use their own words to tell what Mother Owl was doing. Together, determine that the word *searching* means "looking for."

- Provide an example by looking through a drawer, saying: *I am searching for a pen.*

- Have children tell about something real or imagined that they might be searching for. Provide this sentence frame: *I am searching for _____.* (*L.K.5.c*)

Close Reading

- Help children make connections between words and pictures. Display pages 12–13 and read the text aloud. Then prompt:

  How does Mother Owl feel? (*sad*)

  What words tell you that Mother Owl feels sad? (*The words say, "All that day and all that night, she sat in her tree—so sad, so sad, so sad!"*)

  How does the picture show that Mother Owl is sad? (*She is holding her baby owlet in her arms. Her eyes are closed and her head is down.*) (*RL.K.7*)

- Remind children that good readers use evidence in the words and pictures to support their ideas.

Step by Step

- **Reread and discuss the middle.** Read pages 14–23 aloud. Use questions such as these to guide discussion about this part of the story. (RL.K.1; SL.K.1; SL.K.2)

    Pages 14–15: Why does King Lion call a meeting? (*to find out why Mother Owl did not call the sun*)

    Pages 16–17: What does the monkey tell King Lion? (*that it was the crow's fault that the monkey broke the tree limb that killed the owlet*)

    Pages 18–23: What does King Lion hear from each animal? (*that it was another animal's fault that the baby owlet was killed*)

Tip: Help children understand that the events described here are the same events that happened at the beginning, but the animals are describing what happened from last to first instead of first to last.

- **Focus on a key detail.** Direct children to turn to Student Book page 19. Have them draw a picture that shows what the animals do together in this part of the story. Reread pages 14–15 to help them recall the details. (RL.K.3)

- Use the Close Reading activity to help children understand what King Lion does and what role he plays among the other animals.

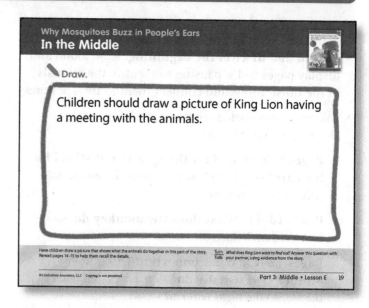

Why Mosquitoes Buzz in People's Ears
In the Middle

✎ Draw.

> Children should draw a picture of King Lion having a meeting with the animals.

Have children draw a picture that shows what the animals do together in this part of the story. Reread pages 14–15 to help them recall the details. **Turn Talk** *What does King Lion want to find out? Answer this question with your partner, using evidence from the story.*

©Curriculum Associates, LLC   Copying is not permitted.   Part 3: Middle • Lesson E   19

- **Have children discuss story evidence.** Read aloud the Turn and Talk activity. Guide partners to have a conversation, beginning as follows:

    What does King Lion want to find out?
    (*why Mother Owl will not wake the sun*)

- As a class, discuss how each animal says its actions are another animal's fault. Emphasize that King Lion wants to find the animal that started the sequence of events. (SL.K.4)

- Work together to identify the most important ideas from this part of the story. Encourage children to use their own words to describe the council meeting.

Tier Two Vocabulary: *trembling*

- Display the first paragraph on page 20. Read it aloud. Underline the word *trembling*.

- Ask children how they think the little rabbit might feel as it talks to the mighty King Lion.

- Guide children to see that the rabbit is probably scared and that its paw is shaking. Work together to decide that the word *trembling* means "shaking from fear." Have children demonstrate the action.

- Then give a personal example. Say: *I tremble in fear when I hear a loud thunderstorm.*

- Have children tell times that they might tremble, such as when they hear a scary story. (L.K.5.c)

Close Reading

- Help children understand what King Lion does in the story. Read aloud pages 14–15. Then prompt:

    What does King Lion want to find out?
    (*why Mother Owl has not called the sun*)

    What does Mother Owl tell King Lion? (*Monkey killed her owlet so she doesn't want to wake the sun.*)

- Move ahead to page 23 and read the second paragraph. Then prompt:

    What is King Lion trying to do? (*find out whose fault it is that Mother Owl won't wake the sun*)

- Help children see that King Lion seems to be in charge of all the other animals.

Step by Step

- **Reread and discuss the end.** Read aloud pages 24–32. Discuss the way the story ends, using questions such as these. (*RL.K.1; SL.K.1; SL.K.2*)

    Page 24: Why wasn't iguana at the meeting?
    (*He did not hear about it because of the sticks in his ears.*)

    Pages 26–27: Why does King Lion laugh when he hears iguana tell about the sticks in his ears?
    (*He realizes the mosquito started all the trouble.*)

> **Tip:** To help children grasp the sequence of the animals' actions, draw a sequence chain showing the order of the animals. As you read King Lion's words, have children tell you which animal comes next.

    Pages 30–32: Why doesn't the mosquito go to the meeting? (*She hides because she feels guilty.*)

- Use the Close Reading activity to identify story evidence that explains why Mother Owl finally calls the sun.

- **Focus on a key detail.** Direct children to turn to Student Book page 20. Have them draw a picture that shows why the other animals cannot find the mosquito. Reread page 30 to help them recall the details. (*RL.K.3*)

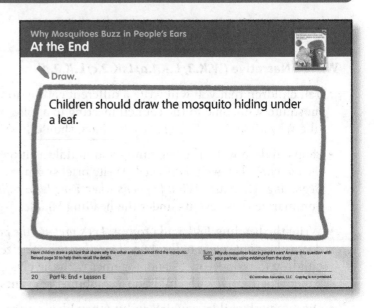

- **Have children discuss story evidence.** Read aloud the Turn and Talk activity. Guide partners to have a conversation, beginning as follows:

    Why do mosquitoes buzz in people's ears?
    (*The story says it's because they feel guilty and are asking if everyone is still angry at them.*)

- Invite children to share ideas with the class.

- **Retell *Why Mosquitoes Buzz in People's Ears.***
Assign each child an animal to play and have them line up in order of story events. Prompt children to retell the story, based on what their characters are doing. Reread parts of the story as needed.

Integrating Foundational Skills

Use these activities to integrate foundational skills into your reading of *Why Mosquitoes Buzz in People's Ears.*

1   Read aloud pages 28–29, tracking the print. Tell children that each word you say is on the page and that each word is made up of letters. Point to several words and have children name the letters. Then ask children to find and read these words: *the, all, she, her.* (*RF.K.1.b; RF.K.1.d; RF.K.3.c*)

2   Say *sun:* /s/ /ŭn/. Then have children segment *big, sat, hide, fell, day.* Say *sun* again. Change /s/ to /b/ and say *bun* together. Change to make *fun* and *run.* Do the same with the other words to make *dig, pig; cat, mat; ride, side; bell, tell; pay, say.* (*RF.K.2.c; RF.K.2.e*)

Close Reading

- Help children look for evidence to explain why Mother Owl finally calls the sun. Display and read aloud pages 28–29. Then prompt:

    What are all the animals shouting?
    (*"Punish the mosquito!"*)

    Why do the animals want to punish the mosquito? (*because she bothered the iguana and started all the events that killed the owlet*)

    How does Mother Owl feel about this? (*She is satisfied to know the mosquito will be punished.*)

    What does Mother Owl do? (*She hoots to wake up the sun.*)

Writing Activity

Write a Narrative *(W.K.3; L.K.1.a; L.K.2.c; L.K.2.d)*

- Tell children that you will write a different ending to the story together. Explain that in this story the mosquito will come to the council meeting to apologize for what she did. Remind children that their story, like *Why Mosquitoes Buzz in People's Ears,* should have a beginning, middle, and end.

- Help children write the beginning and middle as it happened in the book. Ask: *What did the mosquito say to the iguana? Then what happened?* Write brief summaries of the events on chart paper under the heading *Beginning.* Then ask: *What happens when King Lion calls all of the animals together? What does he figure out?* Summarize these events under the heading *Middle.*

- Write the heading *End,* and prompt: *Let's pretend the book ended a different way. Imagine that the mosquito doesn't hide but comes to the council meeting to apologize instead. Tell me what happens next.* Allow several children to propose ideas and, together with the class, agree on two events. Record the events on the chart paper. Then work with children to combine the events from the three columns to write a complete story.

- Discuss with children which ending they liked better, and why.

Speaking and Listening Activity

Hold a Council Meeting *(SL.K.1; SL.K.6)*

- Tell children they will hold a council meeting to figure out why Mother Owl will not wake up the sun.

- Assign a story character to each child. You may wish to assign one character to two or three children so that they can work together to brainstorm ideas.

- Help children proceed with the council just as it happened in the book. Begin with King Lion calling all the animals together and asking: *"Mother Owl, why didn't you wake up the sun?"* Revisit the story as needed to prompt children in their responses.

- Remind children to speak only when it is their turn, to listen carefully to others, and to ask each other questions if they do not understand something.

Language Activity

Nouns and Verbs *(L.K.1.b)*

- Explain to children that *nouns* are words that name a person, place, or thing, and that *verbs* are words that tell about things people or animals do.

- Display this sentence from page 7 of the story: *"The mosquito said, 'I saw a farmer digging yams. . . .'"*

- Work with children to identify the nouns in the sentence. Prompt: *What words name a person or a character who is like a person?* (mosquito, farmer) Underline the words and mark them with an *N.* Continue, asking: *What word names a thing?* (yams) Clarify word meaning as needed.

- Repeat with the verbs, prompting: *Which words tell about what someone does or did?* (said, saw, digging) Underline the words and mark them with a *V.*

- Continue with other simple sentences from the story and repeat the prompts, helping to clarify for children some examples of a "thing."

- Have children take turns using the underlined nouns and verbs in sentences.

Lesson 4 (Student Book pages 49–52)
Identifying Events

CCSS

RL.K.3: With prompting and support, identify . . . major events in a story.

Required Read Alouds: A (*Jamaica's Blue Marker*); E (*Why Mosquitoes Buzz in People's Ears*)

Lesson Objectives

- Recognize that an event is something that happens in a story.

- Understand that a major event is important to the story.

- Identify the major events in a story.

- Understand how thinking about story events can help you better comprehend a story.

The Learning Progression

- **Prior to K:** Children should have a basic understanding of events in a story. They should be able to tell what happens, using pictures as prompts.

- **Grade K: CCSS RL.K.3 expects children to identify major events in a story with prompting and support.**

- **Grade 1:** CCSS RL.1.3 further develops the standard by having children use key details to describe major events in a story. Children are expected to not only identify major events but also use details from the story to tell more about them.

Tap Children's Prior Knowledge

- Tell children that they are going to talk about what happens at school on each day of the week.

- On chart paper, write a heading for each weekday. Point to and read aloud the names of the days.

- Ask children what happens on Monday, and record their ideas beneath the heading *Monday*. Explain that things that happen are called *events*. Then read aloud the list of events they suggested, such as *painting pictures; storytime; puzzles*. Point out that many events happen every day.

- Point to and read one of the events, such as *go to the playground*. Ask: *What happens? (We go to the playground.) What do we do? (We climb on the jungle gym.)* Repeat with a few more events. Do the same for events on the other days of the week.

- Explain that just as events happen in real life, they also happen in stories.

- Tell children that in this lesson, they will learn how to identify events in a story. This will help them understand what happens in the story.

Ready *Teacher Toolbox*   Teacher-Toolbox.com

	Prerequisite Skills	RL.K.3
Ready Lessons		✓
Tools for Instruction		✓
Interactive Tutorials		✓ ✓

Additional CCSS

RL.K.2; RL.K.7; SL.K.1; SL.K.2 *(See page A38 for full text.)*

Step by Step

- **Introduce the standard.** Tell children they will learn to identify the major events in a story.

- Review the chart from the activity on page 49. Remind children that events happen in stories, just like they happen in real life. Then explain that *major events* are the most important events that happen in a story.

- Have children listen carefully as you read aloud a familiar fairy tale, such as *The Three Little Pigs.*

- Divide the fairy tale into three parts: beginning, middle, and end. Reread the beginning, and think aloud as you model how to identify major events.

  I want to figure out the major event in the beginning. First I ask: *What happens at the beginning?* The three pigs each build a house. The first pig builds a house with straw, and the second pig builds his house with sticks. They sing and dance all day. The third pig works hard and builds his house with bricks.

  Next, I ask: *What is the major event? What is the most important thing that happens?* I don't think it is important to know that the pigs sing and dance all day. I could still tell the story without this detail. It is important to know that the three pigs build different kinds of houses. This is a major event.

- Tell children that in their Student Books, they will learn some questions they can ask to identify the major events in a story.

- **Read aloud the Student Book page.** Have children turn to Student Book page 49. Read aloud the page as children listen and follow along.

- Point to the first bullet and reread the question. Then have children listen for what happens as you reread the middle of *The Three Little Pigs. (The wolf sees the pigs and chases them into their houses. He blows down the houses made of straw and sticks. The first two pigs run to the brick house.)*

> **Tip:** Clarify that there can be more than one major event in one part of a story. In fact, in very short tales such as *The Three Little Pigs*, authors tell mostly major events so that the story moves along quickly.

Listen and Learn

Identifying Events

An **event** is something that happens in a story.
Major events are the most important events in a story.

When you are reading or listening to a story, ask:
- What happens in this part of the story?
- What is the major event in this part of the story?

Thinking about events helps you understand a story.

Part 1: Introduction • Lesson 4   49

- Point to the second bullet and reread the question. Prompt children:

  Are all of the events you told important to the story? *(yes)*

  Could I tell the whole story in a way that makes sense without any of those events? *(no)*

- Confirm that all of the events in the middle of the story are major events. Without any one of them, the story wouldn't make sense. Demonstrate this point by quickly retelling the middle and omitting an event.

- Reread the end of the story and repeat the questions. Discuss any events that are not major, particularly why the story would not change if they were left out.

- Tell children that good readers identify major events to better understand what happens in a story. They think about whether an event is important to the story or if the story would be the same without it.

- **Have children demonstrate understanding.** Ask volunteers to share what they have learned so far about identifying major events in a story. Encourage them to identify events from familiar read-alouds.

Step by Step

- **Review Part 1.** Remind children that an *event* is something that happens in a story. Review that major events are the most important events in a story.

- **Revisit the story.** Display *Jamaica's Blue Marker.* Page through the book, using the pictures as prompts to help children recall the story. *(RL.K.2; RL.K.7)*

- **Model identifying events.** Display and read aloud pages 26–27. Think aloud as you model how to identify major events:

  > To identify the events, I ask: *What happens in this part of the story?* First it says that the class has a party with games and cake. Next, Russell tells his mom that everybody made a card for him. Then Jamaica thinks, "Not everybody." She runs and gets her blue marker and gives it to Russell to use at his new school.

  > Next I ask: *Which is a major event? Which event do I need to tell this part of the story?* I don't think it's important to know that everyone eats cake. I could tell the story without this detail. It is important that Jamaica feels bad for not giving Russell a card, so then she gives him her marker. I think this is a major event.

Tip: Help children connect this event to earlier events in the story. Review that Russell previously used the blue marker to wreck Jamaica's picture and Jamaica did not want to make Russell a card.

- Tell children you will model how to complete the Student Book page by identifying a major event in this part of *Jamaica's Blue Marker.*

- **Model completing the Student Book page.** Have children turn to Student Book page 50. Ask: *What is the major event in this part of the story?* Point to each picture and read aloud its caption. Demonstrate writing the letter M to identify the major event.

- Review each picture and ask: *Is this event important to the story? Can I tell the story without this event?* Explain that Russell receiving cards from the class is important, but it is only one part of the major event, which is Jamaica giving Russell her marker because she feels bad for not making him a card.

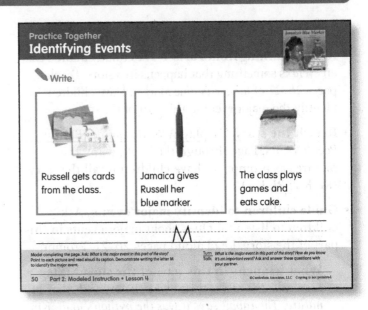

- Use the Close Reading activity to help children use illustrations to identify major events.

- **Have children demonstrate understanding.** Display pages 26–27. Read aloud the Turn and Talk activity. Model what a conversation with a partner should sound like by asking and answering the following questions. *(SL.K.1; SL.K.2)*

  > *What is the major event in this part of the story? How do you know it is an important event? Ask and answer these questions with your partner.* (Jamaica gives Russell her blue marker to keep. This is important because it shows that she will miss him.)

Close Reading

- Display pages 26–27. Ask:

  > **What do the pictures show?** (cake and cups on the desks; Jamaica giving a blue marker to Russell; Russell holding his cards)

  > **Which picture shows something happening?** (the picture of Jamaica giving Russell the marker)

  > **Which picture shows a major event? Explain your answer.** (the picture of Jamaica and Russell; the picture of the cake is just a detail)

- Point out that illustrators can include unimportant details to help readers imagine the setting, but pictures that show people doing something are often clues to a major event.

Step by Step

- **Review learning from Parts 1–2.** Remind children that an *event* is something that happens in a story. Display pages 26–27 of *Jamaica's Blue Marker*. Have children identify the major event in this part of the story.

- **Revisit the story.** Display *Why Mosquitoes Buzz in People's Ears*. Page through the book, using the pictures as prompts to have children recall the story. (RL.K.2; RL.K.7)

- **Guide children to identify major events.** Ask children to listen for clues about major events in this part of the story. Read aloud pages 20–21. Prompt:

  What happens in this part of the story? (*King Lion calls the rabbit to ask why she broke the law of nature. The rabbit says it was the python's fault. King Lion tells the council what he thinks happened.*)

  What is the major event in this part of the story? (*King Lion calls the rabbit to find out why she broke the law of nature.*)

> **Tip:** Explain that a *law of nature* means something that is normal for plants or animals to do. King Lion means that the rabbit doesn't usually go running in the daytime, so he asks her why she did.

- Use the Close Reading activity to help children understand the difference between details and events.

- Tell children that you will work together to complete the Student Book page by identifying the major events in this part of *Why Mosquitoes Buzz in People's Ears*.

- **Guide children to complete the Student Book page.** Have children turn to page 51. Ask: *What is the major event in this part of the story?* Point to each picture and read aloud its caption. Have a volunteer tell where to write the letter *M*.

- Review the Student Book page. Discuss why you wrote an *M* beneath one picture and not the others. Help children see that the other events did not happen in this part of the story.

Practice Together
Identifying Events

Write.

Lion asks Rabbit a question.

The iguana is at the waterhole.

The python looks for a hiding place.

M

Guide children to complete the page. Ask: *What is the major event in this part of the story?* Point to each picture and read aloud its caption. Have a volunteer tell where to write the letter M.
Turn and Talk: With a partner, tell the major event in this part of the story. Tell how you know it is an important event.

©Curriculum Associates, LLC   Copying is not permitted.
Part 3: Guided Practice • Lesson 4   51

- **Have children demonstrate understanding.** Display pages 20–21 of *Why Mosquitoes Buzz in People's Ears*. Read aloud the Turn and Talk activity. (SL.K.1; SL.K.2)

  With a partner, tell the major event in this part of the story. Tell how you know it is an important event. (*King Lion calls the rabbit to find out why he broke the law of nature. This is important because King Lion is trying to figure out why the baby owlet was killed.*)

- Invite children to share their discussions with the class. Encourage them to recall evidence in the text to support their ideas.

Close Reading

- Remind children that an *event* is something that happens. A *detail* is a piece of information. Reread the first two sentences on page 20. Ask:

  What is happening? (*King Lion calls the rabbit.*)

- Work with children to identify this as an event because something is happening. Reread the second sentence. Ask:

  What do we learn about the rabbit here? (*She is standing in front of King Lion. She is timid. Her paw is trembling.*)

- Help children understand that these are details. They tell more information about what is happening, but they do not tell the event.

Step by Step

- **Review learning from Parts 1–3.** Remind children that major events are the most important events in a story. Display pages 20–21 of *Why Mosquitoes Buzz in People's Ears.* Have children recall the major event on these pages.

- **Have children identify major events.** Display and read aloud pages 28–29 of *Why Mosquitoes Buzz in People's Ears.* Tell children they will ask questions to identify a major event in this part of the story.

    What happens in this part of the story? (*All the animals cry, "Punish the mosquito." Mother Owl hoots and the sun comes up.*)

    What is the major event in this part of the story? (*Mother Owl hoots and the sun comes up.*)

- Use the Close Reading activity to help children look carefully at the major event in this part of the story.

- Tell children that they will complete the Student Book page by identifying the major event in this part of *Why Mosquitoes Buzz in People's Ears.*

- **Have children complete the Student Book page independently.** Have children turn to page 52. Ask: *What is the major event in this part of the story?* Point to each picture and read aloud its caption. Have children write the letter M beneath the major event.

> **Tip:** Remind children that the pictures are meant to show one main detail related to the event. They do not match the pictures in the book.

- Review and discuss the Student Book page. Invite volunteers to explain why the other events on the page are not major events in this part of the story. Emphasize that the other events did not happen in this part of the story.

- **Have children demonstrate understanding.** Display pages 28–29 of *Why Mosquitoes Buzz in People's Ears.* Read aloud the Turn and Talk activity. (*SL.K.1; SL.K.2*)

    With your partner, tell the major event in this part of the story. Tell how you know it is an important event. (*Mother Owl calls the sun, and the sun comes up. This is important because most of the story was about the animals worrying that Mother Owl would not wake up the sun ever again.*)

- Invite children to share their discussions with the class. Remind them to take turns speaking and to listen patiently until it is their turn.

- **Have children reflect on their learning.** Invite children to tell why it is important to identify the major events in a story. Help them understand that identifying major events can help them better comprehend what happens in a story.

- Ask volunteers to name the questions they can ask to decide if an event is a major event.

Close Reading

- Display pages 28–29. Use these questions to examine the major event in this part of the story.

    How does Mother Owl feel when she hears "Punish the mosquito!"? (*satisfied*)

    Why does Mother Owl feel better? (*She found out what really happened to her owlet.*)

    What does Mother Owl do to show that she feels better? (*She hoots to wake up the sun.*)

- Discuss how this major event connects to events from earlier in the story, including when Mother Owl found that her baby owlet had been killed.

Assessment and Remediation

If you observe . . .	Then try . . .
Difficulty recognizing an event as something that happens	Using real-life examples. Throughout the day, ask children to identify events. For example, as children learn a song, go to lunch, write their names, or play a game, ask: *What is happening?* Make a list of the day's events and read them together with children. Ask them to name one event from the day.
Difficulty distinguishing an event from other story elements (e.g., characters, setting)	Naming story elements from *Jamaica's Blue Marker* and having children identify which are events. On chart paper, write the following headings: *Characters, Setting, Events.* Review each element. Read aloud the following examples and help children sort them into the appropriate columns: *Mrs. Wirth; the classroom; Jamaica gives Russell a new marker; Jamaica's father; on Friday morning; Jamaica does not make a card.*
Difficulty identifying major events in a story	Presenting a list of events from *Goldilocks and the Three Bears.* For each event ask the following question: *Do I need to tell this event for the story to make sense?* Use the following examples: *Goldilocks ate Baby Bear's porridge. (yes); One morning Goldilocks picked flowers. (no); Goldilocks sat in Baby Bear's chair and it broke. (yes); Goldilocks sat in Papa Bear's chair and it was too hard. (yes); Goldilocks walked into the forest. (no).* Help children see that each example they answered with a *yes* is essential to the story and is a major event.

Connect to the Anchor Standard

R3: *Analyze how and why individuals, events, and ideas develop and interact over the course of a text.*

Throughout the grades, Standard 3 leads students to a deeper understanding of story events. Students will be required to recognize the importance of the sequence of events as well as to compare and contrast events within a story. They will analyze how events, setting, and characters are interconnected. Students might consider questions such as these: *How does one event cause another? What event is the turning point of the story? How do characters' actions determine the course of events?* Use the following activities to help children begin this transition.

- Help children understand how one event in a story can have a big effect on the events that come after it. Recall that initially in *Jamaica's Blue Marker*, Jamaica calls Russell "a mean brat." Discuss why she feels this way. Then read aloud pages 20–21. Discuss the event that changes Jamaica's mind about Russell. Have children explain how Jamaica thinks about Russell differently after learning that he is moving. (SL.K.1)

- Read aloud page 9 of *Why Mosquitoes Buzz in People's Ears.* Ask: *What makes the python hide in the rabbit's hole? What makes the rabbit run out of her hole?* Discuss the two events and why they happen. Ask children to tell how each character feels. Help them notice that the two characters' feelings are the same. Point out other events in the story where animals feel afraid, and discuss why. (SL.K.2)

Lesson 5 (Student Book pages 53–56)
Retelling Stories

CCSS

RL.K.2: With prompting and support, retell familiar stories, including key details.

Required Read Aloud: *C (Chrysanthemum)*

Lesson Objectives

- Identify important events and key details in a story.
- Recognize that story events happen in sequence.
- Retell the important events of a story in order.
- Understand how retelling a story can help readers remember important events and key details.

The Learning Progression

- **Prior to K:** Children should have a basic understanding of characters and events. They should also be able to act out a sequence of events.

- **Grade K: CCSS RL.K.2 requires children to retell familiar stories, including key details, with prompting and support.**

- **Grade 1:** CCSS RL.1.2 advances the standard by having children retell stories and then use that information to show their understanding of the story's central message or lesson.

Tap Children's Prior Knowledge

- Tell children they will think about the order in which things happen: first, next, and last.

- Print the numerals 1, 2, and 3 on large cards. Ask for three volunteers. Call one child to come and stand at the front of the room. One at a time, call the two other children to do the same.

- Ask the class: *Who came up first?* After children respond, hand card 1 to the appropriate child and ask him or her to hold it up. Ask: *Who came up next?* (Hand out card 2.) *Who came up last?* (Hand out card 3.)

- Use the word *after* as needed to help children understand the word *next*. For example, say: *Who came up after [name 1]? Yes, [name 2] was next. He/She came up after [name 1].*

- Explain that it is often helpful to tell about things that happened in the correct order. Say: *[Child 1] came up first. [Child 2] came up next. [Child 3] came up last.*

- Repeat the activity, using four volunteers and four numbered cards. Ask: *Who came up first? Who came up next? Who came up next? Who came up last?*

- Tell children that in this lesson, they will learn how to retell a story by naming the events in the order in which they happen.

Ready *Teacher Toolbox*   Teacher-Toolbox.com

	Prerequisite Skills	RL.K.2
Ready Lessons		✓
Tools for Instruction	✓ ✓	✓
Interactive Tutorials	✓ ✓	

Additional CCSS

RL.K.7; SL.K.1; SL.K.2 (*See page A38 for full text.*)

Step by Step

- **Introduce the standard.** Tell children they will learn how to retell a story. Explain that retelling a story will help them remember the important events.

- Read aloud the following story:

    Lily couldn't find her cat, Turbo. She looked under the bed. She looked in the closet. At last, Lily found Turbo in the laundry basket, fast asleep.

- Review that a *key detail* is an important piece of information. Give examples from the story: *Lily can't find her cat, Turbo. Turbo was fast asleep.* Then review that an *event* is something that happens. Help children identify the events. (*Lily looks under the bed and in the closet. She finds him in the laundry basket.*)

- Think aloud about how you begin to retell a story:

    When I retell a story, I remember the most important details and events. Then I tell them in the order that they happen in the story.

- Have children listen carefully as you reread the story. Prompt them to recall the order of events:

    Start with key details: who is in the story and what is going on? (*Lily. She can't find her cat, Turbo*).

    What happens at the beginning of the story? Where does Lily look first? (*under the bed*)

    What happens next? Where is the next place she looks? (*in the closet*)

    What happens last, or at the end? (*Lily finds Turbo sleeping in the laundry basket.*)

- Model how to piece together the details and events into a complete retelling, using the words *beginning, first, next,* and *end.*

    In the beginning, Lily can't find her cat, Turbo. First she looks under the bed. Next she looks in the closet. At the end, Lily finds Turbo sleeping in a laundry basket.

Tip: It may seem repetitive to use *in the beginning* and *first,* but *first* is a sequence word that tells when something happens. You can use *In the beginning* to describe an event or to give context details, as in this retelling. Provide plenty of repeated practice to help children understand the subtle difference.

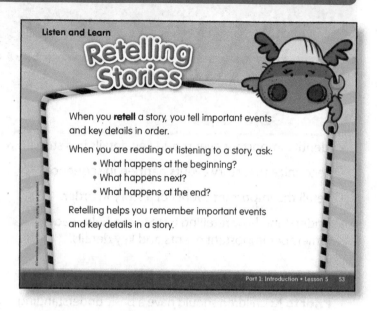

- Tell children that in their Student Books, they will learn questions they can ask about the order of events in a story.

- **Read aloud the Student Book page.** Have children turn to Student Book page 53. Read aloud the page as children listen and follow along.

- Point to and reread each question. Reread the story, and guide children to do a shared retelling by prompting them for each event in order: *What is going on at the beginning? What happens first? What happens next? What happens at the end?*

- Help children understand that good readers retell stories to help them remember important events and key details.

- **Have children demonstrate understanding.** Call on volunteers to share what they have learned so far about retelling a story, including the questions they can ask to identify key details. Encourage them to tell why readers retell stories in order.

Step by Step

- **Review Part 1.** Remind children that to retell a story, they should ask and answer the following questions: *What happens at the beginning? What happens next? What happens at the end?*

- **Revisit the story.** Display *Chrysanthemum.* Have children recall the names of the characters. Tell them you will work together to retell this story throughout the lesson.

- **Model retelling part of a story.** Explain that you will model retelling the beginning of *Chrysanthemum.* Display and read aloud pages 3–10. Think aloud:

  To retell this part of the story, I will start by asking: *What happens at the beginning?* **I'll reread and listen for important details and events.** (Reread pages 3–7.) **So what happens? Chrysanthemum is born. Her parents give her the name** *Chrysanthemum.* **She loves her name.**

  Tip: Pause to demonstrate how you consolidated several sentences into one. Use the repetition of the phrase "she loved" on pages 6–7 to show children how the same point is being emphasized, and so it only needs to be included once in the retelling.

- Reread pages 8–10. Continue thinking aloud:

  What happens next? Chrysanthemum goes to school in a great mood. What happens after that? Everyone giggles when they hear Chrysanthemum's name. That makes her feel pretty bad about her name.

- Use the Close Reading activity to help children understand a key detail in the retelling. (*RL.K.7*)

- Model combining the events into one retelling:

  In the beginning, a little girl is born and her parents give her the name *Chrysanthemum.* **She loves her name. But then she starts school, and all the kids laugh at her name. This makes Chrysanthemum feel bad about her name.**

- Tell children you will model how to complete the Student Book page by retelling in order the important events from this part of *Chrysanthemum.*

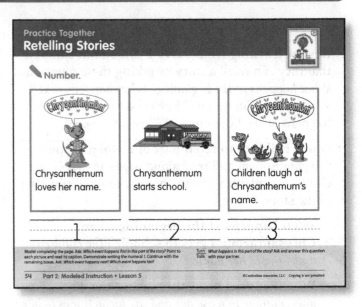

- **Model completing the Student Book page.** Have children turn to Student Book page 54. Ask: *Which event happens first in this part of the story?* Point to each picture and read its caption. Demonstrate writing the numeral 1. Continue with the remaining boxes. Ask: *Which event happens next? Which event happens last?*

- **Have children demonstrate understanding.** Read aloud the Turn and Talk activity. Model having a conversation with a partner by asking and answering the question below. (*SL.K.1; SL.K.2*)

  What happens in this part of the story? Ask and answer this question with your partner. (*Chrysanthemum loves her name, but then she goes to school and the kids laugh at it. She doesn't love her name anymore.*)

Close Reading

- Tell children that pictures often give clues about important details to include in a retelling. Display and read aloud page 10. Ask:

  What are the mice doing and saying to Chrysanthemum? (*pointing, laughing, and saying mean things about her name*)

  How does Chrysanthemum look? (*sad*)

  Why are the details on this page important to include in a retelling? (*They show why Chrysanthemum doesn't like her name anymore, even though she used to love it.*)

Step by Step

- **Review learning from Parts 1–2.** Remind children that they can retell a story by asking these questions: *What happens at the beginning? What happens next? What happens at the end?* Review with children what happens at the beginning of *Chrysanthemum.*

- **Guide children to retell part of a story.** Display *Chrysanthemum* and read aloud pages 16–21. Guide children to identify events in order to retell this part of the story. Prompt:

  What happens at the beginning when Chrysanthemum gets to school? *(The children make fun of her name.)*

  What happens next, throughout the day? *(The kids continue to tease her and say mean things to her.)*

  How does this make Chrysanthemum feel about her name? *(sad and upset)*

  What happens at the end that makes Chrysanthemum feel better? *(Her parents tell her that her name is perfect and do things to cheer her up.)*

- Use the Close Reading activity to remind children that a good retelling includes events and details.

- Guide children to combine the details in their responses into one retelling. Help them use the words *first, next,* and *last.* (First, Chrysanthemum gets to school and the children tease her about her name. Next, they tease her all through the day until she decides she doesn't like her name anymore. Last, Chrysanthemum's parents cheer her up and tell her that her name is perfect.)

  > **Tip:** Use the pictures on pages 16–21 to help children recall key events. Point to each picture and ask: *What is happening here? (RL.K.7)*

- Tell children that you will work together to complete the Student Book by retelling the events in order in this part of *Chrysanthemum.*

- **Guide children to complete the Student Book page.** Have children turn to Student Book page 55. Ask: *Which event happens first in this part of the story?* Point to each picture and read its caption. Have a volunteer tell where to write the numeral 1. Continue with the remaining events. Ask: *Which event happens next? Which event happens last?*

- **Have children demonstrate understanding.** Display pages 16–21. Read aloud the Turn and Talk activity. (*SL.K.1; SL.K.2*)

  ***What happens in this part of the story?* Ask and answer this question with your partner.** *(Chrysanthemum starts to feel better about her name, but when she gets to school the kids tease her all day. She decides again that she doesn't like it. Her parents tell her it is perfect and try to cheer her up.)*

- Invite partners to share their retellings with the class. Help them point to details in the story that support the details they chose to include.

Close Reading

- Remind children that a good retelling involves not only events, but also details such as characters' feelings. Display and reread page 16. Prompt:

  How does Chrysanthemum feel in this part of the story? *(She is starting to feel better.)*

  What clues tell you this? *(She wears comfortable clothes and starts writing her name again.)*

- Display and reread page 17. Prompt:

  Chrysanthemum "wilted." What does that mean? *(She went from happy to sad again.)*

- Recall with children that the story is about how Chrysanthemum feels about her unusual name. Explain that for this reason, it is important to include details about how she feels in the retelling.

Step by Step

- **Review learning from Parts 1–3.** Remind children that they can retell a story by telling events and key details in order. Display pages 16–21 of *Chrysanthemum*. Help them retell the details and events in this part of the story.

- **Have children retell part of a story.** Display and read aloud pages 27–31 of *Chrysanthemum*. Tell children they will practice retelling this part of the story. Prompt:

  What happens first in this part of the story? *(The kids continue to tease Chrysanthemum about her name. They tell Mrs. Twinkle how silly it is.)*

  What happens next? What does Mrs. Twinkle say? *(Mrs. Twinkle says her name is long, she is named after a flower, and she likes Chrysanthemum as a name for her baby.)*

  What happens next? What do the girls do? *(They all pretend they have flower names.)*

  What happens last? How does Chrysanthemum feel? *(Chrysanthemum feels proud. She loves her name again.)*

- Use the Close Reading activity to help children look closely at the turning point in the story.

  Tip: As needed, display and reread pages 24–26 to help children recall why Mrs. Twinkle's opinion is so important to the girls in the class.

- **Have children complete the Student Book page independently.** Have children turn to Student Book page 56. Ask: *Which event happens first in this part of the story?* Point to each picture and read its caption. Have children write the numeral 1. Continue with the remaining events. Ask: *Which event happens next? Which event happens last?*

- Discuss the answers to the Student Book page. Ask children to explain why they placed the events in this order, using evidence from the story.

- **Have children demonstrate understanding.** Display pages 27–31 of *Chrysanthemum*. Read aloud the Turn and Talk activity. *(SL.K.1; SL.K.2)*

What happens in this part of the story? Ask and answer this question with your partner. *(The girls at school tell Mrs. Twinkle how silly Chrysanthemum's name is, but Mrs. Twinkle thinks it's perfect. Then the girls all wish they had flower names, and Chrysanthemum is happy again.)*

- Invite partners to share their retellings with the class. Help them point to details in the story that support the details they chose to include.

- **Have children reflect on their learning.** Invite children to tell why readers retell stories. Encourage them to explain why it is important to tell events and key details in order.

Close Reading

- Help children look carefully at a big event in the story. Display and reread page 30. Prompt:

  What are the girls doing in the top picture? *(looking at Chrysanthemum and smiling)*

  It says they looked at her "longingly." *Longingly* **means "really wanting something." What do the girls do that shows they really want a name like Chrysanthemum's?** *(They give themselves made-up flower names.)*

  Explain why the girls change their minds about being named after a flower. *(They think Mrs. Twinkle is perfect and if she is named after a flower, and likes her name, then it is a good thing.)*

Assessment and Remediation

If you observe . . .	Then try . . .
Difficulty identifying key events	Having children distinguish between examples and non-examples. Choose a familiar topic, such as throwing a birthday party. Provide three sentences: two that are important to telling about the topic and one that is not. For example, say: *I made a special cake for the party. I decorated the house with bright balloons. I threw paper scraps in the wastebasket.* Have children listen to the sentences and ask themselves *Is this important to the story about [topic]?* Help them determine why the non-example is not a key event.
Difficulty telling events in sequence	Using a hands-on activity. On each of three sentence strips, write a major event from the beginning, middle, and end of a familiar story, such as *The Fox and the Crow.* Read the sentences in order. Then mix up the strips. Ask: *What happens at the beginning of the story? What happens next? What happens at the end of the story?* Have children help you sequence the events. Display the sentences in the correct order and reread to confirm.
Difficulty retelling a story	Scaffolding using picture cards. Use a set of three to five picture cards that represent the events in a brief story. Have children identify the illustration on each card. Then hold up the first card and prompt: *What happened in the beginning?* Have children begin their responses with the word *First.* Continue, asking *What happened next?* and *What happened last?* until children have told every event. Then challenge them to use the picture cards to retell the story without any prompts.

Connect to the Anchor Standard

R2: *Determine central ideas or themes of a text and analyze their development; summarize the key supporting details and ideas.*

Throughout the grades, Standard 2 progresses students from recounting story events and key details to synthesizing this information in order to interpret central ideas, messages, and themes. Students will learn to analyze stories in a wide range of cultural traditions and examine dramas and poems. In later grades, they will move beyond retelling texts to summarizing them. Students may ponder questions such as these: *What message or lesson is the author trying to convey? How does the message apply to real life? What are the themes in this text? How can I summarize this text?* Use the following activities to help children begin this transition.

- Explain that an author often writes a story to give a message. Tell children that one message in *Chrysanthemum* is that everyone is unique and should be proud of what makes them different and special. Reread pages 27–31. Have children tell how Chrysanthemum comes to feel this way about her unusual name. *(SL.K.1; SL.K.2)*

- Explain that when readers summarize a story, they tell only the most important ideas in just a few sentences. Prompt children to build a summary of *Chrysanthemum* by asking the following questions: *What does Chrysanthemum love? (her name) What makes Chrysanthemum sad? (The girls at school tease her about her unusual name.) How does Mrs. Twinkle surprise everyone? (She says she is named after a flower.) How does Chrysanthemum feel then? (proud)* Work with children to put all of their answers together into a brief summary of the story.

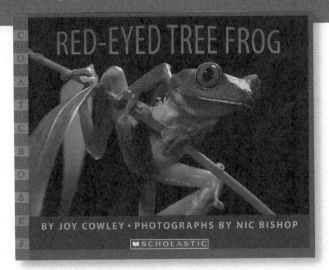

RED-EYED TREE FROG

BY JOY COWLEY • PHOTOGRAPHS BY NIC BISHOP

SCHOLASTIC

Lesson Objectives

You will read aloud *Red-Eyed Tree Frog,* which children will revisit in later lessons. With prompting and support, children will:

- Identify the main topic of an information book.
- Ask and answer questions about key details.
- Retell key details to describe sections of the book.

About the Text

Summary

In the rain forest, a hungry red-eyed tree frog wakes up in the evening, ready to look for food. While it searches, it tries not to be eaten by other nighttime animals. At last, the frog finds a meal. As morning comes, the frog finds a leaf to rest on and goes to sleep once again.

Information Book: Narrative Nonfiction

- Explain that nonfiction books tell facts and details about people, animals, or things that exist in real life.
- Tell children that narrative nonfiction books, such as *Red-Eyed Tree Frog,* are similar to stories: they have a beginning, middle, and end. Explain that this book is also like a story in that it has a problem and a solution.

Critical Vocabulary

- Prior to reading, briefly define the following words:

  evening (p. 2) the part of the day when the sun is going down and it is starting to get dark

  near (p. 13) close to; not far away

  lands (p. 20) comes to rest; stops

  shuts (p. 26) closes

- As you read, pause to point to the words as you encounter them, and review their definitions.

Word Bank

- Display a word bank of the Critical Vocabulary.
- Add other important words from the book, such as *hungry, poisonous,* and *morning,* on subsequent readings.

New Concepts: Nocturnal Animals

- Explain that there are many animals that rest or sleep during the day and look for food at night. Tell children that these animals are called *nocturnal* animals.
- Cats, owls, and foxes are some animals that children might recognize as nocturnal. As you read the book, have children think about why being nocturnal might be helpful to the red-eyed tree frog.

Ready *Teacher Toolbox*   *Teacher-Toolbox.com*

	Prerequisite Skills	RI.K.2
Ready Lessons		✓
Tools for Instruction	✓	✓
Interactive Tutorials	✓	

CCSS Focus

RI.K.2 *With prompting and support, . . . retell key details of a text.*

ADDITIONAL STANDARDS: RI.K.1; RI.K.3; RI.K.7; RF.K.2.d, e; RF.K.3.a, d; W.K.2; SL.K.1; SL.K.2; SL.K.4; SL.K.5; SL.K.6; L.K.1.a; L.K.2.b, c; L.K.5.c *(See page A38 for full text.)*

Step by Step

- **Introduce and explore *Red-Eyed Tree Frog*.** Read aloud the title and the name of the author, Joy Cowley. Read aloud Nic Bishop's name. Explain that he took the photographs in the book.

- Display the book cover and ask children what animal they think this book is about and why. (*It is about a red-eyed tree frog. The photo shows a frog, it has red eyes, and the title names it.*)

- Turn the pages, asking children what they see. Provide animal names as needed. Ask children to find the red-eyed tree frog throughout. Tell children to think about what each picture shows about the frog and/or the other animals in the photo.

> **Tip:** Point out the photos that cross over two pages (pages 2–3, 14–15, 16–17, 18–19, 26–27, 28–29). Guide children to look across both pages to be sure they understand what is happening in the entire photo.

- Explain that as you read aloud, children should listen closely to hear what the red-eyed tree frog and the other animals in the book are doing. Remind children to look closely at the photos as they listen.

- **Read aloud *Red-Eyed Tree Frog*.** As you read, pause to define challenging vocabulary and give children opportunities to look closely at the photographs.

- **Guide a review of the book.** Direct children to turn to Student Book page 21. Have them circle the picture that shows what the book *Red-Eyed Tree Frog* is mostly about. Point to and name each picture (*a red-eyed tree frog; an animal that lives in a shell; a swimmer; a fish*).

- Then have children draw one important thing they learned from the book. For example, they might draw what a red-eyed tree frog will not eat.

- **Have children discuss text evidence.** Read aloud the Turn and Talk activity. Have partners tell each other about one important thing they learned from this book. Help children use their pictures and evidence from the book to support their ideas. (*SL.K.1; SL.K.2; SL.K.4; SL.K.5*)

Red-Eyed Tree Frog
Explore the Book

Circle.

Draw.

Children might draw an iguana, an ant, a katydid, or a caterpillar.

Have children circle the picture that shows what the book *Red-Eyed Tree Frog* is mostly about. Point to and name each picture (*a red-eyed tree frog; an animal that lives in a shell; a swimmer; a fish*). Then have children draw one important thing they learned from the book. For example, they might draw what a red-eyed tree frog will not eat.

Turn Talk Tell your partner one important thing you learned from this book. Use your picture and evidence from the book to support your ideas.

©Curriculum Associates, LLC   Copying is not permitted.

Part 1: Explore the Book • Lesson F   21

- Guide their discussion with prompts such as this:

  How does the red-eyed tree frog feel when it wakes up? (*It feels hungry.*)

- Invite children to share other information they learned about red-eyed tree frogs, as well as any other animals in the book, in class discussion.

- Ask children whether they have more questions about red-eyed tree frogs after listening to the text, such as *What other things does a red-eyed tree frog eat?* or *Where is the rain forest?* Discuss where you might look to find answers to these questions.

- Refer to the *Did You Know?* section on pages 30–31 as needed to answer some of children's questions.

ELL Support: Animal Names

- Explain that you will point to and name the animals in the book. Display the cover, point, and say: *This is a red-eyed tree frog. It is a special kind of frog.* Have children repeat the name with you.

- Display page 4, point, and say: [top photo] *This is a macaw.* [bottom photo] *This is a toucan.* [both photos] *These are two kinds of birds.* Have children repeat the names.

- Continue with the other animals in the book. Help children find and name the red-eyed tree frog and the other animals that reappear.

- Have volunteers choose a page from the book and name the animals they find there.

Step by Step

- **Reread to learn about the red-eyed tree frog waking up.** Explain that children will listen and look for details about when the frog wakes up and what it does while it is awake. Instruct them to listen and look closely as you reread pages 2–9.

- **Have children identify details.** Use questions such as these to guide discussion. (*RI.K.1; SL.K.1; SL.K.2*)

    Pages 2–5: Where do the animals live? (*a rain forest*)

    Page 5: What does the frog do all day? (*It sleeps.*)

    Page 6: When does the frog wake up? (*evening*)

    Page 6: What does the frog want to do? (*It wants to eat. It feels hungry.*)

    Page 7: What does the frog *not* eat? (*an iguana*)

    Pages 8–9: Why does the frog hop onto another branch? (*The frog thinks the iguana might try to eat it.*)

    Tip: Explain that the word *another* on page 9 means "different." Guide children to see that the frog hops to a different branch to move away from the iguana.

- Use the Close Reading activity to help children find evidence about why the frog hops away.

- **Focus on a key detail.** Direct children to turn to Student Book page 22. Have them draw a picture that shows what the red-eyed tree frog does during the day. Reread page 5 to help them recall the details. (*RI.K.3*)

Red-Eyed Tree Frog
Waking Up

Draw.

Children should draw a sleeping red-eyed tree frog.

Have children draw a picture that shows what the red-eyed tree frog does during the day. Reread page 5 to help them recall the details.

Turn Talk: *When does the red-eyed tree frog wake up? What does it do when it is awake? Answer these questions with your partner, using evidence from the book.*

22   Part 2: Key Details • Lesson F   ©Curriculum Associates, LLC Copying is not permitted.

- **Have children discuss text evidence.** Read aloud the Turn and Talk activity. Guide partners to have a conversation, beginning as follows:

    When does the red-eyed tree frog wake up? (*It wakes up in the evening.*)

    What does it do when it is awake? (*It looks for food to eat.*)

- Invite children to share their ideas with the class.

- Work with children to identify the most important details from this part of the book. Encourage them to use evidence from the book as well as their drawings to help explain their ideas. (*SL.K.4; SL.K.5*)

Tier Two Vocabulary: *wait*

- Display pages 8–9. Read them aloud. Underline the word *wait*.

- Ask children if the frog stays by the iguana. (*no*) Ask what evidence shows this. (*It hops away.*) Guide children to see that the phrase *does not wait* means the frog goes away; it doesn't stay where it is.

- Work together to decide that the word *wait* means "to stay; to *not* go away" and that *does not wait* means the opposite of that: "to go away; to *not* stay."

- Provide an example, such as: *Sometimes I am late, and the bus driver does not wait for me.*

- Have children discuss how they feel when they have to wait/don't have to wait to do something. (*L.K.5.c*)

Close Reading

- Discuss evidence that tells why the frog hops away. Display pages 8–9, and read them aloud. Prompt:

    What question do the words ask? (*"Do iguanas eat frogs?"*) **Do the words tell the answer?** (*no*)

    What doesn't the frog "wait to find out"? (*whether the iguana will eat it or not*)

    What does the frog do instead of waiting to find out if iguanas eat frogs? (*It hops away.*)

    Why does the frog hop away? (*If the iguana does eat frogs, the frog doesn't want to be eaten.*)

- Help children see that the frog hops away because it doesn't know if the iguana wants to eat it or not.

Step by Step

- **Reread to learn how a red-eyed tree frog stays safe.** Explain that children will listen and look for details about how the frog stays safe as it looks for food. Instruct them to listen as you reread pages 10–19.

> **Tip:** If time allows as you reread pages 10–12, explain that ants can bite and that katydids are big and spiny, which makes them hard for the frog to swallow. (See the *Did You Know?* section, page 31.)

- **Have children identify details.** Use questions such as these to guide discussion. (RI.K.1; SL.K.1; SL.K.2)

   Pages 10–12: What animals will the frog not eat? (*ant, katydid, caterpillar*)

   Pages 13–15: What hungry animal is near the frog? (*a boa snake*)

   Pages 16–17: What does the snake do with its tongue? (*It flicks its tongue, tasting frog in the air.*)

   Pages 18–19: What does the frog do when the snake is near? (*It jumps away from the snake.*)

- Use the Close Reading activity to discuss evidence that shows how the frog is in danger and gets away.

- **Focus on a key detail.** Direct children to turn to Student Book page 23. Have them draw a picture that shows how a red-eyed tree frog gets away from a hungry animal. Reread pages 16–19 to help them recall the details. (RI.K.3)

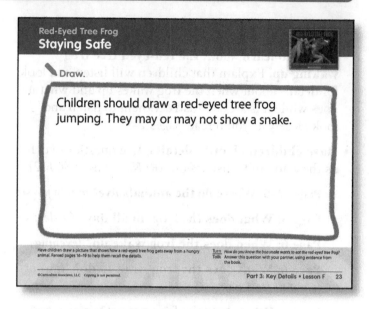

- **Have children discuss text evidence.** Read aloud the Turn and Talk activity. Guide partners to have a conversation, beginning as follows:

   How do you know the boa snake wants to eat the red-eyed tree frog? (*The words say that the boa is hungry and that it can taste frog in the air. The picture shows the snake trying to catch the frog.*)

- Work with children to discuss how the frog stays safe. (*It jumps away from the snake. It doesn't eat insects that are dangerous or poisonous.*) Encourage them to use evidence from the book as well as their drawings to help explain their ideas. (SL.K.4; SL.K.5)

Tier Two Vocabulary: *slips*

- Display pages 14–15. Read aloud page 14. Underline the word *slips*.

- Ask children if the snake is moving. (*yes*) Guide children to see that the words *slips* and *slithers* are action words (verbs) that tell how the snake moves.

- Ask: *Does a snake bump and bounce? Or does it slide and stay flat as it moves?* Together, decide that *slips* means "moves in a smooth, sliding way."

- Provide an example, such as, *My cat slips under the couch to hide when he hears thunder.* Have children give other examples of *slips.* If there is an opportunity, discuss other meanings of *slips* that children may know as well. (L.K.5.c)

Close Reading

- Discuss word and picture evidence that explains how the frog is in danger and how it escapes. Display pages 16–19 and read them aloud. Prompt:

   What evidence tells that the frog is in danger? (*Words: "It tastes frog in the air. Look out, frog!" Picture: The snake's tongue is touching the frog.*)

   What does the frog do? (*It jumps away.*)

   Does the frog take a big jump or a little jump? What tells you this? (*The picture shows the frog taking a big jump. Its legs are stretched out, and the frog is high in the air.*)

- Discuss how looking at the words and pictures together helps readers learn details about events.

Step by Step

- **Reread to learn what the red-eyed tree frog eats and when it sleeps.** Explain that children will listen and look for details about what the frog eats and when it sleeps. Instruct children to listen closely as you reread pages 20–29.

- **Have children identify details.** Use questions such as these to guide discussion. (RI.K.1; SL.K.1; SL.K.2)

   Page 20: Why is the frog on a leaf? (*It lands there after jumping away from the boa snake.*)

   Pages 21–23: What animal is near the frog now? (*a moth*)

   Pages 21–23: What does the frog do with the moth? (*It eats the moth.*)

   Tip: As needed, explain that the phrase *no longer hungry* on page 24 means "not hungry anymore." Discuss the detail that the frog was hungry when it woke up, but now it isn't hungry anymore.

   Pages 25–27: Where does the frog go to sleep? (*on a leaf*)

   Pages 28–29: When does the frog go to sleep? (*as morning comes*)

- **Focus on a key detail.** Direct children to turn to Student Book page 24. Have them draw a picture that shows something a red-eyed tree frog will eat. Reread pages 21–23 to help them recall the details. (RI.K.3)

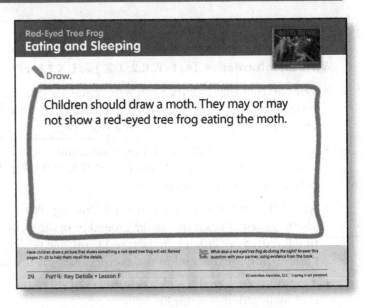

- **Have children discuss text evidence.** Read aloud the Turn and Talk activity. Guide partners to have a conversation, beginning as follows:

   What does a red-eyed tree frog do during the night? (*It looks for food to eat and tries to stay safe.*)

- Encourage children to look back at their drawings on the Student Book pages to recall any details about what the frog does at night. (SL.K.4; SL.K.5)

- **Review *Red-Eyed Tree Frog*.** Use the prompts in the Book Review to revisit and record important details from the book. Use the words and the photographs throughout the book to help children recall important details about the red-eyed tree frog. (RI.K.7)

Integrating Foundational Skills

Use these activities to integrate foundational skills into your reading of *Red-Eyed Tree Frog*.

1   Say *soon*. Ask: *What is the beginning sound?* (*/s/*) Repeat with these words: *go, day, red, not, jump, far, see.* Then say: *Change the /s/ in soon to /m/: moon.* Have children repeat. Use the other words to make *so, no; say, way; bed, fed; dot, pot; bump, lump; car, tar; bee, key.* (RF.K.2.d, e)

2   Write *look*. Have children say the sound for the letter *l* (*/l/*). Write *book*. Have children tell which letter is different from *look* (*b*), say that sound (*/b/*), and then say both words as you point to each one. Continue with: *go/no; will/fill/hill; red/bed; jump/bump/lump.* (RF.K.3.a, d)

Book Review

- As children review key details from *Red-Eyed Tree Frog*, record their answers on chart paper. Keep the chart on hand for later revisiting.

   Where does the frog live? (*in the rain forest*)

   When does the frog sleep? (*all day*)

   When does the frog wake up? (*in the evening*)

   What does the frog eat? (*moths*)

   What doesn't the frog eat? (*iguanas, ants, katydids, caterpillars*)

   What does the frog do to stay safe from a hungry snake? (*The frog jumps to get away.*)

Writing Activity

Write an Informative Text (W.K.2; L.K.1.a; L.K.2.b, c)

- Tell children that together you will create a chart of the information they learned in *Red-Eyed Tree Frog*. First, ask children to name the topic that all the information is about. Write the topic at the top of a large piece of chart paper: *The Red-Eyed Tree Frog*.

- Explain that you will ask children questions and record their answers in the chart. Group the information into three columns, with these heads: *Where It Lives; What It Looks Like; What It Does*. Write the column heads and read them aloud.

- Ask children questions such as the following: *Where does the red-eyed tree frog live? Does it live underground or above ground? Does it live on the ground or in the trees?* Record children's answers in the first column. (*in the rain forest; above ground; in the trees*) Continue with questions about what the frog looks like and what it does both during the day and in the evening. Record responses in the second and third columns.

- As children respond, call on volunteers to share the pen. Ask them to write single letters and simple VC and CVC words that they know.

- After completing the chart, reread it together with children. Children may also want to draw pictures to accompany the information in the chart.

Speaking and Listening Activity

Act It Out (SL.K.4; SL.K.6)

- Have small groups of children act out the narrative in three sections: pages 2–9, 10–19, and 20–29.

- Ask one child from each group to narrate as the other children in the group act out the story line. Have each group discuss what the narrator should say. Be sure groups include the time of day in their narration.

- Give children time to practice before presenting their section to the larger group. Observe and offer advice as children practice, guiding them to collaborate and helping them clarify their ideas.

- As time permits, have groups rotate through each section of the book, changing narrators and other parts as they do so.

Language Activity

Recognize End Punctuation (L.K.2.b)

- Have children practice identifying end punctuation in *Red-Eyed Tree Frog*. Display and read aloud page 12. Point out and name each punctuation mark. Explain what each mark tells about the words. Have children identify each mark.

- Reread the question on page 12 two ways: once as a statement, once as a question. Have children clap when they hear it read as a question.

- Display and read aloud page 16. Discuss how end punctuation affects meaning by rereading "Look out, frog" three ways: first as written (with an exclamation point), then with a period, and then with a question mark. Use voice inflection to indicate the different types of punctuation.

- Have children identify which punctuation mark you are "using" each time.

- Page through *Red-Eyed Tree Frog*, having children identify end punctuation and tell its meaning. Then ask them to say new sentences and tell what punctuation mark their sentence should have.

What's It Like to Be a Fish?

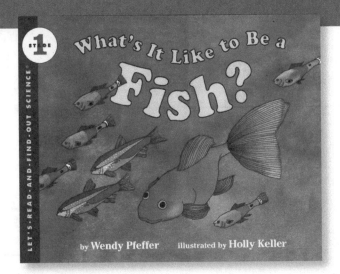

What's It Like to Be a Fish?
by Wendy Pfeffer illustrated by Holly Keller

Lesson Objectives

You will read aloud *What's It Like to Be a Fish?* which children will revisit in later lessons. With prompting and support, children will:

- Identify the main topic of an information book.
- Ask and answer questions about key details.
- Retell key details to describe sections of the book.

About the Text

Summary

This book explains where fish live, what a fish's body is like, how fish swim and breathe, and what fish eat. It also discusses keeping a fish as a pet and includes directions for how to set up a goldfish bowl.

Information Book: Science

- Explain that an information book tells facts and details about a topic, and that a science text tells facts about a science topic such as animals or space.
- Display information books from the classroom library on various topics. Guide children to identify the science texts and tell what they are probably about.

Critical Vocabulary

- Prior to reading, briefly define the following words:

  fins (p. 10) parts of a fish's body used for swimming

  scales (p. 12) hard, clear pieces like plates that cover the skin of a fish

  gills (p. 17) parts of a fish's body used for breathing

  oxygen (p. 17) a gas in water and in air that fish and people need to live

- As you read, pause to point to the words as you encounter them, and review their definitions.

Word Bank

- Display a word bank of the Critical Vocabulary.
- Add other important words from the book, such as *slime* and *breathe*, on subsequent readings.

New Concepts: Underwater Animals

- Explain that many animals and plants live underwater, either in salt water (oceans) or in fresh water (most lakes, rivers, and ponds). Some live close to the top of the water, while others live deep below the surface.
- As you read *What's It Like to Be a Fish?* have children listen for all the things that a fish needs and uses in order to be able to live underwater.

Ready Teacher Toolbox		Teacher-Toolbox.com
	Prerequisite Skills	**RI.K.2**
Ready Lessons		✓
Tools for Instruction	✓	✓
Interactive Tutorials	✓	

CCSS Focus

RI.K.2 *With prompting and support, . . . retell key details of a text.*

ADDITIONAL STANDARDS: RI.K.1; RI.K.3; RI.K.7; RF.K.1.d; RF.K.2.d, e; RF.K.3.c; W.K.3; SL.K.1; SL.K.2; SL.K.4; SL.K.5; SL.K.6; L.K.1.a, f; L.K.2.b, c; L.K.4.a; L.K.5.c *(See page A38 for full text.)*

Step by Step

- **Introduce and explore *What's It Like to Be a Fish?*** Read aloud the title and the name of the author, Wendy Pfeffer. Read aloud the name of the illustrator, Holly Keller. Explain that she drew the pictures.

- Display the book cover and ask children what kind of animals they see. (*They are fish. They don't all look the same, so they are probably different kinds of fish.*)

- Turn the pages of the book and think aloud:

    The title says this book is about fish. I wonder what I will learn about fish. As I turn the pages, I see lots of pictures with labels. I'll be sure to read the labels when I read those pages.

    Some labels have lines leading to different parts of the picture (page 11); **these kinds of pictures are called *diagrams*. I see other diagrams that have arrows** (pages 17–18). **The arrows show how one thing is connected to another. I will look closely at all of these pictures to find out the information they give about fish.**

> **Tip:** Explain that the labels give many types of details: they name different kinds of fish, they name parts of a fish, and they provide action and environmental details about fish. Readers can use words and pictures to understand more information about the fish.

- Explain that as you read aloud, children should listen closely to find out information about fish: where they live, what a fish's body is like, how fish swim and breathe. Remind them to look closely at the illustrations and diagrams as they listen.

- **Read aloud *What's It Like to Be a Fish?*** As you read, pause to define challenging vocabulary and give children opportunities to look closely at the pictures.

- **Guide a review of the book.** Direct children to turn to Student Book page 25. Have them circle the picture that shows what the book *What's It Like to Be a Fish?* is mostly about. Point to and name each picture (*a red-eyed tree frog; an animal that lives in a shell; a swimmer; a fish*).

- Then have children draw one important thing they learned from the book. For example, they might draw a fish that has scales.

- **Have children discuss text evidence.** Read aloud the Turn and Talk activity. Have partners tell each other about one important thing they learned from this book. Help children use their pictures and evidence from the book to support their ideas. (*SL.K.1; SL.K.2; SL.K.4; SL.K.5*)

- Guide their discussion with prompts such as this:

    How do scales help a fish to swim?
    (*Scales are smooth and slick and help a fish slide through the water.*)

- Invite children to share other information they learned about fish in class discussion. Discuss other questions they may have and where they might look to find answers to those questions.

ELL Support: Diagram a Fish

- Draw a simple fish on chart paper. Label these parts: *head, tail, body, eyes, mouth, fins, scales, gills.* (See pages 11 and 18 as needed.) Point to and name each part as you label it.

- Point to the fish's head and say: *This is the fish's head.* Repeat the name with children: *head.* Continue for each labeled part of the fish.

- Point to each part of the fish and ask the group: *What part of the fish is this?* After reviewing each part of the fish a few times, call on individual children to identify different parts of the fish.

- Draw a new fish. Have children tell you how to label it, prompting them as needed.

Step by Step

- **Reread to learn about a fish's body.** Explain that children will listen and look for details about a fish's body. Instruct them to listen and look closely as you reread pages 10–13.

- As you read, pause at page 11 to count the number of fins (*seven*) and the types of fins (*five*) that a fish has.

- **Have children identify details.** Use questions such as these to guide discussion. (*RI.K.1; SL.K.1; SL.K.2*)

  Page 10: What parts of a fish help it to swim? (*its sleek body, its fins*)

  Page 10: Which fin pushes a goldfish through the water? (*its tail fin*)

  Page 10: As a fish swims, what does it use its fins for? (*to steady, steer, or stop it*)

  Page 12: What covers a fish's skin? (*scales that are covered with slime*)

  Page 12: What are two ways that scales and slime help a fish? (*help it swim; help keep it healthy*)

  Tip: Rather than the terms *caudal, dorsal,* and so on, help children describe the fins using easier position words (*at the back; on top; in front on the bottom; in the middle on the bottom; in back on the bottom*).

- Use the Close Reading activity to find evidence that explains how scales and slime keep a fish healthy.

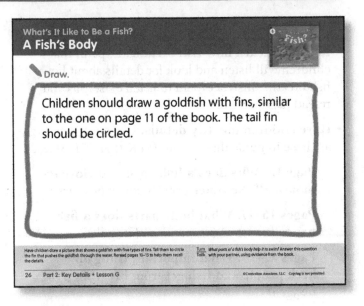

- **Focus on a key detail.** Direct children to turn to Student Book page 26. Have them draw a picture that shows a goldfish with five types of fins. Tell them to circle the fin that pushes the goldfish through the water. (*tail fin*) Reread pages 10–13 to help them recall the details. (*RI.K.3*)

- **Have children discuss text evidence.** Read aloud the Turn and Talk activity. Guide partners to have a conversation, beginning as follows:

  What parts of a fish's body help it to swim? (*its sleek body shape, fins, scales, slime*)

- Help children identify important details in these pages and support their ideas with evidence. (*SL.K.4*)

Tier Two Vocabulary: *delicate*

- Display the last paragraph on page 12. Read aloud the second sentence. Underline the word *delicate*.

- Ask children what the word *delicate* tells about in the sentence. (*the fish's skin*) Discuss what the sentence says the scales do. (*They protect the fish's skin from cuts and scrapes.*) Talk about the meaning of *protect*: "to keep from being hurt."

- Work together to decide that the word *delicate* here means "needing to be protected; easily hurt."

- Provide an example: *People's eyes are delicate.*

- Have children tell about other things that are delicate, using complete sentences. (*L.K.1.f; L.K.5.c*)

Close Reading

- Discuss evidence that tells how scales and slime keep a fish healthy. Display the last paragraph on page 12, and read it aloud. Then prompt:

  What do a fish's scales protect it from? (*getting cuts and scrapes on its skin*)

  What happens to germs before they can make a fish sick? (*Germs get stuck in the fish's slime and are washed away.*)

  What do these details about scales and slime help us understand? (*how they keep a fish healthy*)

- Discuss how looking for details helps readers understand important ideas in a book.

Step by Step

- **Reread to learn how fish breathe.** Explain that children will listen and look for details about how fish breathe. Instruct them to listen closely as you reread pages 16–18.

- **Have children identify details.** Use questions such as these to guide discussion. *(RI.K.1; SL.K.1; SL.K.2)*

  Page 16: Why does a fish open and close its mouth all the time? *(This is how it breathes.)*

  Pages 16–17: What body parts does a fish use to breathe? *(its mouth and its gills)*

  Pages 17–18: What important thing do both people and fish get from breathing? *(oxygen)*

> **Tip:** Use the diagrams on pages 17 and 18 to help children compare and contrast how people and fish breathe. Also explain that some underwater animals, such as whales, breathe with lungs, as people do.

- Use the Close Reading activity to show that comparing two things helps readers understand details better.

- **Focus on a key detail.** Direct children to turn to Student Book page 27. Have them draw a picture that shows a fish. Tell them to circle the part of the fish that opens and closes when the fish breathes. Reread pages 16–18 to help them recall the details. *(RI.K.3)*

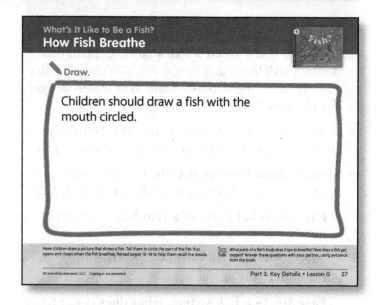

What's It Like to Be a Fish?
How Fish Breathe

Draw.

Children should draw a fish with the mouth circled.

Have children draw a picture that shows a fish. Tell them to circle the part of the fish that opens and closes when the fish breathes. Reread pages 16–18 to help them recall the details.
Turn and Talk: What parts of a fish's body does it use to breathe? How does a fish get oxygen? Answer these questions with your partner, using evidence from the book.

©Curriculum Associates, LLC   Copying is not permitted.   Part 3: Key Details • Lesson G   27

- **Have children discuss text evidence.** Read aloud the Turn and Talk activity. Guide partners to have a conversation, beginning as follows:

  What parts of a fish's body does it use to breathe? *(It uses its mouth and gills to breathe.)*

  How does a fish get oxygen? *(The fish opens and closes its mouth to let water flow over its gills, and its body takes oxygen from the water.)*

- Work with children to discuss how a fish breathes and how this is different from and the same as how people breathe. Encourage them to use evidence from the book as well as their drawings to help explain their ideas. *(SL.K.4; SL.K.5)*

Tier Two Vocabulary: *flows*

- Display the first four sentences on page 18. Read them aloud. Underline the word *flows*.

- Reread the words ". . . the water flows over the gills." Tell children that here, the word *flows* tells about something the water does. Ask what the sentence says the water does. *(It flows over the gills.)*

- Ask children to describe how water moves: *Is water easy to stop once it's moving? Does it move around or over things easily?* Together, decide that *flows* means "always moving; moving steadily."

- Provide an example of other things that flow. Say: *The milk flows over the cereal.* Have children give other examples. *(L.K.5.c)*

Close Reading

- Discuss how comparing helps readers understand details better. Read aloud pages 17–18. Prompt:

  What do fish use to breathe? *(mouth and gills)*

  What do people use to breathe? *(mouth/nose and lungs)*

  What do both people and fish need when they breathe? *(oxygen)*

  Where do fish get oxygen from? *(water)*

  Where do people get oxygen from? *(air)*

- Have children explain what is the same and what is different about how fish and people breathe.

Step by Step

- **Reread to learn what fish eat.** Explain that children will listen and look for details about the things that pet fish and wild fish eat. Instruct children to listen closely as you reread pages 20–23.

- **Have children identify details.** Use questions such as these to guide discussion. *(RI.K.1; SL.K.1; SL.K.2)*

   Page 20: What do pet goldfish eat? *(fish flakes made of flies, fish, shrimp, crab, oats, corn, carrots, and vitamins)*

   Page 21: Explain whether the fish in the picture are pets or fish in the wild. *(They are pets. They are eating fish flakes, not something in the wild.)*

   Pages 22–23: What do wild fish eat? *(tiny plants and animals, worms, crabs, shrimp, or other fish)*

   Pages 22–23: Explain whether the fish in the picture are pets or fish in the wild. *(They are fish in the wild. They are feeding themselves, not being fed by someone. They are eating other fish.)*

   Tip: Explain that the food chain includes all animals and plants, not just fish and what they eat. Discuss how people are part of the food chain as well.

- **Focus on a key detail.** Direct children to turn to Student Book page 28. Have them draw a picture that shows a fish and something that the fish eats. Reread pages 20–23 to help them recall the details. *(RI.K.3)*

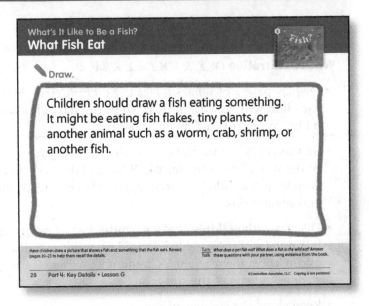

- **Have children discuss text evidence.** Read aloud the Turn and Talk activity. Guide partners to have a conversation, beginning as follows:

   What does a pet fish eat? *(A pet fish eats fish flakes.)*

   What does a fish in the wild eat? *(A fish in the wild might eat tiny plants and animals, worms, crabs, shrimp, or other fish.)*

- Invite children to share their ideas with the class.

- **Review *What's It Like to Be a Fish?*** Use the prompts in the Book Review to revisit and record important details from the book. Use the words and illustrations throughout the book to help children recall important details about fish. *(RI.K.7)*

Integrating Foundational Skills

Use these activities to integrate foundational skills into your reading of *What's It Like to Be a Fish?*

1 Say *fin*. Ask: *What is the final sound in* fin? *(/n/)* Continue with *bag, hot, hide, lake, sit, feed, let*. Then say: *Change the final sound /n/ in* fin *to /t/. Say the new word*: fit. Have children repeat. Use the other words to make *back, bad, bat; hog, hop; hike, hive; lane, late; sick, sip; feet; led, leg, less.* *(RF.K.2.d, e)*

2 Display the title. Have children find and read these words: *Like, to, Be, a*. Ask them to identify capital and lowercase letters in the words. Display page 10. Point out and have children read these words: *a, is, for, your, you, on, out, from, the*. *(RF.K.1.d; RF.K.3.c)*

Book Review

- As children review key details from *What's It Like to Be a Fish?* record their answers on chart paper. Keep the chart on hand for later revisiting.

   What body parts help a fish to swim? *(its sleek body shape, fins, scales, slime on its scales)*

   What do fish eat? *(Pet fish eat fish flakes. Wild fish eat tiny plants and animals, worms, crabs, shrimp, or other fish.)*

   How does a fish breathe? *(It opens and closes its mouth, water flows over its gills, its body takes in oxygen, water flows back out through its gills.)*

   How do fish rest? *(They move very, very slowly.)*

Writing Activity

Write a Narrative (*W.K.3; L.K.1.a; L.K.2.b, c*)

- Display page 7 of *What's It Like to Be a Fish?* Tell children that together you will write a narrative about what the child will do with his fish. To begin, have children choose a title for their narrative, such as *A Home for a Fish*. Write the title on chart paper.

- Remind children to think about the facts they have learned about fish and how these facts will be important in the story. For example, ask: *What will the boy's fish live in? What will the fish eat? What will the boy do to keep his fish healthy?* As needed, reread pages 30–32 and other pages from the book to guide children's ideas and suggestions.

- Discuss with children that a narrative has a beginning, middle, and end. Ask them to dictate sentences to begin the story. As needed, formulate children's ideas into complete sentences. Have children share the pen, asking them to write letters, punctuation marks, and complete words as appropriate. Continue with the middle and end of the story.

- Read aloud the completed story.

- Post the story in the classroom. Children may want to create illustrations to add to the story.

Speaking and Listening Activity

Describe Fish (*SL.K.4; SL.K.5; SL.K.6*)

- Have partners or small groups of children work together to describe fish.

- Tell children that each pair or group of children will work together to draw a fish, label what kind of fish it is, and present the fish to the class.

- Explain that children can choose any kind of fish to draw. Display *What's It Like to Be a Fish?* and help pairs or groups choose one of the many specific fish shown in the book's illustrations.

- Provide chart paper, markers and crayons. As children work together, prompt them to draw specific parts of the fish's body. Help them notice the colors of the fish.

- Ask each group to choose one child to present their fish to the class. Encourage other group members to contribute as needed to clarify and answer any questions other children might have about their fish.

Language Activity

Multiple-Meaning Words (*L.K.4.a*)

- Tell children that many words have more than one meaning. Explain that listening to the word in a sentence and finding clues helps us know what the word means.

- Display page 9 of *What's It Like to Be a Fish?* Read aloud the first sentence.

- Point out the word *pet*. Explain that one clue to its meaning is the word *goldfish*. Explain that when the word *pet* is used to describe an animal, it means "an animal that people take care of."

- Ask children if they know another meaning of the word *pet*. (*"to pat or rub gently"*) Ask them to demonstrate and use the word in a sentence. Then guide children to use *pet* in two different sentences that each shows the different meanings of the word.

- Help children practice using other multiple-meaning words from the book, such as *can* and *watch* (page 9); *right* (page 10); *swing* and *wave* (page 14); *flies* (page 20).

Asking Questions

CCSS

RI.K.1: With prompting and support, ask and answer questions about key details in a text.

Required Read Alouds: *F (Red-Eyed Tree Frog); G (What's It Like to Be a Fish?)*

Lesson Objectives

- Recognize question words.
- Understand that most questions begin with question words.
- Ask questions about words and pictures to identify key details in information books.
- Understand why asking and answering questions helps readers comprehend information books.

The Learning Progression

- **Prior to K:** Children should have a basic understanding of the concepts of questions and answers. Children should also be able to answer open-ended questions with prompting and support.

- **Grade K: CCSS RI.K.1 expects children to ask and answer questions about key details in a text with prompting and support.**

- **Grade 1:** CCSS RI.1.1 advances the standard by having children ask and answer questions about key details in a text more independently.

Tap Children's Prior Knowledge

- Review with children what they have learned about words they can use to ask questions. Help them recall the following question words: *who, where, what, when, why, how.*

- Display a classroom board game. Tell children that asking questions can help them learn about playing the game.

- Model asking questions about the game. For example, ask: *Who has played this game? When did you play?*

- Hold up different game pieces and ask questions about them such as these: *Where do you place this piece? Why do you need these cards? What are the small cubes used for? When do you pick up a card? How do you move your piece?*

- Work with children to provide a brief answer to each question. Then invite them to ask their own questions about the game. Remind them of the words they can use to begin their questions.

- Tell children that in this lesson, they will learn how to ask questions about details in an information book. Explain that answering the questions will help them understand important information in the book.

Ready *Teacher Toolbox*   Teacher-Toolbox.com

	Prerequisite Skills	RI.K.1
Ready Lessons		✓
Tools for Instruction		✓
Interactive Tutorials		

Additional CCSS

RI.K.2; RI.K.7; SL.K.1; SL.K.2 *(See page A38 for full text.)*

Step by Step

- **Introduce the standard.** Tell children they will learn how to ask and answer questions about key details in information books. Explain that asking questions and finding the answers helps readers understand important pieces of information.

- Ask children to listen carefully as you read the following informational text:

  Ducks go dabbling in ponds. They move their heads in and out of the water. Ducks dabble when they are looking for food. They dabble to find fish in the water.

- Model asking a question about the text. Think aloud:

  I will ask questions to make sure I understand what I read. I ask: *Where do ducks dabble?* I will read again. (Reread the first sentence.) **I read that ducks dabble in ponds.**

- Continue thinking aloud as you ask questions about the text:

  I have another question: *How do ducks dabble?* I will read again to find the answer. (Reread the second sentence.) **They move their heads in and out of the water. That's how ducks dabble.**

- Tell children that asking questions and finding answers helped you understand key details about ducks. Review that a *key detail* is an important piece of information.

- Tell children that in their Student Books, they will learn about questions they can ask to help them understand key details in an information book.

- **Read aloud the Student Book page.** Have children turn to Student Book page 57. Read aloud the page as children listen and follow along.

- Point to and reread each question word. Then point to the word *Where*, and invite a volunteer to tell the *where* question you asked about the text. Repeat with the word *How*.

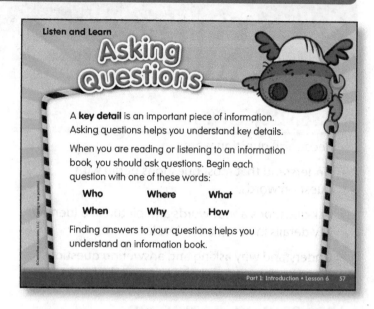

Listen and Learn

Asking Questions

A **key detail** is an important piece of information. Asking questions helps you understand key details.

When you are reading or listening to an information book, you should ask questions. Begin each question with one of these words:

Who	**Where**	**What**
When	**Why**	**How**

Finding answers to your questions helps you understand an information book.

Part 1: Introduction • Lesson 6   57

- Reread the passage, and guide children to practice using other question words from the Student Book page to ask and answer questions about dabbling ducks. Use the following questions for support as needed.

  What do ducks do in the pond? (*They go dabbling.*)

  When do ducks dabble? (*when they are looking for food*)

  Why do ducks dabble? (*to find fish to eat*)

  Tip: No information in the passage answers a *who* question. Explain that some books tell about things like ducks and some tell about people. Tell children they can ask *who* questions to find out about people.

- Help children understand that good readers ask questions about key details in a book. Finding answers to these questions helps readers understand important information in the book.

- **Have children demonstrate understanding.** Ask volunteers to share what they have learned so far about asking and answering questions about key details in a book. Encourage them to give examples of questions they can ask, using familiar information read-alouds in the classroom.

Step by Step

- **Review Part 1.** Remind children they can ask questions about key details to understand important information in a book. Help them recall question words they can use: *who, what, where, when, why, how.*

- **Revisit the book.** Display *Red-Eyed Tree Frog.* Page through the book, using the pictures as prompts to help children recall it. *(RI.K.2; RI.K.7)*

- **Model asking and answering questions.** Explain that you will model asking and answering questions about the information book. Display and read aloud pages 20–24. Think aloud:

  > **There are a lot of details about the tree frog on these pages. I will ask questions to see if I understand what I read.** (Reread page 20.) **First I will ask:** *Where is the frog?* **The words say "the frog lands on a leaf."** (Point to the picture on page 21.) **This picture shows the frog sitting on a leaf. Now I know where the frog is: on a leaf.**

  Tip: Some children may be confused by the image of the frog on page 20. Explain that the photograph was taken from underneath the leaf. The picture shows the frog's shadow as the frog lands on the leaf.

- Display and reread pages 22–23. Think aloud:

  > **I want to find out more about the tree frog. I will ask:** *What does the tree frog eat?* **The picture shows a moth in the frog's mouth. The words say "Crunch, crunch, crunch." I know crunching is an eating sound. This detail helps me understand that the frog is eating a moth.**

- Use the Close Reading activity to help children understand that sometimes the answer to a question can be found on a different page.

- Tell children you will model how to complete the Student Page by asking and answering questions about this part of *Red-Eyed Tree Frog.*

- **Model completing the Student Book page.** Have children turn to page 58. For the first item, ask: *Where is the red-eyed tree frog?* Point to and name each picture *(on a rock; on a branch; on a leaf).* Demonstrate circling the correct answer. Continue with the second item. Ask: *What does the red-eyed tree frog eat?* *(ant; moth; katydid)*

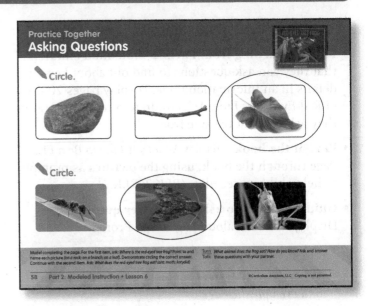

- **Have children demonstrate understanding.** Display pages 21–24. Read aloud the Turn and Talk activity. Model what a conversation with a partner should sound like by asking and answering the questions below. *(SL.K.1; SL.K.2)*

  > **What animal does the frog eat? How do you know? Ask and answer these questions with your partner.** *(The frog eats a moth. The words tell that it is a moth and the pictures show that it is a moth.)*

- For additional support, point to the picture on page 23 and ask: *What does the frog have in its mouth?* Have partners think together about the answer.

Close Reading

- Explain to children that thinking about details in a different part of the book can help them answer some questions.

- Display and reread page 24. Explain that the words "no longer" tell that the frog was hungry before but is not now. Ask: *Why isn't the frog hungry now?*

- Turn back to pages 22–23. Ask:

  > **What do the pictures show?** *(the frog catching and eating the moth)*

  > **What do the words say?** *("crunch crunch crunch")*

  > **Why isn't the frog hungry now?** *(because it ate the moth)*

Step by Step

- **Review learning from Parts 1–2.** Remind children that they can ask questions to find out about key details in an information book. Display pages 20–24 of *Red-Eyed Tree Frog.* Ask children to recall questions they asked about the tree frog.

- **Revisit the book.** Display *What's It Like to Be a Fish?* Page through the book, using the pictures as prompts to help children recall it. (RI.K.2; RI.K.7)

- **Guide children to ask and answer questions.** Display and read aloud pages 5–9. Prompt:

  What lives in water? *(fish)*

  Where can fish live? *(in lakes, ponds, aquariums, and even plastic bags)*

- Guide children to use the picture on page 7 to answer the following question:

  When do fish live in a plastic bag? *(when they leave a pet store)*

Tip: To help children understand that the picture on page 7 shows a pet store, ask them to identify the animals in the picture. Explain that these animals are for sale in the pet store.

- Display and reread pages 8–9. Guide children to ask and answer questions beginning with *what* and *where.* Use the following questions for support as needed.

  What is in the bowl? *(a castle; plants; rocks)*

  Where can a pet goldfish hide in the bowl? *(behind a plant; in the castle)*

- Use the Close Reading activity to help children notice when authors give information by using descriptive language.

- Tell children you will work together to complete the Student Book page by answering questions about key details in this part of *What's It Like to Be a Fish?*

- **Guide children to complete the Student Book page.** Have children turn to page 59. For the first item, ask: *Where can a pet goldfish live?* Point to and name each picture (in a goldfish bowl; in a swimming pool; in the ocean). Have a volunteer tell which picture to circle. Continue with the second item. Ask: *Where can a pet goldfish hide?* (in water plants; in rocks; in a castle) Guide children to circle two pictures.

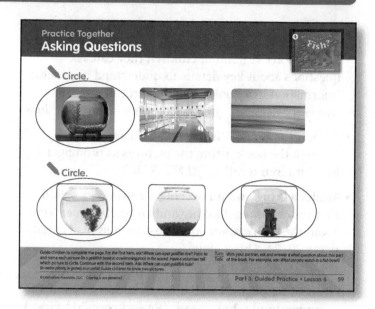

Practice Together
Asking Questions

Circle.

Circle.

Guide children to complete the page. For the first item, ask: *Where can a pet goldfish live?* Point to and name each picture (in a goldfish bowl in a swimming pool in the ocean). Have a volunteer tell which picture to circle. Continue with the second item. Ask: *Where can a pet goldfish hide?* (in water plants; in gravel; in a castle) Guide children to circle two pictures.

Turn Talk: With your partner, ask and answer a *what* question about this part of the book. For example, ask: *What can you watch in a fish bowl?*

©Curriculum Associates, LLC   Copying is not permitted.   Part 3: Guided Practice • Lesson 6   59

- Discuss the answers to the Student Book page. Help children point to evidence in the book that supports the correct answers.

- **Have children demonstrate understanding.** Display pages 8–9 of *What's It Like to Be a Fish?* Read aloud the Turn and Talk activity. (SL.K.1; SL.K.2)

  With your partner, ask and answer a *what* question about this part of the book. For example, ask: *What can you watch in a fish bowl?* *(fish hiding in the water plants)*

- Invite partners to share their *what* questions and answers with the class.

Close Reading

- Tell children that an author sometimes uses descriptive words to give details that answer *how* questions.

- Display and reread pages 8–9. Ask: *How do goldfish move around in their bowl?*

- Guide children in identifying the descriptive words *slip* and *glide.* Prompt:

  What word does the author use to tell how fish move "over and under the castle"? *(slip)*

  What word does the author use to tell how fish move "in their underwater world"? *(glide)*

- Discuss how identifying the descriptive words helps readers better understand how goldfish move.

Step by Step

- **Review learning from Parts 1–3.** Remind children that they can ask and answer questions to find out key details in an information book. Display pages 8–9 of *What's It Like to Be a Fish?* Have children recall questions they asked about where fish live and hide on these pages.

- **Have children ask questions independently.** Display and read aloud pages 26–27 of *What's It Like to Be a Fish?* Tell children they will practice asking and answering questions about this part of the book.

- Have children ask questions beginning with *what, why,* and *how.* Use the following questions for support as needed.

  What part of a fish is always moving? (*its fins*)

  Why are a fish's eyes always open? (*because fish do not have eyelids*)

  How can you take care of a goldfish's eyes? (*by keeping the fish out of the sun*)

  Tip: The author uses the phrase "as you do" on pages 26–27. Children may benefit from a discussion comparing how they sleep to how fish rest and telling why they need eyelids but fish do not.

- Use the Close Reading activity to provide practice with using picture evidence to ask and answer questions about key details.

- Tell children they will complete the Student Book page by answering questions about key details in this part of *What's It Like to Be a Fish?*

- **Have children complete the Student Book page independently.** Have children turn to page 60. For the first item, ask: *Why are a fish's eyes always open?* Point to and name each picture (*fish have no eyelids; fish have eyelids; fish have no fins*). Have children circle their answers. Continue with the second item. Ask: *How can you take care of a goldfish's eyes?* (*put fish in the sun; remove fish from the bowl; keep fish out of the sun*)

- Discuss the answers to the Student Book page. Help children find evidence in the book that supports the correct answers.

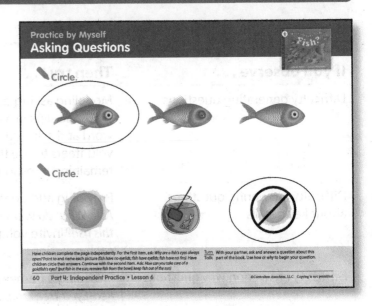

- **Have children demonstrate understanding.** Display pages 26–27 of *What's It Like to Be a Fish?* Read aloud the Turn and Talk activity. (SL.K.1; SL.K.2)

  With your partner, ask and answer a question about this part of the book. Use *how* or *why* to begin your question. (*Why don't goldfish need tears? [The water keeps their eyes washed.]*)

- **Have children reflect on their learning.** Invite children to share questions they have asked about key details in an information book. Invite volunteers to answer the questions, telling evidence from the book to support their answers.

- Have children tell why asking and answering questions helps them understand key details.

Close Reading

- Remind children that readers often need to look for clues in pictures to answer questions about details in an information book.

- Display pages 26–27. Point to each fish. Guide children to use evidence in the pictures to answer the following questions:

  Page 26: How are these fish different? (*One has a long tail. One has spots.*)

  Page 27: Where are the fins on the Common Goldfish? (*on top of it; on its sides; at the back*)

- Invite children to use evidence in the pictures to ask and answer their own questions about details.

Assessment and Remediation

If you observe . . .	Then try . . .
Difficulty generating questions	Modeling asking questions. Write each question word on a slip of paper and place the slips in a bag. Have a volunteer choose a slip of paper. Read the word and ask a question using the word, such as *Where is my pen?* Call on volunteers to use this question word to ask other questions. Repeat with the remaining question words in the bag.
Difficulty answering questions about key details	Providing additional practice. Display the cover of *What's It Like to Be a Fish?* Ask: *What do you see? How many fish are here? Where are the fish? What color is this fish?* Invite volunteers to point to the detail(s) in the picture and answer each question.
Difficulty answering *why* questions	Providing a framework. Give an example of a *why* question related to *Red-Eyed Tree Frog,* such as: *Why does the frog eat a moth?* Tell children they can answer a *why* question by putting the words in a sentence with the word *because.* Say: *Why does the frog eat a moth? The frog eats a moth because . . .* Help children find evidence in the text to complete the sentence. Continue with more *why* questions. Provide sentence frames for children to use as they look for evidence in the words and pictures.

Connect to the Anchor Standard

R1: *Read closely to determine what the text says explicitly and to make logical inferences from it; cite specific textual evidence when writing or speaking to support conclusions drawn from the text.*

Throughout the grades, Standard 1 builds toward an increasingly sophisticated analysis of details in the text. Early readers learn to ask simple questions and to find answers presented explicitly in the words and pictures. In later grades, readers transition to asking and answering more complex questions, leading them to make logical inferences supported by text evidence. Students might ask questions such as these: *What does the author want me to understand? What questions can I ask to help me understand this information? What details in the book help me answer my questions? Are the answers to questions right in the words and pictures or do I need to make an inference?* Use the activities shown to help children begin this transition.

- Display pages 10–14 and 22 of *Red-Eyed Tree Frog.* Point out that even though the title is *Red-Eyed Tree Frog,* other animals appear in the book. Have children identify some other animals. Ask: *Why does the author include other animals? How do these animals interact with the frog?* Point out that the author wants readers to know what happens when the frog encounters other animals in the rain forest. Discuss that some animals do not bother the frog, some are enemies, and others might be food. (*SL.K.1; SL.K.2*)

- Guide children to make an inference. Display and read aloud pages 20–21 of *What's It Like to Be a Fish?* Have children describe what is happening on page 21. Ask: *Why do the fish eat so quickly?* Reread the third sentence on page 20, and point out the words *race, snap,* and *gulp.* Discuss the picture clue on page 21. Ask children what information these clues help them understand. (*The fish are very hungry.*)

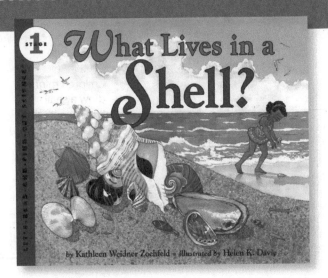

by Kathleen Weidner Zoehfeld • Illustrated by Helen K. Davie

Lesson Objectives

You will read aloud *What Lives in a Shell?* which children will revisit in later lessons. With prompting and support, children will:

- Identify the main topic of an information book.
- Ask and answer questions about key details.
- Retell key details to describe sections of the book.

About the Text

Summary

This book tells about different land and sea animals that have a shell for a home. Readers learn how a shell grows as the animal grows, how the shell keeps the animal safe, and how the animal takes its shell wherever it goes.

Information Book: Science

- Explain that a science book tells facts about a science topic such as the ocean, the land, or animals. Explain that *What Lives in a Shell?* is about animals that live in shells.
- Help children notice ways that this book is different from and also like another science book, *What's It Like to Be a Fish?*

Critical Vocabulary

- Prior to reading, briefly define the following words:

  safe (p. 6) without danger; not able to be harmed

  grows (p. 8) gets bigger

  enemy (p. 13) an animal or person that wants to hurt another animal or person

  outgrows (p. 19) gets too big to fit in something

- As you read, pause to point to the words as you encounter them, and review their definitions.

Word Bank

- Display a word bank of the Critical Vocabulary.
- Add other important words from the book, such as *home, opening,* and *armor,* on subsequent readings.

New Concepts: Animal Homes

- Tell children that animals have homes just like people do. Ask children to name animal homes, such as a bird's nest, a fox's den, or a fish's fishbowl.
- Explain that an animal's home might be found on land, underground, in an ocean or a pond, or high in a tree. Discuss that, wherever a home is, it helps keep an animal safe and warm. As you read, have children listen closely to learn about the different animals in the book that live in a shell.

Ready *Teacher Toolbox*   Teacher-Toolbox.com

	Prerequisite Skills	RI.K.2
Ready Lessons		✓
Tools for Instruction	✓	✓
Interactive Tutorials	✓	

CCSS Focus

RI.K.2 *With prompting and support, . . . retell key details of a text.*

ADDITIONAL STANDARDS: RI.K.1; RI.K.3; RI.K.7; RF.K.2.d, e; RF.K.3.b, d; W.K.1; SL.K.1; SL.K.2; SL.K.4; SL.K.5; SL.K.6; L.K.1.a, f; L.K.2.b, c; L.K.5.a, b, c *(See page A38 for full text.)*

Step by Step

- **Introduce and explore *What Lives in a Shell?*** Read aloud the title and the name of the author, Kathleen Weidner Zoehfeld. Read aloud the name of the illustrator, Helen K. Davie. Explain that she drew the pictures in the book.

- Display the book cover and ask children what they see. (*many kinds of shells; beach; ocean; girl picking up shells*)

- Turn the pages, asking children what they see. Help them find and name different animals that have shells. Discuss different features of shells that children notice, such as colors, shapes, and textures.

- Explain that as you read aloud, children should listen closely to find out information about shells and the different kinds of animals that have shells. Remind them to look closely at the illustrations and diagrams as they listen.

- **Read aloud *What Lives in a Shell?*** As you read, pause to define challenging vocabulary and give children opportunities to look closely at the illustrations.

> **Tip:** Pause briefly at the beginning and end of the following sections to discuss the topic each tells about: pages 4–13 (*snails*); pages 14–17 (*turtles*); pages 18–27 (*shells at the beach*); pages 28–32 (*finding shells*).

- **Guide a review of the book.** Direct children to turn to Student Book page 29. Have them circle the picture that shows what the book *What Lives in a Shell?* is mostly about. Point to and name each picture (*a red-eyed tree frog; an animal that lives in a shell; a swimmer; a fish*).

- Then have children draw one important thing they learned from the book. For example, they might draw a snail hiding in its shell from a bird.

- **Have children discuss text evidence.** Read aloud the Turn and Talk activity. Have partners tell each other about one important thing they learned from this book. Help children use their pictures and evidence from the book to support their ideas. (*SL.K.1; SL.K.2; SL.K.4; SL.K.5*)

- Guide their discussions with prompts such as this:

  What does a crab do when it outgrows its shell? (*It pulls itself out of the old shell and has a new one underneath.*)

- Invite children to share other information they learned about shells and animals that live in shells in class discussion.

- Ask children if they have more questions about what lives in a shell after listening to the text, such as *What do snails eat?* and *What other animals live in a shell?* Discuss where you might look to find answers to these questions.

ELL Support: Shells

- If possible, bring some shells to class for children to see and feel. Help children describe the different colors, shapes, and textures of the shells.

- Display pages 24–25. Read them aloud.

- Guide children to name colors, shapes, and textures that describe the shells. Ask questions such as: *Is this shell red or brown? Is it round or oval? Does it look bumpy or smooth?* Model how to respond in complete sentences, such as: *This shell is _____.* Have children repeat the questions and answers with you.

- Have children ask each other questions about the shells and respond using appropriate words that tell about the colors, shapes, and textures.

Step by Step

- **Reread to learn how a shell is a home.** Explain that children will listen and look for details about how a shell is a home for some animals. Instruct them to listen and look closely as you reread pages 4–9.

- **Have children identify details.** Use questions such as these to guide discussion. (*RI.K.1; SL.K.1; SL.K.2*)

  Page 5: What is the shell for? (*It is a home for the animal that made it.*)

  Pages 6–7: Name some different kinds of homes. (*house, apartment, nest, tunnel, cave*)

  Page 8: What happens to a snail's shell as the snail grows? (*The snail's shell grows, too.*)

  Pages 6–8: How do homes help people and animals? (*Homes help people and animals stay safe.*)

- Use the Close Reading activity to help children use word and picture evidence to see how a snail's shell grows with the snail.

Tip: Examine the diagram on page 9. Point out the snail's features. Explain that its foot looks different from a person's foot, as do its eyes, head, nose, and mouth.

- **Focus on a key detail.** Direct children to turn to Student Book page 30. Have them draw a picture that shows one home that is not a shell and one home that is a shell. Reread pages 5–8 to help them recall the details. (*RI.K.3*)

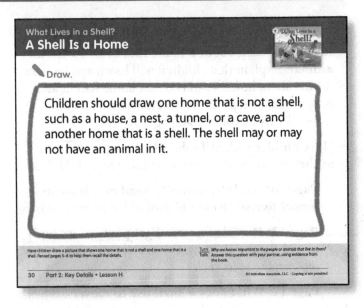

What Lives in a Shell?
A Shell Is a Home

✎ Draw.

Children should draw one home that is not a shell, such as a house, a nest, a tunnel, or a cave, and another home that is a shell. The shell may or may not have an animal in it.

Have children draw a picture that shows one home that is not a shell and one home that is a shell. Reread pages 5–8 to help them recall the details.

Turn Talk *Why are homes important to the people or animals that live in them?* Answer this question with your partner, using evidence from the book.

30 Part 2: Key Details • Lesson H   ©Curriculum Associates, LLC Copying is not permitted.

- **Have children discuss text evidence.** Read aloud the Turn and Talk activity. Guide partners to have a conversation, beginning as follows:

  Why are homes important to the people or animals that live in them? (*Homes keep people and animals safe.*)

- Invite children to share their ideas with the class.

- Work with children to identify the most important details from this part of the book. Encourage them to use evidence from the book as well as their drawings to help explain their ideas. (*SL.K.4*)

Tier Two Vocabulary: *hollow*

- Display the second-to-last paragraph on page 5. Read it aloud. Underline the word *hollow*.

- Ask children what the word *hollow* tells about in the sentence. (*the inside of the shell*) Talk about what else the sentence says about the inside of the shell. (*that it is "like a cup"*) Discuss how a shell and a cup are alike.

- Work together to decide that a cup and a shell are both used to hold something, which means they both can be empty. Explain that *hollow* means "empty."

- Provide an example: *A straw is hollow.* Have children tell about other things that are hollow, using complete sentences. (*L.K.1.f; L.K.5.c*)

Close Reading

- Discuss word and picture evidence to see how a snail's shell grows with the snail. Display page 8. Read it aloud. Then prompt:

  When does a snail get its shell? (*when it is born*)

  What words tell what happens as a snail grows? (*The words say "its shell grows with it."*)

  What do the five pictures in the middle of the page show? (*They show a snail getting bigger and its shell getting bigger with it.*) (*RI.K.7*)

- Discuss how connecting word and picture details helps readers understand ideas in a book.

Step by Step

- **Reread to learn about a home that moves with an animal.** Explain that children will listen and look for details about how a snail takes its home with it and how its shell keeps the snail safe. Instruct them to listen closely as you reread pages 10–13.

- **Have children identify details.** Use questions such as these to guide discussion. *(RI.K.1; SL.K.1; SL.K.2)*

   Pages 10–11: Why doesn't a snail ever leave its home? *(because it takes its shell with it wherever it goes)*

   Page 12: How does a snail get parts of its body out of its shell? *(It sticks its head and its foot out of the opening in its shell.)*

   Page 12: What does a snail use to move? *(its foot)*

   Page 13: What does a snail do instead of run away from its enemies? *(It pulls its head and foot inside its shell.)*

   Page 13: How does its shell keep a snail safe? *(Its shell keeps enemies from eating the snail.)*

- Use the Close Reading activity to find evidence that tells how a snail stays safe from enemies.

- **Focus on a key detail.** Direct children to turn to Student Book page 31. Have them draw a picture that shows a snail that is taking its home with it as it moves. Reread pages 11–12 to help them recall the details. *(RI.K.3)*

What Lives in a Shell?
A Home That Moves

✎ Draw.

> Children should draw a snail that has its head and its foot out of the shell.

Have children draw a picture that shows a snail that is taking its home with it as it moves. Reread pages 11–12 to help them recall the details.

Turn
Talk *How does a snail move? Why doesn't it leave its home?* Answer these questions with your partner, using evidence from the book.

©Curriculum Associates, LLC Copying is not permitted.   Part 3: Key Details • Lesson H   31

- **Have children discuss text evidence.** Read aloud the Turn and Talk activity. Guide partners to have a conversation, beginning as follows:

   How does a snail move? *(It uses its foot to inch along slowly.)*

   Why doesn't it leave its home? *(Its shell goes with it wherever it goes, so it never leaves its home.)*

- Invite children to share their ideas with the class.

- Work with children to discuss how having its home with it wherever it goes helps a snail when it can't run away from enemies. Encourage them to use evidence from the book as well as their own drawings to explain their ideas. *(SL.K.4; SL.K.5)*

Tier Two Vocabulary: *pokes*

- Display the first sentence on page 12. Read it aloud. Underline the word *pokes*.

- Ask children what the snail is doing in the pictures on page 12. *(coming out of its shell)* Discuss that the snail *pokes* out its head and foot, so the word *pokes* tells about what the snail does with its head and foot so it can get out of its shell.

- Work with children to talk about other words that might tell what the snail is doing. Together, decide that *pokes* means "pushes," "sticks out," or "stretches."

- Provide an example: *The cat pokes it paw out of the box.* Have children give other examples. *(L.K.5.c)*

Close Reading

- Help children find evidence about how a snail stays safe from enemies. Read aloud pages 12–13. Prompt:

   Why is a bird a snail's enemy? *(It eats snails.)*

   Does a snail run away from enemies? Why or why not? *(No, it can't run. It moves only slowly.)*

   What do the words say a snail does if an enemy comes around? *("It pulls its head and foot inside its shell.")*

   How does going into its shell help the snail? *(It keeps it safe from being eaten.)*

- Discuss how finding evidence can help readers answer questions about details in a book.

Step by Step

- **Reread to learn about a shell that fits.** Explain that children will listen and look for details about how a crab's shell fits its body. Instruct them to listen closely as you reread pages 18–19.

- **Have children identify details.** Use questions such as these to guide discussion. *(RI.K.1; SL.K.1; SL.K.2)*

    Page 18: What does a crab's shell cover? *(It covers the crab's ten legs, two claws, and the rest of its body.)*

    Pages 18–19: How does a crab's shell keep it safe? *(It is hard and fits its whole body like a suit of armor.)*

    Tip: Help children understand what a suit of armor is by asking them to imagine their own clothes turning into metal and wearing them that way. Explain that a crab's shell is not as heavy as metal, but it is very hard.

    Page 19: When a crab outgrows its shell, what does it do? *(It pulls itself out of its shell.)*

    Page 19: Where is the crab's new shell? *(It is underneath the old shell.)*

    Page 19: How is a crab and its shell like you and a shirt you've outgrown? *(As you both grow and get bigger, the crab's shell and your shirt both get too tight.)*

- **Focus on a key detail.** Direct children to turn to Student Book page 32. Have them draw a picture that shows an animal whose shell fits it like a suit of armor. Reread pages 18–19 to help them recall the details. *(RI.K.3)*

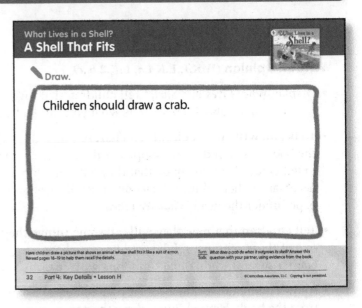

- **Have children discuss text evidence.** Read aloud the Turn and Talk activity. Guide partners to have a conversation, beginning as follows:

    What does a crab do when it outgrows its shell? *(It pulls itself out of the shell that is too tight. There is a new shell underneath the old one.)*

- **Review What Lives in a Shell?** Use the prompts in the Book Review to revisit and record important details from the book. Use the words and illustrations throughout the book to help children recall important details about shells and the different animals that live in them. *(RI.K.7)*

Integrating Foundational Skills

Use these activities to integrate foundational skills into your reading of *What Lives in a Shell?*

1 Say *big*. Ask: *What is the middle sound in big?* /ĭ/ Continue with *fun, not, pat, like, head.* Then say: *Change the middle sound /ĭ/ in big to /ŭ/. Say the new word: bug.* Have children repeat. Use the other words to make *fan, fin; nut, net; pet, pit, pot; lake, leak; had, hid.* *(RF.K.2.d, e)*

2 Write *run* and read it with children. Write *ran*. Have children tell which letter is different. Say its sound, /ă/, and read each word as you point to it. Continue with *top/tip; cave/cove; like/lake; fit/fat; not/nut/net; big/bag/bug.* *(RF.K.3.b, d)*

Book Review

- As children review key details from *What Lives in a Shell?* record their answers on chart paper. Keep the chart on hand for later revisiting.

    What are some animals that live in shells? *(snails, turtles, crabs, clams, oysters, scallops)*

    How do snails and turtles stay safe? *(They pull all parts of their bodies into their shells.)*

    How are the shells of snails and crabs the same? *(They keep the animals safe; they go wherever the animals go.)*

    Why does a hermit crab live in empty shells? *(Its shell is too soft to keep it safe from enemies.)*

Writing Activity

Write an Opinion *(W.K.1; L.K.1.a; L.K.2.b, c)*

- Display *What Lives in a Shell?* Tell children that together you will write a class opinion about the book. Explain that an *opinion* about a book tells what you think about it. It includes reasons that explain your ideas.

- To begin, write the book title on chart paper. Tell children that first they will tell some things they liked about the book. Ask children to complete this sentence: *I liked _____ because _____.* As children respond, guide them to tell details from the book that they felt were important, helpful, or interesting. Page through the book as necessary to help children remember details. Gather several "liked" opinions and record them on the chart paper under the head *What We Liked.*

- Tell children that now they will tell some things they didn't like about the book. Ask children to complete one of these sentences: *I did not like _____ because _____. I think the book would have been better if _____.* Gather several "didn't like" opinions with reasons and record them under the head *What We Didn't Like.*

- Allow children to formulate their own sentences as appropriate, making sure they include some information from the book. Have children share the pen, writing letters, punctuation marks, and words as appropriate.

- Have children dictate a final thought to end the opinion piece. Explain that they might tell whether they think other children would enjoy reading this book or not and why.

- Post the chart in the classroom. Divide the class into two groups. Help one group share the "likes" and the other group the "didn't likes."

Speaking and Listening Activity

Discuss Movable Homes *(SL.K.1; SL.K.4; SL.K.6)*

- Tell children they will have a discussion about homes that go with animals wherever they go. Explain that they will use evidence from *What Lives in a Shell?* to discuss these questions: *What is good about having a movable home? What is bad about it?*

- Have children work in small groups. Have each group discuss a few ideas they want to share with the class. Help them draw or write down these ideas to refer to during the discussion.

- Before the discussion begins, review rules such as listening carefully, taking turns to speak, and staying on topic. Remind children not to simply tell about their own ideas but to respond to the ideas and comments of others.

- As children speak, clarify that they should ask questions if they do not understand something.

- After the discussion, have children give a brief summary of the ideas they talked about.

Language Activity

Opposites *(L.K.5.a, b)*

- Explain to children that a good way to understand a word is to think about another word that has the opposite, or completely different, meaning. Discuss the opposites *up/down, tall/short,* and *run/walk* to help children understand this concept.

- Read aloud this sentence from page 23 of the book: "He throws away the old shell and crawls into the new one." Help children identify the opposites in the sentence. *(old/new)* Explain that the words *old* and *new* tell how the hermit crab's first shell is different from the second shell. Have children use *old* and *new* in sentences.

- Continue in the same way with some or all of these examples from the book: *in/out* (page 10); *bumpy/smooth, rounded/flat* (page 14); *slow/fast* (pages 16–17); *hard/soft* (page 22); *big/small* (page 23); *plain/fancy* (page 32).

- Have children take turns telling what they have learned about opposites.

Main Topic

CCSS

RI.K.2: With prompting and support, identify the main topic and retell key details of a text.

Required Read Alouds: *G (What's It Like to Be a Fish?);* H *(What Lives in a Shell?)*

Lesson Objectives

- Understand that a main topic is what an information book or part of an information book is all about.

- Understand that key details are pieces of information that tell about the main topic.

- Identify the main topic and key details in an information book.

- Understand how identifying the main topic and key details helps readers comprehend a text.

The Learning Progression

- **Prior to K:** Children should be able to recall important facts from an informational text after listening to it read aloud. Additionally, with support, they should be able to describe the main topic orally or represent it through drawing.

- **Grade K: CCSS RI.K.2 requires that children identify the main topic and retell key details of a text with prompting and support.**

- **Grade 1:** CCSS RI.1.2 builds on the standard by having children work more independently to identify the main topic and key details of a text.

Tap Children's Prior Knowledge

- Tell children that you will work with them to make a list of things that go together.

- On a sheet of chart paper, write the words *swing set* and *slide.* Invite children to suggest other words that might fit in this group. *(monkey bars; seesaw; tunnels)*

- When the list is complete, ask children to give it a title. Prompt: *Where can we find all of these things? What would we call this group?* Work together to title the list *Things at a Playground.*

- Discuss with children what the title helps them understand. Explain that it tells the *main topic,* or what the list is mostly about.

- Repeat the activity with classroom objects or daily activities such as morning meeting, storytime, and lunch. For each group, help children select a title that tells what the group is mostly about.

- Tell children that in this lesson, they will learn how to tell what an information book, or part of that book, is all about. They will also learn to retell important information from the book.

Ready *Teacher Toolbox*		Teacher-Toolbox.com
	Prerequisite Skills	**RI.K.2**
Ready Lessons		✓
Tools for Instruction	✓	✓
Interactive Tutorials		

Additional CCSS

RI.K.1; RI.K.7; SL.K.1; SL.K.2 (See page A38 for full text.)

Step by Step

- **Introduce the standard.** Tell children they will learn to identify the main topic of a book, as well as how to retell key details. Explain that identifying the main topic helps them understand what they are reading.

- Tell children that you are going to read aloud an informational paragraph. Have them listen for what the paragraph is all about.

  Our shadows do what we do. Jump up and your shadow jumps up. Clap and your shadow claps. Wave an arm, and your shadow's arm waves, too.

- Make sure that children understand the meaning of *shadow.* Then prompt:

  What is this paragraph all about? *(shadows)*

  Explain your answer. *(Every sentence is about shadows and what they do.)*

- Remind children that in the activity on page 85, they learned how to name the main topic of a list by thinking about how all the things on the list were connected. Explain that the sentences in a paragraph are connected, too. The main topic of this paragraph is *shadows.*

> **Tip:** Point out that in this example, the main topic is stated in the first sentence. Explain that this is often, but not always, where the main topic will be in a text.

- Have children listen again for details about shadows as you reread the text. Then prompt:

  What did you learn about shadows from this paragraph? *(Shadows do what we do. They do things like jump, clap, and wave if we do those things, too.)*

- Explain that these are the key details, or important ideas, that tell more about the main topic.

- Tell children that in their Student Books, they will learn questions they can ask to identify the main topic and key details of an information book.

- **Read aloud the Student Book page.** Have children turn to Student Book page 61. Read aloud the page as children listen and follow along.

Listen and Learn

Main Topic

The **main topic** is what a book, or part of a book, is all about.

When you are reading or listening to an information book, ask:
- What is this book all about?
- What are the key details?

The main topic is what the key details are all about.

Part 1: Introduction • Lesson 7   61

- Point to the first bullet and reread the question. Remind children that when they ask what a book or part of a book is all about, the answer is the main topic. Invite a volunteer to repeat the main topic of the paragraph you read earlier. *(shadows)*

- Point to the second bullet and reread the question. Remind children that key details tell more about the main topic. Invite volunteers to share what they learned about shadows from the paragraph. Reread it as needed.

- Help children understand that good readers ask these questions when they listen to or read an information book. Answering the questions will help them tell what the book is all about and what important information they can learn from it.

- **Have children demonstrate understanding.** Call on volunteers to share what they have learned so far about identifying the main topic and key details of an information book. Display basic information books from the classroom library and invite children to use the title and cover photograph to identify the main topic of each.

Part 2: Modeled Instruction

Step by Step

- **Review Part 1.** Remind children that the *main topic* is what a book is all about. Key details are important pieces of information about the main topic.

- **Revisit the book.** Display *What's It Like to Be a Fish?* Page through the book, using the pictures as prompts to have children recall information. *(RI.K.7)*

- **Model identifying the main topic and key details.** Explain that you will model identifying the main topic and key details of one part of the book. Display page 10, and read aloud the second paragraph. Then think aloud:

  To find the main topic, I ask: *What is this paragraph all about?* I will reread and listen to the details. Then I will think about how they are connected. (Reread) **Most of the sentences tell about what a fish uses to swim. This is how they are connected. I think the main topic is *A fish's body is perfect for swimming.***

> **Tip:** Emphasize that there can be more than one way to state a main topic. Suggest other ways to phrase this topic, such as the following: *A fish is a great swimmer; A fish's body helps it to swim.*

- Continue thinking aloud about key details:

  Next I ask: *What are the key details?* I can ask another way: *What makes a fish's body perfect for swimming?* (Reread, pausing each time you read a key detail.) I see: its sleek body is the perfect shape—that's one detail. It uses its fins—that's another. And its tail pushes it through the water. Each of these details tells me why a fish's body is so good for swimming.

- Use the Close Reading activity to find out how the diagram provides more information about the topic.

- Tell children you will model how to complete the Student Book page by identifying the main topic and key details in this part of *What's It Like to Be a Fish?*

- **Model completing the Student Book page.** Have children turn to page 62. Read aloud the main topic: *A fish's body is perfect for swimming.* Then reread the second paragraph on page 10. Each time you read a key detail, pause to model circling the corresponding picture *(fish body; fish fins; fish tail).*

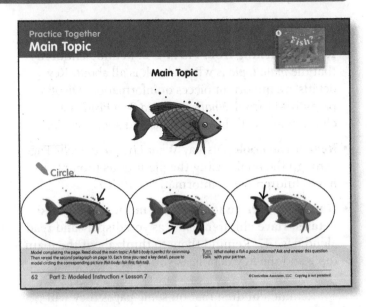

- **Have children demonstrate understanding.** Display pages 10–11. Read aloud the Turn and Talk activity. Model what a conversation with a partner should sound like by asking and answering the question below. *(SL.K.1; SL.K.2)*

  What makes a fish a good swimmer? Ask and answer this question with your partner. *(a sleek body; fins; a tail)*

- Help children locate evidence in the words and pictures that support the answer to the question.

Close Reading

- Display page 11. Explain that a *diagram* is a picture with labels that has a main topic. Point to each fin and read its label. Count the fin labels together. Ask:

  How many different kinds of fins does a goldfish have? *(five)*

  What is this diagram mostly about? *(a goldfish's different fins)*

  How could we say the main topic of this diagram in a full sentence? *(A goldfish has many different kinds of fins.)*

- Emphasize that just as they used details in the words to identify the main topic of the paragraph, children can also use details in the pictures to identify the main topic of a diagram.

Step by Step

- **Review learning from Parts 1–2.** Remind children that the *main topic* is what a book is all about. Key details are important pieces of information. Display pages 10–11 from *What's It Like to Be a Fish?* Ask children to recall the main topic and some key details.

- **Revisit the book.** Display *What Lives in a Shell?* Page through the book, using the pictures as prompts to have children recall information. (RI.K.7)

- **Guide children to identify the main topic and key details.** Have children listen as you display and read aloud page 17. Remind them to think about the main topic and the key details as you read.

> **Tip:** Remind children that on some pages they will hear the main topic at the beginning of the page. Provide a clue that this time, they should listen for the main topic at the end of the page.

- Prompt children as follows:

    What frightens the turtle? *(the cat)*

    Why doesn't the turtle run away? *(because the turtle cannot run as fast as the cat)*

    How can the turtle hide from the cat? *(It pulls its head, legs, and tail into its shell.)*

    What keeps the turtle safe? *(its shell)*

    What is the main topic of this page? *(A turtle stays safe in a shell.)* (RI.K.1)

- Explain to children that you will work together to complete the Student Book page by identifying the main topic and key details in this part of *What Lives in a Shell?*

- **Guide children to complete the Student Book page.** Have children turn to page 63. Read aloud page 17, and help children decide what all the key details are about. *(A turtle stays safe in a shell.)* Then as you reread page 17, guide children to circle the corresponding picture as you read a key detail. *(The turtle is afraid of the cat; the turtle cannot run fast; the turtle pulls its head, legs, and tail into its shell.)*

- Check that children have circled all three pictures. Then discuss how each detail helps tell more about a turtle staying safe in its shell.

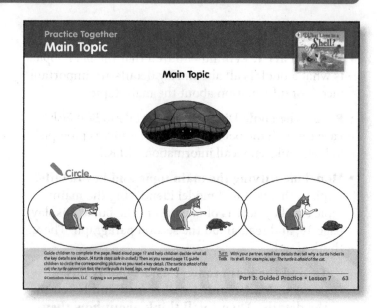

- **Have children demonstrate understanding.** Display pages 16–17 of *What Lives in a Shell?* Read aloud the Turn and Talk activity. (SL.K.1; SL.K.2)

    With your partner, retell key details that tell why a turtle hides in its shell. For example, say: The turtle is afraid of the cat. *(The turtle cannot run as fast as the cat. The turtle is safe in its shell when the cat tries to pat it with its paw.)*

- Invite partners to share their discussions with the class. Help children find evidence in the book to support their ideas.

- Use the Close Reading activity to help children focus on key details in words and pictures.

Close Reading

- Tell children that they can find key details in both words and pictures. Display and read aloud page 16. Then prompt:

    What details did we learn about the turtle from the words? *(It has four legs. It pokes its head, legs, and tail through its shell. It is slow.)*

- Then display the picture. Ask:

    Which of these details can we see in the picture? *(four legs; the cat and the frog are jumping over the turtle, showing how slow the turtle is)*

- Discuss how the pictures help children better understand the key details written in the words.

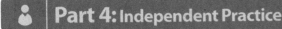
Step by Step

- **Review learning from Parts 1–3.** Remind children that the *main topic* is what a book is all about and that key details are pieces of information. Ask children for examples of a main topic and key details they have identified in *What Lives in a Shell?*

- **Have children identify the main topic and key details.** Display and read aloud pages 22–23 of *What Lives in a Shell?* Tell children to listen for key details and then use them to identify the main topic. Prompt:

   Why can't the hermit crab use its own shell to stay safe from enemies? *(Its shell is too soft.)*

   What happens when a hermit crab gets too big for its shell? *(It finds a new one that fits.)*

   What is the main topic of this part of the book? *(A hermit crab lives in an empty snail shell.) (RI.K.1)*

- Use the Close Reading activity to focus on key details that are connected through words and pictures.

- Tell children that they will complete the Student Book page by identifying the main topic and key details in this part of *What Lives in a Shell?*

- **Have children complete the Student Book page independently.** Have children turn to Student Book page 64. Read aloud pages 22–23, and state the main topic: *A hermit crab lives in an empty snail shell.* Then, as you reread the pages, have children circle the corresponding picture as you read a key detail (*a hermit crab's body is soft; a hermit crab cannot stay safe from enemies; a hermit crab outgrows its shell*).

> **Tip:** Remind children that on the previous two Student Book pages, they circled all three pictures. Have them listen carefully for details in the words that match each of the pictures on this page.

- Review and discuss the Student Book page. Help children locate evidence in the text to confirm why they circled each picture.

- **Have children demonstrate understanding.** Display pages 22–23 of *What Lives in a Shell?* Read aloud the Turn and Talk activity. *(SL.K.1)*

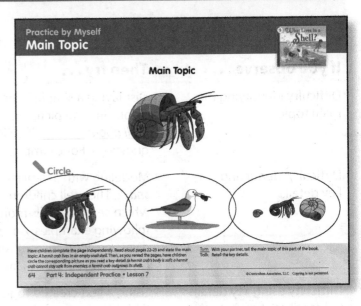

Practice by Myself
Main Topic

Main Topic

✎ Circle.

Have children complete the page independently. Read aloud pages 22–23 and state the main topic: *A hermit crab lives in an empty snail shell.* Then, as you reread the pages, have children circle the corresponding picture as you read a key detail *(a hermit crab's body is soft; a hermit crab cannot stay safe from enemies; a hermit crab outgrows its shell)*. **Turn Talk** With your partner, tell the main topic of this part of the book. Retell the key details.

64   Part 4: Independent Practice • Lesson 7   ©Curriculum Associates, LLC   Copying is not permitted.

With your partner, tell the main topic of this part of the book. Retell the key details.
(A hermit crab lives in an empty snail shell. His own shell is too soft to keep him safe. He finds an empty snail shell that fits.)

- If partners need support, ask: *Where does the hermit crab live? Why does it need an empty shell?*

- **Have children reflect on their learning.** Invite children to tell how they can listen or look for key details in an information book. They can use the key details to answer the question *What is the book all about?* This will help them name the main topic.

Close Reading

- Review that words and pictures can work together to tell key details. Display page 23. Have children look closely at each small picture and its number.

- Read aloud from "After a while..." through "looks for a bigger one." Point to picture 1, and ask:

   What is this hermit crab doing? Does this picture go with the words we just read?

- Continue helping children connect details and pictures as follows: "too small" with 2; "one he likes" with 3; "throws away old, crawls into new" with 4; "new shell is home" with 5.

Assessment and Remediation

If you observe . . .	Then try . . .
Difficulty identifying the main topic	Displaying a simple information book on a single topic. Page through the book, displaying the pictures. Ask children to complete this sentence frame: *This book is all about* _____. If children need additional support, ask them *either/or* questions. For example: *Is this book about trucks or dinosaurs? How do you know?*
Difficulty identifying key details	Modeling with a familiar topic. Say the following sentence: *An apple is a healthy snack.* Then tell children you will say pairs of sentences. They should tell you which sentence tells more about an apple being a healthy snack. See the following examples: *An apple is green. An apple gives you good energy. (An apple gives you good energy.); An apple is good for your heart. An apple is round. (An apple is good for your heart.)* Invite children to offer examples and non-examples.
Difficulty using key details to identify the main topic	Using a text created together. Ask children to name different kinds of pets. Write their ideas to complete this sentence frame: *A [name of animal] can be a pet.* After several kinds of pets have been named, read the sentences. Work with children to generate the main topic that tells what all the sentences are about. Write the sentence: *There are many kinds of pets.* Review that the names of the animals are all key details that tell about the main topic.

Connect to the Anchor Standard

R2: *Determine central ideas or themes of a text and analyze their development; summarize the key supporting details and ideas.*

Throughout the grades, Standard 2 leads students from determining the main topic and key details of a text to analyzing and explaining how key details support one or more main ideas. Students learn to examine texts closely in order to identify multiple main ideas along with their supporting details. From this, they determine the central idea of a text. Students might ask questions such as these: *How do the main ideas and supporting details of each section lead to an understanding of the central idea of the entire text? How can I use the main ideas and details to summarize the text?* Use the following activities to help children begin this transition.

- Explain to children that they can use the main topic and key details to *summarize*, or tell about a book in their own words. Read aloud page 9 of *What's It Like to Be a Fish?* Work with children to identify the key details. (*A goldfish can move around a castle. It can hide in the plants. It can swim in the water.*) Discuss what all of these details are about. (*A goldfish can live in a bowl.*) Then ask them to tell about the details in their own words. (SL.K.1)

- Guide children to identify multiple main topics in a book and then the main topic of the entire book. Read aloud page 8 of *What Lives in a Shell?* Ask: *What is this page all about?* (a land snail) Repeat for page 14 (a turtle); and page 19 (a crab). Ask children to tell what is alike about all these animals. (*They all live in shells.*) Guide them to understand that this is the main topic of the entire book. Use the title to emphasize this point. (SL.K.2)

Lesson 8 (Student Book pages 65–68)

CCSS

RI.K.3: With prompting and support, describe the connection between two individuals, events, ideas, or pieces of information in a text.

Describing Connections

Required Read Alouds: *F (Red-Eyed Tree Frog); G (What's It Like to Be a Fish?)*

Lesson Objectives

- Understand that events and ideas in a text are connected to one another.

- Use words that describe time-order connections.

- Use words that describe cause-and-effect connections.

- Recognize that describing connections between events and ideas in a text can help you understand important information.

The Learning Progression

- **Prior to K:** Children should be able to ask and answer questions about informational text that is read aloud. They should also be able to tell about or act out a simple sequence of events.

- **Grade K: CCSS RI.K.3 expects children to describe the connection between two individuals, events, ideas, or pieces of information in a text with prompting and support.**

- **Grade 1:** CCSS RI.1.3 advances the standard by having children describe the connection between two individuals, events, ideas, or pieces of information in a text more independently.

Tap Children's Prior Knowledge

- Tell children they are going to learn about how two events are connected, or fit together. Remind them that an *event* is something that happens. Have children share some things they do at bedtime.

- Choose a common activity, such as brushing teeth. Say: *First, you squeeze toothpaste onto your toothbrush. Then you brush your teeth.* Have children pantomime each step. Say: *These two events are connected. The second event—brushing your teeth, comes right after the first event—squeezing the toothpaste onto your brush.*

- Talk about turning off the lights next. Say: *You push the light switch. Then the lights go off. Why did the lights go off? (because you pushed the light switch)* Guide children to see that these events are connected because the first one made the second one happen.

- Review with children that they have learned about two types of connections: one event happens right after another event, and one event happens because of another event. Invite them to share additional examples of these connections in their daily lives.

- Tell children that in this lesson, they will learn how to describe the connections between events or ideas in an information book.

Ready *Teacher Toolbox*		*Teacher-Toolbox.com*
	Prerequisite Skills	**RI.K.3**
Ready Lessons		✓
Tools for Instruction		✓ ✓
Interactive Tutorials		✓ ✓

Additional CCSS

RI.K.2; RI.K.7; SL.K.1; SL.K.2 *(See page A38 for full text.)*

Part 1: Introduction

Step by Step

- **Introduce the standard.** Tell children they will learn how to identify and describe connections between events in an information book.

- Remind children that an *event* is something that happens. Recall that events can be connected in different ways. Review the examples from the activity on page 91.

- **Read aloud the Student Book page.** Have children turn to Student Book page 65. Read aloud the introduction as children listen and follow along.

- Read aloud the description of a time-order connection. Then say:

  > **Time order is one kind of connection. We use this phrase to tell about when one event *follows* another, which means one event happens right after another. Look at these pictures: they show a time-order connection. First it is daytime. Then it is nighttime. Nighttime follows daytime.**

  Tip: If children are having trouble with the concept of events following each other, use familiar examples of other things that follow in time order, such as hours of the day, days of the week, and months of the year.

- Have children practice describing the connection between daytime and nighttime. Encourage them to use the word *then* as they describe the connection.

- Discuss additional examples of time-order connections between events, such as making a sandwich and eating it or painting a picture and hanging it on the wall. Point out that each example has one action that follows another.

- Read aloud the description of a cause-and-effect connection. Say:

  > **Cause and effect is another kind of connection. We use this phrase to tell about when one event *causes* another, which means one event makes another one happen. Look at these pictures: they show a cause-and-effect connection. In the first picture, it is raining. So then what happens in the next picture because it rained? The ground gets all wet.**

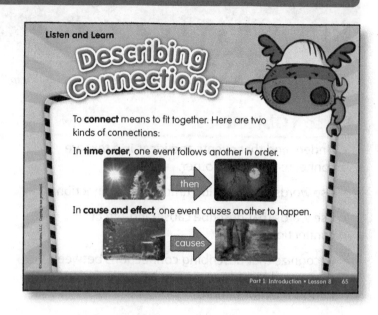

Listen and Learn

Describing Connections

To **connect** means to fit together. Here are two kinds of connections:

In **time order**, one event follows another in order.

then

In **cause and effect**, one event causes another to happen.

causes

Part 1: Introduction • Lesson 8   65

- Have children practice describing the connection between the rain and the wet ground. Encourage them to practice describing it in the following ways:

  The rain causes the ground to get wet.

  The ground gets wet because of the rain.

- Discuss additional examples of cause-and-effect connections, such as missing the bus and arriving late for school, going to bed late and yawning throughout the next day, or planting a seed and growing a flower. Point out that each example has one action that causes the other action to happen.

- Help children understand that good readers describe connections between events so they can understand the information they read. Point out that information can be connected in other ways, but this lesson will only focus on time order and cause and effect.

- **Have children demonstrate understanding.** Have children share what they have learned so far about describing connections between events. Encourage them to provide additional examples of both time-order and cause-and-effect connections from their own experiences.

Step by Step

- **Review Part 1.** Remind children that they can describe connections between events. Review that they have learned how to describe time-order and cause-and-effect connections.

- **Revisit the book.** Display *What's It Like to Be a Fish?* Page through the book, using the pictures as prompts to have children recall what it is about. *(RI.K.2; RI.K.7)*

- **Model describing connections.** Explain that you will model describing a connection in an information book. Display and read aloud the first three sentences on page 20. Think aloud:

  > **These sentences give me information about how fish eat. So what do they do? They "race to the top of the bowl, snap at their food, and gulp it down." How are these events connected to each other? Let me think: they race to the top. That happens first. Then they snap at the food and gulp it down. We can think of these as one event because they snap and gulp at the same time.** (Mimic the action.) **So that happens second. The second event happens right after the first one. These events are connected by time order.**

  Tip: Quickly think aloud as you confirm your answer and check whether the events are connected by cause and effect. Determine that the fish did not gulp down the food *because* they raced to the top, so the events are not connected by cause and effect.

- Use the Close Reading activity to help children break apart multiple details within one sentence.

- Tell children you will model how to complete the Student Book page by describing a connection between two events in *What's It Like to Be a Fish?*

- **Model completing the Student Book page.** Have children turn to Student Book page 66. Point to and name each picture (*goldfish racing to the top; goldfish gulping down food*). Model using the clue word *then* to describe the connection. Then ask: *How do you describe the connection when one event follows another one?* Model circling the correct answer.

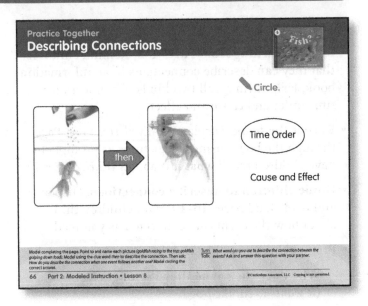

- **Have children demonstrate understanding.** Display page 20. Read aloud the Turn and Talk activity. Model a conversation that partners might have by asking and answering the question below. *(SL.K.1; SL.K.2)*

  > *What word can you use to describe the connection between the events? Ask and answer this question with your partner.* (then)

- Have children practice describing the connection using the words *time order* and *then*. Invite them to explain why the example on page 20 is not a cause-and-effect connection.

Close Reading

- Help children unpack sentences that have several details in them. Reread the third sentence on page 20. Ask:

  > **What three actions are the fish doing in this sentence?** *(racing, snapping, and gulping)*

- Define any unfamiliar words. Then invite different volunteers to demonstrate each action.

- Guide children to understand that even though the actions are written together in one sentence, the author is telling about three different things.

- Have children describe the connection between the three actions, using the word *then*.

Step by Step

- **Review learning from Parts 1–2.** Remind children that they can describe connections in an information book. Help them recall two kinds of connections: time order and cause and effect.

- **Revisit the book.** Display *Red-Eyed Tree Frog.* Page through the book, using the pictures as prompts to have children recall what it is about. *(RI.K.2; RI.K.7)*

- **Guide children to describe connections.** Display and read aloud pages 16–19. Have children think about how the events are connected as you read.

- Prompt children to identify the connection:

  Why does the snake flick its tongue?
  (It wants to eat the frog.)

  So what does the frog do? *(It jumps.)*

  What makes the frog jump? *(The frog jumps because the snake flicks its tongue. The frog wants to get away from the hungry snake.)*

  The snake flicks its tongue and causes the frog to jump. How can we describe the connection between these two events? *(cause and effect)*

> **Tip:** Some children might correctly argue that these events are also connected by time order. As children demonstrate understanding of each distinct kind of connection, you should explain that most events connected by cause and effect are also connected by time order. Provide several examples to clarify.

- Use the Close Reading activity to help children look for connections in the words and pictures.

- Tell children you will work together to complete the Student Book page by describing the connection in this part of the book.

- **Guide children to complete the Student Book page.** Have children turn to page 67. Point to and name each picture *(snake flicking its tongue; frog jumping).* Guide a volunteer to use the clue word *causes* to describe the connection. Then ask: *How do you describe the connection when one event causes another?* Read the answer choices, and guide children to circle the correct one.

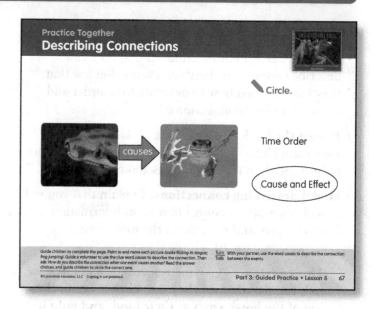

- Allow children to explain how these events are also connected by time order as appropriate.

- **Have children demonstrate understanding.** Display pages 16–19 of *Red-Eyed Tree Frog.* Read aloud the Turn and Talk activity. *(SL.K.1; SL.K.2)*

  With your partner, use the word *causes* to describe the connection between the events. *(The snake flicks its tongue. This causes the frog to jump.)*

- Invite partners to share their descriptions of the cause-and-effect connection with the class. Encourage them to also practice describing the connection using the word *because.* *(The frog jumps because the snake flicks its tongue.)*

Close Reading

- Help children look for clues about how events are connected in the words and pictures. Display and reread pages 16–17. Prompt:

  Why does the snake flick its tongue? *(It is hungry and wants to eat the frog.)*

  What details in the picture show you this? *(The snake has its tongue out toward the frog.)*

  Which words say that the frog should try to get away? *("Look out, frog!")*

- Turn the page, and help children describe the cause-and-effect connection between the snake's actions and the frog's response.

Step by Step

- **Review learning from Parts 1–3.** Have children review the words they use to describe cause-and-effect connections and time-order connections. Then display pages 16–19 of *Red-Eyed Tree Frog* and have children review how the events are connected.

- **Have children describe connections.** Display pages 21–24 of *Red-Eyed Tree Frog.* Tell children they will describe how the events are connected in this part of the book.

- Provide context for this part of the book. Briefly return to page 6 and remind children that the red-eyed tree frog is hungry and looking for food. Then turn to pages 21–24, and read them aloud. Prompt:

  What does the frog see on the leaf? (*a moth*)

  What does the frog do? (*It eats the moth.*)

  How does the frog feel after eating the moth? (*It is not hungry anymore.*)

  Why doesn't the frog feel hungry anymore? (*because it ate the moth*)

  Tip: If the wording becomes too confusing for children, rephrase "the frog does not feel hungry anymore" to say "the frog feels full." Use this language in the *causes* and *because* sentence frames.

- Tell children that they will complete the Student Book page by describing the connection between events in this part of *Red-Eyed Tree Frog.*

- **Have children complete the Student Book page independently.** Have children turn to Student Book page 68. Point to and name each picture (*frog eating a moth; frog is not hungry*). Have a volunteer use the clue word *causes* to describe the connection. Then ask: *How do you describe the connection when one event causes another?* Read the answer choices, and have children circle the correct one.

- Discuss the answer to the Student Book page. If children wish to describe the connection as time order, have them use evidence to explain why.

- **Have children demonstrate understanding.** Display pages 21–24 of *Red-Eyed Tree Frog.* Read aloud the Turn and Talk activity. (*SL.K.1; SL.K.2*)

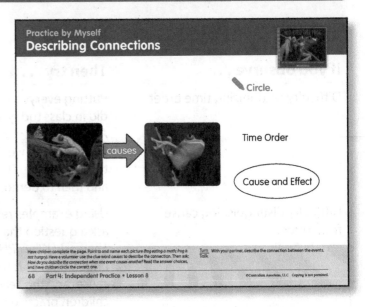

With your partner, describe the connection between the events. (*The frog eats the moth. This causes the frog to not feel hungry anymore.*)

- Use the Close Reading activity to help children make an additional cause-and-effect connection.

- **Have children reflect on their learning.** Invite children to tell why readers describe connections between events in an information book. Emphasize that describing connections helps them pay closer attention to what happens, in what order, and why. This helps them remember important details.

Close Reading

- Tell children that they can make connections between events in different parts of a book.

- Display and read aloud pages 5–6. Ask:

  What do we learn about the frog here? (*It is hungry and wants to eat.*)

- Return to pages 21–23 and read them aloud. Ask:

  Why is the frog eating a moth? (*because it is hungry*)

- Emphasize that describing this connection helps readers understand more about the frog and the reasons for its behavior throughout the book.

Assessment and Remediation

If you observe . . .	Then try . . .
Difficulty recognizing time order	Putting everyday events in time order. Have children tell three things they did in class today. Write each event on a sentence strip and read it aloud. Ask: *What did we do first?* As children respond, post the sentence strip. Ask: *Then what did we do?* Place the second strip below the first. Repeat for the third sentence. Then read the sentences with children, using the words *first* and *then* to demonstrate the time-order connection.
Difficulty distinguishing cause from effect	Using examples related to rules children are familiar with. For instance, ask a question that requires children to raise their hands. Call on one child. Then ask: *Why did I call on you? (because I raised my hand)* Lead children to understand that the first event—the child raising his/her hand—is the cause, and the second event—getting called on—is the effect. Help children practice describing the cause and the effect.
Difficulty identifying cause-and-effect connections	Providing practice by asking *why* questions that children will know the answers to. For instance, ask: *Why did we wear our coats outside today? (because it is cold out); Why did I move to this side of the room? (because it is time for math lessons); Why is the board empty? (because you erased it)* For each example, help children rephrase the events so they understand that the first event caused the second one. For example: *It is cold out. This caused us to wear our coats today. The cold is the cause. Wearing our coats is the effect.*

Connect to the Anchor Standard

R3: *Analyze how and why individuals, events, and ideas develop and interact over the course of a text.*

Throughout the grades, Standard 3 advances students' understanding of connections and relationships among ideas in text. Students in early grades examine and describe connections between two discrete pieces of information in a text. In later grades, students are engaged in more complex explorations of how ideas are connected in scientific, historical, and technical texts. Students learn to ask questions such as these: *Why is this idea critical to the one that follows? How does this event affect each event that follows? Why is it important that the author connected these ideas in this way? Why is it important that the author included these particular ideas in this series of ideas?* Use the following activities to help children begin this transition.

- Help children understand why it is important to recognize how events in a series are related. Read aloud the second paragraph on page 17 of *What's It Like to Be a Fish?* Explain that to understand the way people breathe, you must be able to connect the events in order. Ask: *What is the first event? What happens to the air you breathe in? What does your body do with the oxygen? What does your body do next?* (SL.K.1; SL.K.2)

- Guide children to see the impact of one event on others. Read aloud page 12 of *Red-Eyed Tree Frog.* Ask: *What does the frog do when it sees the caterpillar?* Discuss how this event affects subsequent events— the frog is not poisoned, and so lives on. The rest of the book tells about what the frog does. Have children consider an alternate cause and effect. Ask: *If the frog had eaten the caterpillar, how might the rest of the book have been different?*

Lesson 9 (Student Book pages 69–72)

CCSS

RL.K.4: Ask and answer questions about unknown words in a text.

Unknown Words

Required Read Alouds: D (*Stone Soup*); E (*Why Mosquitoes Buzz in People's Ears*)

Lesson Objectives

- Ask questions about unknown words in stories.

- Use evidence from the story to answer questions about unknown words and determine their meanings.

- Understand why determining the meanings of unknown words helps readers comprehend stories.

The Learning Progression

- **Prior to K:** Children are able to distinguish between spoken words they recognize and spoken words they do not understand.

- **Grade K: CCSS RL.K.4 expects children to ask and answer questions about unknown words in a story.**

- **Grade 1:** CCSS RL.1.4 advances the standard by having children identify sensory words or phrases in stories or poems.

Tap Children's Prior Knowledge

- Ask children what they do when they hear new or unfamiliar words. Invite them to share some ways they learn the meanings of new words.

- Explain that one way to learn a new word is to listen for information that gives clues about its meaning. Another way is to look at a picture or visual aid that shows what it means.

- Point to your elbow and say: *This is my elbow. My elbow is in the middle of my arm. My elbow is where my arm bends.* Discuss the word and visual clues you used to convey the meaning of *elbow*.

- Sing "Head, Shoulders, Knees, and Toes" with children. Have them act out the words of the song.

- Choose body parts from the song and work with children to help show and tell what they mean. For example, point to your head and say: *My head is on top of my shoulders. My head has my hair and face on it.* Review the word and visual clues that would help someone understand the meaning of each word.

- Tell children that in this lesson, they will learn how to use word and picture clues to figure out the meanings of new or unknown words they hear or read in stories.

Ready *Teacher Toolbox*   *Teacher-Toolbox.com*

	Prerequisite Skills	RL.K.4
Ready Lessons		✓
Tools for Instruction	✓ ✓	✓
Interactive Tutorials		

Additional CCSS

RL.K.2; RL.K.7; SL.K.1; SL.K.2 (*See page A38 for full text.*)

Step by Step

- **Introduce the standard.** Tell children that when they read or listen to stories, there may be words they do not know or understand. Explain that they will learn strategies for finding the meaning of an unknown word.

- Draw or post a picture of a puppy wearing a harness. Then read aloud the following story. Ask children to notice and remember any words they do not know.

  Jim's puppy, Mocha, always pulled on her leash, so his mom bought a harness. Jim slipped the straps of the harness over Mocha's head. He buckled the straps under her neck. He hooked the leash to the harness. Now Jim and Mocha could walk. No more pulling!

- Have children name words in the story they do not know. (*Possible responses include* leash, harness, slipped, buckled, hooked.)

- Choose one of the words, such as *harness*. Discuss the word with children, as follows:

  How can we find out what a *harness* might be? Let's check for clues in the words. (Reread) **We know Mom buys it. We know it has straps and it goes over the dog's head and buckles under her neck. Jim hooks the leash to it. These are all good clues. Does the picture show us what a *harness* is?** (Point) **Yes, this dog is wearing something that has straps, and the leash is hooked to it. This must be the harness.**

- Invite children to suggest a meaning for *harness*. Together, define it as "straps an animal wears to help the owner keep control of it." Have children use the word in a different sentence to demonstrate understanding of its meaning.

- Tell children that in their Student Books, they will learn some questions they can ask to help them understand words in a story they do not know.

- **Read aloud the Student Book page.** Have children turn to Student Book page 69. Read aloud the page as children listen and follow along.

- Reread each question. Tell children they will practice looking for word and picture clues for another unknown word in the story, such as *leash*.

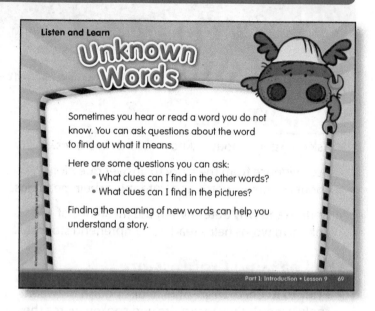

Listen and Learn

Unknown Words

Sometimes you hear or read a word you do not know. You can ask questions about the word to find out what it means.

Here are some questions you can ask:
- What clues can I find in the other words?
- What clues can I find in the pictures?

Finding the meaning of new words can help you understand a story.

Part 1: Introduction • Lesson 9   69

- Reread the story, having children listen carefully for sentences that contain the word *leash*. Then invite them to repeat clues from the story. (*Mocha pulls on the leash. The leash is hooked to the harness.*) Next have them point to the leash in the picture.

- Work together with children to define *leash* as "a strap attached to a dog to keep it close to its owner."

Tip: Tell children that sometimes there aren't enough clues in the words or pictures to tell the meaning of a word. In these cases, children can think of whether they have heard the word another time, ask someone what it means, or ask for help looking it up in a children's dictionary.

- Help children understand that good readers notice when they do not understand a word and they look for clues to figure out the word's meaning.

- **Have children demonstrate understanding.** Call on volunteers to share what they have learned so far about asking questions about unknown words. Ask them to tell the questions they can ask themselves when they listen to or read a word they do not know.

- Encourage children to tell how noticing unfamiliar words and figuring out their meanings will help them better understand a story.

Step by Step

- **Review Part 1.** Review with children the questions they can ask to find out meanings of unknown words.

- **Revisit the story.** Display *Stone Soup*. Page through the book, using the pictures as prompts to have children recall the story. *(RL.K.2; RL.K.7)*

- **Model asking questions about unknown words.** Explain that you will model figuring out the meaning of a word in this story. Display and read aloud page 7. Reread the first sentence, and think aloud:

  I notice a word I don't know—*trudged*. The words say "[t]hree soldiers trudged down a road." The picture shows the soldiers walking down the road. That makes me think *trudged* tells about the *way* the soldiers are walking.

  Are there other clues? The words say "[b]esides being tired, they were hungry." Maybe *trudge* tells how people walk when they are tired and hungry. I know how that might look.

  Tip: Invite volunteers to demonstrate what trudging looks like. Help them to clarify the movement, and briefly brainstorm some places you might trudge to. For example, say: *He trudged toward the dentist's office. She trudged upstairs to clean her messy room.*

- Display pages 8–9 and read aloud page 8. Model how to determine the meaning of *village*. Think aloud:

  The words say "ahead of them they saw the lights of a village." The picture shows what the soldiers see ahead of, or in front of them. It is a small group of houses and buildings nestled close together. A village must be like a small town.

- Use the Close Reading activity to look for additional clues to the meaning of *village*.

- Tell children you will model how to complete the Student Book page by identifying pictures that show unknown words in *Stone Soup*.

- **Model completing the Student Book page.** Have children turn to page 70. For the first item, ask: *Which picture shows someone trudging?* Demonstrate circling the correct picture. Continue with the second item. Ask: *Which picture shows a village?* Discuss the evidence that helped you choose each correct picture.

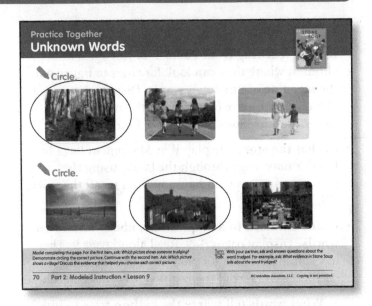

Practice Together
Unknown Words

Circle.

Circle.

Model completing the page. For the first item, ask: *Which picture shows someone trudging?* Demonstrate circling the correct picture. Continue with the second item. Ask: *Which picture shows a village?* Discuss the evidence that helped you choose each correct picture.

Turn Talk: With your partner, ask and answer questions about the word trudged. For example, ask: *What evidence in Stone Soup tells about the word trudged?*

70 Part 2: Modeled Instruction • Lesson 9   ©Curriculum Associates, LLC Copying is not permitted.

- **Have children demonstrate understanding.** Display pages 7–9 of *Stone Soup*. Read aloud the Turn and Talk activity. Model what a conversation with a partner should sound like by asking and answering the question below. *(SL.K.1; SL.K.2)*

  With your partner, ask and answer questions about the word *trudged*. For example, ask: What evidence tells about the word trudged? (*The soldiers are trudging down a road so it seems to be a way of walking. They are on their way home from war and they are tired and hungry. These details make me think they would not be walking very quickly.*)

Close Reading

- Guide children to look for additional word clues to help them figure out the meaning of *village*. Reread page 8. Prompt:

  What are the soldiers wishing for as they walk? (*a good dinner and a bed to sleep in*)

  Once they see the village, what do the soldiers hope they'll find there? (*a bite to eat and a loft to sleep in*)

  Where can you usually find food to eat and a bed to sleep in? (*at a house*)

- Revisit the picture clues from your modeling, and help children understand that the soldiers are pleased to see a village because there will be homes there, and they expect to be invited in.

Step by Step

- **Review learning from Parts 1–2.** Review with children where they can look for clues to figure out the meaning of unknown words. Display pages 8–9 of *Stone Soup*. Have children tell the meaning of *village* and the clues they used to figure it out.

- **Revisit the story.** Display *Why Mosquitoes Buzz in People's Ears*. Page through the book, using the pictures as prompts to have children recall the story. (RL.K.2; RL.K.7)

- **Guide children to ask questions about unknown words.** Display pages 8–9. Read aloud page 9. Then have children listen for clues about the meaning of *burrow* as you reread the last two paragraphs. Prompt:

  What words tell where the python tries to hide? (*"The first likely place he found was a rabbit hole."*)

  What does the rabbit see? (*the big snake coming into her burrow*)

  Where is the rabbit in the picture? (*in a hole underground*)

  > **Tip:** Since the illustrations in this story are not traditional, you may need to point out the sun on page 8 and the tree on page 9 to help children gain the perspective to see that the rabbit is underground.

- Decide together that a *burrow* is a hole in the ground where the rabbit lives. Clarify that a rabbit is only one type of animal that lives in a burrow. Some other examples are chipmunks, foxes, and groundhogs.

- Use the Close Reading activity to guide children in finding the meaning of *scurried* in the same paragraph.

- Tell children you will work together to complete the Student Book page by identifying pictures that show unknown words in *Why Mosquitoes Buzz in People's Ears*.

- **Guide children to complete the Student Book page.** Have children turn to page 71. For the first item, ask: *Which picture shows a burrow?* Guide children to circle the correct picture. Continue with the second item. Ask: *Which picture shows someone scurrying?* Discuss the evidence that helped children choose each correct picture.

- **Have children demonstrate understanding.** Display pages 8–9 of *Why Mosquitoes Buzz in People's Ears*. Read aloud the Turn and Talk activity. (SL.K.1; SL.K.2)

  > ***What evidence in the book tells about the word scurried? Ask and answer this question with your partner.*** (*The words say the rabbit bounded, or ran, away. The picture shows the rabbit looking over her shoulder and then running out of her burrow.*)

- Invite partners to share their ideas with the class. Then encourage children to use *scurry* in other sentences that demonstrate its meaning.

Close Reading

- Guide children in understanding the word *scurried*. Read aloud the last paragraph on page 9. Ask:

  What action does the word *scurried* describe? (*the way the rabbit moves when she sees the snake*)

  What do the words say about how the rabbit feels? (*She is terrified, or scared.*)

  How would you move if you were scared? (*I would run away quickly.*)

  What does the picture show about the rabbit? (*She is running out and away from the snake.*)

- Decide together that *scurried* means "ran away quickly or in a rush."

Step by Step

- **Review learning from Parts 1–3.** Review strategies to figure out the meaning of unknown words. Display pages 8–9 of *Why Mosquitoes Buzz in People's Ears*. Have children tell the meaning of *burrow* and the clues they used to figure it out.

- **Have children ask questions about unknown words.** Display and read aloud pages 10–11 of *Why Mosquitoes Buzz in People's Ears*.

- Reread the first two sentences on page 10. Point out the words "crying kaa, kaa, kaa!" Ask children what *crying* usually means. *(weeping)* Explain that here, *crying* has a different meaning. Read the next sentence. Ask:

    What is the crow's duty, or job? *(He spreads the alarm in case of danger.)*

    How does someone speak when there is danger? *(They speak loudly and quickly. They yell.)*

    When the crow is *crying*, what is he doing? *(shouting to the others to tell them there is danger)*

- Read aloud the last paragraph on page 11. Point to the word *limb*. Explain that an arm or leg can be called a *limb*, but that is not its meaning here. Prompt:

    What word clues tell you about a *limb*? *(It is in the treetops. It can break.)*

    What picture clues tell you about a *limb*? *(The monkey is holding a tree branch that is breaking off.)*

    What does *limb* mean? *(a tree branch)*

> **Tip:** Emphasize that some words have more than one meaning, such as *crying* and *limb*. Readers use word and picture clues to figure out which meaning is the correct one in the story.

- **Have children complete the Student Book page independently.** Have children turn to page 72. For the first item, ask: *Which picture shows someone crying out?* Have children circle the correct picture. Continue with the second item. Ask: *Which picture shows a limb?* Have children discuss the evidence that helped them choose each correct picture.

- Use the Close Reading activity to provide additional practice with using text clues to understand an unknown word.

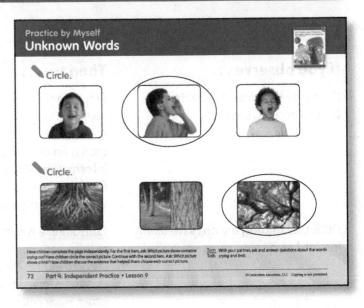

Practice by Myself
Unknown Words

Circle.

Circle.

Have children complete the page independently. For the first item, ask: Which picture shows someone crying out? Have children circle the correct picture. Continue with the second item. Ask: Which picture shows a limb? Have children discuss the evidence that helped them choose each correct picture.

Turn With your partner, ask and answer questions about the words
Talk crying and limb.

72 Part 4: Independent Practice • Lesson 9 ©Curriculum Associates, LLC Copying is not permitted.

- **Have children demonstrate understanding.** Display pages 10–11 *Why Mosquitoes Buzz in People's Ears*. Read aloud the Turn and Talk activity. (SL.K.1; SL.K.2)

    With your partner, ask and answer questions about the words *crying* and *limb*. *(What is the crow crying? [kaa, kaa, kaa] Where does the monkey land? [on a dead limb])*

- **Have children reflect on their learning.** Invite children to tell why it is important to ask questions when they do not understand words in a story. Have them name the types of clues they can use to find the meaning of an unknown word.

Close Reading

- Read aloud pages 10–11. Help children understand the meaning of the made-up words *kili wili* by looking at the other words around it.

    What action do the made-up words *kili wili* describe? *(how the monkey is moving)*

    What other word clues tell what the monkey is doing? *(screeching, leaping, crashing)*

    Why does the monkey act this way? *(He is in a hurry to warn the other animals.)*

    From these clues, what do you think *kili wili* means in this story? *(in a hurry; not carefully)*

Assessment and Remediation

If you observe . . .	Then try . . .
Difficulty locating text evidence for unknown words	Practicing with a created text. Read aloud these sentences: *Dad turns the oven to a very high temperature. He broils the fish. We eat the cooked fish hot out of the oven.* Work together to define *broil*. Help children establish that *broil* is an action word. Then have them look for other words that give information. Prompt: *What is Dad cooking in? How hot is the oven? What is the fish like when it comes out of the oven?* Help them define *broil* as "cooking at a very high temperature."
Difficulty finding a word's meaning in word or picture clues	Consulting a reference book. Read aloud page 7 of *Stone Soup,* and ask children to tell what *country* means. Read aloud the words around it and say: *I see they are on a road in the country, and that the country is strange, but there aren't enough clues here for me to know what a country is. The picture does not give many details either.* Have children suggest possible meanings. Then demonstrate how to look up the word in a children's dictionary. Read aloud each definition, and find the one that makes sense in the context of *Stone Soup.*
Difficulty defining unknown words	Providing the word in a different context. For instance, if children cannot define *entertain*, say: *My nephews are coming over today. I got lots of books, toys, and movies to entertain them. I hope they have fun!* Help children find the word clues in your sentences *(books, toys, movies, fun)* and then have them tell the word's meaning. Use the word in additional sentences to clarify as needed.

Connect to the Anchor Standard

R4: *Interpret words and phrases as they are used in a text, including determining technical, connotative, and figurative meanings, and analyze how specific word choices shape meaning or tone.*

Throughout the grades, Standard 4 builds students' awareness of authors' precise word choices in texts. As students become increasingly conscious of an author's deliberate role in shaping a text, they change focus from identifying a word's denotative meaning in the early grades to analyzing the nuances of its connotative meaning in later grades. As students examine the impact of word choice on texts, they might consider questions such as these: *How do the author's word choices shape the tone of the text? How does the author use metaphors and similes? How do these word choices affect the reader's experience?* Use the following activities to help children begin this transition.

- Help children analyze figurative language. Read aloud page 33 of *Stone Soup,* and point out the phrase "fit for the king." Explain that *fit for* means "good enough for." Ask: *What would a king expect soup to taste like? Why does this description excite the peasants? Why do the soldiers say this instead of simply saying the soup is delicious?* Discuss how the figurative language makes the peasants think the soup is incredibly special and rare. *(SL.K.1; SL.K.2)*

- Guide children to understand how an author's word choice can tell a lot about a character. Read aloud page 20 of *Why Mosquitoes Buzz in People's Ears.* Discuss the words the author uses to describe the rabbit and her actions: *timid, trembling, uncertainly.* Ask: *What do these words tell you about how the rabbit feels? How do you think the author wants you to feel toward the rabbit?* Lead children to see that the author wants readers to feel sympathy for the rabbit.

Lesson 10 (Student Book pages 73–76)

Types of Texts

CCSS

RL.K.5: Recognize common types of texts (e.g., storybooks, poems).

Required Read Alouds: *Projectable 1 ("The Owl and the Pussy-Cat"); Projectable 2 ("How to Make Play Dough"); D (Stone Soup)*

Lesson Objectives

- Understand that there are different types of texts.

- Identify the features of various texts, including poems, stories, and recipes.

- Recognize that knowing what type of text you are reading can help you better comprehend it.

The Learning Progression

- **Prior to K:** Children should be familiar with books and understand that people read or listen to them. They should also be able to describe content features such as pictures or characters.

- **Grade K: CCSS RL.K.5 introduces the idea that there are different types of texts, with the expectation that children can readily recognize familiar genres such as poems and stories.**

- **Grade 1:** CCSS RL.1.5 expects children to distinguish between different types of text and describe specific differences between literary texts and informational texts (fiction and nonfiction), based on listening to and reading a wide range of texts.

Tap Children's Prior Knowledge

- Gather a variety of books from the classroom library, including fiction stories, information books, books with poems, and books with procedural instructions. Sort the books into piles based on genre.

- Tell children that there are many different kinds of books. Readers read each type of book for a different reason, and sometimes in different ways.

- Point to one pile of books, such as information books. Model looking for ways the books are the same. Read the titles and beginning of each book aloud. Say: *All of these books go together in one group. How are they alike? I notice these all have photographs and are all about real, not made-up, things.*

- Guide children to recognize similar features in each group of books. Use prompts such as these: *Do these books all have drawings? Do these books all have characters? Do these books all tell how to do something in numbered steps?*

- Help children describe each group together, naming features that make them alike.

- Explain that a book or any other piece of writing is called *text*. Tell children that in this lesson, they will learn to recognize three different types of texts: poems, stories, and recipes.

Ready *Teacher Toolbox*		*Teacher-Toolbox.com*
	Prerequisite Skills	**RL.K.5**
Ready Lessons		✓
Tools for Instruction		
Interactive Tutorials		✓ ✓

Additional CCSS

RL.K.2; RL.K.7; SL.K.1; SL.K.2 *(See page A38 for full text.)*

Step by Step

- **Introduce the standard.** Tell children they will learn about different types, or kinds, of texts. Explain that understanding what type of text they are reading will help them know why they are reading it.

- Gather a few books each from the following groups: stories, children's poems, and recipes for children.

- Recall the activity from page 103, and tell children they will now help you sort books into three groups. Work together to sort the books into their genres.

Tip: Children will notice that books could also be sorted into different groups, such as books with drawings versus photographs. Confirm that different kinds of books often share characteristics, and help them focus on key characteristics of each type.

- Create a three-column chart with the following heads: *Stories, Poems, Recipes.*

- Point to the group of stories and guide children to name characteristics that are alike. Prompt:

  This pile has stories in it. What is the same about all of these books? (*They tell a story with characters, a setting, and events. They have pictures that someone drew.*) Record their observations in the chart under *Stories.*

- Point to the group of poems. Read from a poem or two as needed. Then prompt:

  This pile has books of poems in it. What is the same about the poems? (*There are many different poems in the book. The poems are shorter than stories. They are written in short lines. Some have words that rhyme.*) Record their observations in the chart under *Poems.*

- Point to the group of recipe books. Flip through the pages and read aloud from two recipes. Then prompt:

  This pile has recipes in it. What is the same about the recipes? (*They have lists of ingredients and directions written in steps. They show pictures of what is being made.*) Record their observations in the chart under *Recipes.*

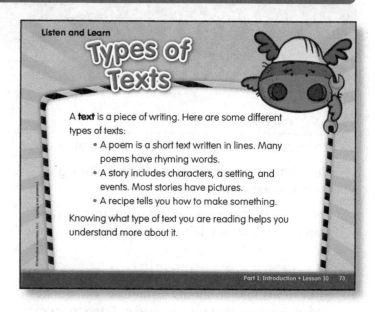

Listen and Learn

Types of Texts

A **text** is a piece of writing. Here are some different types of texts:

- A poem is a short text written in lines. Many poems have rhyming words.
- A story includes characters, a setting, and events. Most stories have pictures.
- A recipe tells you how to make something.

Knowing what type of text you are reading helps you understand more about it.

Part 1: Introduction • Lesson 10   73

- Tell children that in their Student Books, they will learn some clues to help them identify the type of text they are listening to or reading.

- **Read aloud the Student Book page.** Have children turn to Student Book page 73. Read aloud the page as children listen and follow along.

- Point to the first bullet, and reread the statement. Invite a volunteer to select a poem (or book of poems) from the piles of texts and prompt the child to tell why the poem fits the description. Reread portions of text as needed for support.

- Repeat with the second and third bullets. Then invite children to give examples of other books they know that could be added to each pile.

- Discuss with children how identifying the type of text they are reading will help them understand more about it. For example, say:

  If I am reading a recipe, I know that I should pay attention to the directions so that I do the steps in the right order.

- **Have children demonstrate understanding.** Call on volunteers to share what they have learned so far about different types of text. Prompt children to identify a few examples of each type of text.

Step by Step

- **Review Part 1.** Remind children that they listen to and read many different types of texts. Review the piles of texts from the previous activity and have children share characteristics they have in common.

> **Tip:** Children may think that the word *text* means an entire book. Explain that a *text* is a piece of writing that can be a whole book or just a short passage.

- **Read "The Owl and the Pussy-Cat."** Display Projectable 1 on page 163. Read aloud the title and then the poem, tracking the print.

- **Model how to recognize a poem.** Remind children that a poem is one type of text. Explain that you will model some ways to recognize a poem. Think aloud:

  > **I can see that this text is not nearly as long as a book. Plus, the writing looks different.** (Point to individual lines.) **These are called *lines*. Poems are written in lines instead of sentences. See how each line begins with a capital letter, but not every line ends with a punctuation mark? This is because lines in poems do not follow the same rules as sentences in a story.**

- Use your finger to track a few lines. Point to the capital letters that begin each line. Then continue:

  > **Also, many poems have words that *rhyme*, or end with the same sound. Let's listen again for rhyming words.** (Reread lines 1–4.) **I hear *sea*, *honey*, and *money*. These words rhyme because they all end with the /ē/ sound. I also hear *boat* and *note*. These words rhyme too: they make the /ōt/ sound. These features help me know that "The Owl and the Pussy-Cat" is a poem.**

- Use the Close Reading activity to examine another stanza of the poem with children.

- Tell children you will model how to complete the Student Book page by telling what type of text "The Owl and the Pussy-Cat" is.

- **Model completing the Student Book page.** Have children turn to page 74. For the first item, ask: *What type of text is "The Owl and the Pussycat"?* Point to and name each picture (*recipe; story; poem*). Demonstrate circling the correct answer. Continue with the second item. Ask: *What type of text often has rhyming words? (recipe; story; poem)*

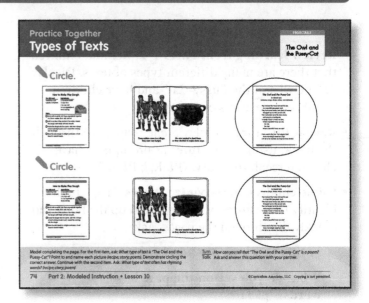

- **Have children demonstrate understanding.** Display "The Owl and the Pussy-Cat." Read aloud the Turn and Talk activity. Model what a conversation with a partner should sound like by asking and answering the question below. (*SL.K.1; SL.K.2*)

  > **How can you tell that "The Owl and the Pussy-Cat" is a poem?** Ask and answer this question with your partner. ("The Owl and the Pussy-Cat" *is shorter than a book, is written in lines, and has rhyming words, so it is a poem.*)

- Share and discuss other familiar poems. As you display and read each poem, guide children to recognize and point out the features of poems.

Close Reading

- Read the second stanza from "The Owl and the Pussy-Cat." Clarify any challenging vocabulary, such as *fowl* and *tarried*. Then prompt:

  > **What rhyming words do you hear in the first line?** (*Owl* and *fowl*)

  > **What rhyming words do you hear in the third line?** (*married* and *tarried*)

  > **What do you notice when you look at the lines?** (*They are all different lengths.*)

- Discuss how the rhyming words and uneven lines make the poem fun to read aloud and listen to. Invite children to repeat each line after you.

Step by Step

- **Review learning from Parts 1–2.** Remind children that there are many different types of texts. Display "The Owl and the Pussy-Cat" and have children recall some features of a poem.

- **Revisit the story.** Display *Stone Soup*. Page through the book, using the pictures as prompts to have children recall the story. *(RL.K.2; RL.K.7)*

- **Guide children to recognize stories.** Help children identify the features of a story. Hold up the book and quickly flip through the pages. Ask:

  Is this text long or short? *(long)*

  What do you see on the page besides words? *(pictures)*

- Refer to the features of a story on Student Book page 73. Then have children listen for details about characters, setting, and events as you read aloud pages 7–9 of *Stone Soup*. Prompt:

  Who are the characters? *(the soldiers; the peasants)*

  What is the setting? *(a strange country)*

  What event is happening? *(The soldiers are walking toward a village looking for food and a place to sleep.)*

  What type of text is *Stone Soup*? *(a story)*

> **Tip:** Emphasize that even though *Stone Soup* has the word *soup* in the title, and the characters talk about making soup, it is not a recipe.

- Use the Close Reading activity to help children understand how words and pictures work together to tell a story.

- Explain to children that you will work together to complete the Student Book page by telling what type of text *Stone Soup* is.

- **Guide children to complete the Student Book page.** Have children turn to page 75. For the first item, ask: *What type of text is* Stone Soup? Point to and name each picture *(recipe; story; poem)*. Have a volunteer tell which picture to circle. Continue with the second item. Ask: *What type of text has characters, a setting, and events? (recipe; story; poem)*

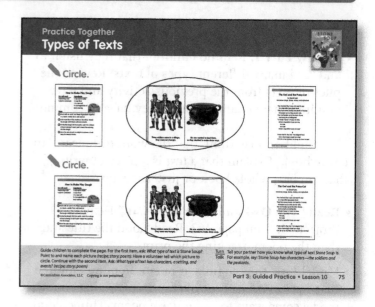

- **Have children demonstrate understanding.** Display *Stone Soup*. Read aloud the Turn and Talk activity. *(SL.K.1; SL.K.2)*

  Tell your partner how you know what type of text *Stone Soup* is. For example, say: *Stone Soup* has characters—the soldiers and the peasants.

- Invite partners to share their ideas with the class. Help children point to examples of the features in *Stone Soup* that show it is a story.

- Share and discuss other familiar stories. Display each book and page through it, guiding children to recognize the features of stories.

Close Reading

- Review that most stories have words and pictures. Explain that the pictures help readers see what the words describe. Display and read aloud pages 18–19 of *Stone Soup*. Then prompt:

  What is happening in this part of the story? *(The soldiers are telling the peasants they are going to make stone soup.)*

  What can you see in the pictures? *(the three soldiers; one soldier is talking; the peasants are looking at and listening to the soldiers)*

- Discuss how the pictures support the words. Ask children to tell what they learned about the soldiers and peasants from the picture that the words did not describe.

Step by Step

- **Review learning from Parts 1–3.** Remind children that they have learned some features of poems and stories. Have them tell how they can recognize the difference between "The Owl and the Pussy-Cat" and *Stone Soup*.

- **Read "How to Make Play Dough."** Display Projectable 2 on page 165. Read aloud the title and then the text, tracking the print.

- **Guide children to recognize a recipe.** Tell children that you will guide them in finding the features of a recipe. Ask:

  What information do you get from this text? *(what you need to make play dough; how to make it)*

  Which part tells you what tools and ingredients you need? *(There are lists at the top titled* You will need *and* Ingredients.)

  Which part tells you how to make play dough? *(There are instructions labeled* Steps. *They tell how to make the play dough.)*

  How do you know what to do first? *(Each step has a number. You follow the steps in order.)*

  What kind of text is this? *(a recipe)*

  Tip: Help children understand that while most recipes tell how to make food, some recipes are for nonedible items, such as bubble solution or finger paint.

- Use the Close Reading activity to help children understand why some recipes have illustrations.

- Tell children that they will complete the Student Book page by telling what type of text "How to Make Play Dough" is.

- **Have children complete the Student Book page independently.** Have children turn to page 76. For the first item, ask: *What type of text is "How to Make Play Dough"?* Point to and name each picture *(recipe; story; poem)*. Have children circle their answer. Continue with the second item. Ask: *What type of text tells how to make something? (recipe; story; poem)*

- **Have children demonstrate understanding.** Display "How to Make Play Dough." Read aloud the Turn and Talk activity. *(SL.K.1; SL.K.2)*

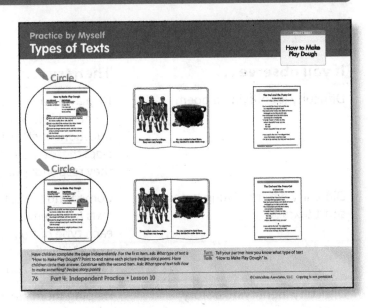

Tell your partner how you know what type of text "How to Make Play Dough" is. *(It tells how to make something and has a list of ingredients and tools you need, so it is a recipe.)*

- Discuss with children recipes they have used at home and in class. Ask: *What might happen if you did not follow the steps in order?*

- **Have children reflect on their learning.** Invite children to describe the different features of a poem, story, and recipe, and discuss how some features can be present in more than one type of text. Emphasize that recognizing what type of text they are reading helps readers make sense of the text.

Close Reading

- Explain that like a story, a recipe may sometimes have an illustration. Display "How to Make Play Dough" and point to the illustration. Ask:

  What does this picture show? *(play dough and a hand print)*

  Why do you think this picture is here? *(It shows readers what play dough looks like.)*

- Guide children to understand that illustrations in recipes tell more about what is being made. Discuss whether the recipe would give enough information without the picture.

Assessment and Remediation

If you observe . . .	Then try . . .
Difficulty identifying a poem	Displaying and reading aloud a short, familiar poem, such as "Twinkle, Twinkle, Little Star." Help children focus on the key features by asking questions such as these: *Is this text short or long? What does the first line say? Does the text have rhyming words? Which words rhyme?* To support children as they respond, point to each feature and reread the poem as needed.
Difficulty differentiating types of short texts	Comparing texts. Display a poem and a recipe side-by-side. Say: *One of these texts is a poem and the other is a recipe.* Help children recall the features of each type of text. Then read aloud both texts. Ask: *Which text has rhyming words? Which text has numbered steps?* Have children identify the correct text to answer each question.
Difficulty identifying a story	Helping them create a story. Provide the sentence starter *Once upon a time,* and have children decide who the characters will be and what will happen. Jot down notes as they brainstorm so you can help them recall their ideas. Craft the story together. Then point to the elements that made it a story, such as the characters, setting, and events. Choose a short, familiar classroom story and work together to identify those same elements.

Connect to the Anchor Standard

R5: *Analyze the structure of texts, including how specific sentences, paragraphs, and larger portions of the text (e.g., a section, chapter, scene, or stanza) relate to each other and the whole.*

Throughout the grades, Standard 5 leads students from identifying types of texts to an understanding of the underlying structures of texts. By delving into a text at the sentence and paragraph level, students are able to see these elements as the underpinnings of sections, chapters, and stanzas. In turn, students learn how these multiple parts within a text are related and connected with the purpose of forming a whole work. Students may ask questions such as these: *What are the features of this text? How did the author organize this text? How does each part of the text relate to the part that comes next? How does each part relate to the whole text?* Use the following activities to help children begin this transition.

- Guide children to see the purpose of the beginning and end of a story. Display and read aloud pages 7–9 of *Stone Soup.* Review the information the beginning tells: the setting, the characters, and the problem. Display and read aloud pages 44–47. Explain that the end usually wraps up the story, explaining how the characters' problem is solved. Ask: *How are the beginning and the end of* Stone Soup *connected?* (SL.K.1; SL.K.2)

- Use "The Owl and the Pussy-Cat" to help children understand how stanzas work together to form one piece. Display and read aloud the poem. Explain that the Owl and the Pussy-Cat are introduced in the first stanza. Talk about what they do. Point out that the next two stanzas have the same characters. Help children connect the events in these stanzas. Point out that together, the three stanzas tell what the Owl and the Pussy-Cat do.

Authors and Illustrators

CCSS

RL.K.6: With prompting and support, name the author and illustrator of a story and define the role of each in telling the story.

Required Read Alouds: A (*Jamaica's Blue Marker*); B (*The Art Lesson*); E (*Why Mosquitoes Buzz in People's Ears*)

Lesson Objectives

- Name the author of a story.
- Name the illustrator of a story.
- Define the roles of authors and illustrators in creating a story.

The Learning Progression

- **Prior to K:** Children should have a basic understanding of the concepts of *author* and *illustrator*. They should recognize that the name of the author and the illustrator usually appear on the cover of a book.

- **Grade K: CCSS RL.K.6 requires children, with prompting and support, to identify the author and illustrator of a story and the role of each in creating the story.**

- **Grade 1:** CCSS RL.1.6 further develops the standard by expecting children to identify who is telling the story at various points. Children are expected to begin thinking about whose point of view the story represents.

Tap Children's Prior Knowledge

- Tell children that they will help you write a story and then draw pictures to go with the words. Post a sheet of chart paper. At the top, write a story title and the first sentence, such as the following: ***Our New Dog Zoe.*** *Zoe and I go to the dog park every Sunday.*

- Invite children to contribute to the story. Call on a volunteer to dictate a sentence, and record it on the chart paper. Repeat until the story is about four sentences long.

- Read the story aloud. Then ask a volunteer to draw a picture on the chart paper. Explain that the picture should show an important detail in the story, such as the dog Zoe playing at the dog park.

- When the drawing is complete, ask: *Who thought of the words in the story?* Be sure children understand that even though you printed the words, it was the volunteers who made up the sentences.

- Then ask: *Who drew the picture?* Point out that writing and drawing are different jobs that were done by different children.

- Tell children that in this lesson, they will learn about the job of the person who writes stories and the job of the person who draws the pictures for stories.

Additional CCSS

RL.K.2; RL.K.7; SL.K.1; SL.K.2 (*See page A38 for full text.*)

Step by Step

- **Introduce the standard.** Tell children they will learn about the author and illustrator of a story. Explain that an author and illustrator work together to tell a story.

- Post a piece of chart paper. Invite a volunteer to share a story about something fun and exciting he or she did recently. Capture the story in three to four sentences, saying the words aloud as you record them.

- Post a second sheet of chart paper on top of the first. Ask children to suggest a title for the story. Remind them that a story title should hint as to what the story will be about. Record the title at the top of the paper in big letters.

- Brainstorm with children what the picture on the book cover should look like, based on the details in the story. Ask a volunteer to come draw the picture.

- Tell children that your book cover is almost complete, except for two more details. Prompt:

  Who wrote this story? Who thought of the words that I wrote down?

- Record the child's name beneath the title after the words *Written by.* Say:

  [Child's name] is the author of this story. Remember that the *author* is the person who thinks of a story and usually the person who writes it down.

- Emphasize that in this case, you merely helped while children learn to write, but that does not make you the author. Continue:

  We find the author's name on the cover of the book. Sometimes the book cover will say *written by* like it does here. Other times, the author's name will appear by itself.

- Display a few familiar classroom books that list the author's name in a variety of ways, such as by itself, preceded by the words *by* or *written by,* and located at different places on the cover.

- Ask children to tell who drew the picture for the book cover. Record the child's name after the words *illustrated by.* Remind children that many stories have *illustrators,* or someone who draws the pictures. Their names also go on the cover.

- Tell children that in their Student Books, they will learn questions they can ask about the author and illustrator of a story.

- **Read aloud the Student Book page.** Have children turn to Student Book page 77. Read aloud the page as children listen and follow along.

- Point to your class book cover and have children review the author and illustrator. Provide different sentence frames to help children talk about the roles of each. For example:

  The author of [title] is _____.

  [Title] is written by _____.

  [Title] is illustrated by _____.

- Explain that good readers understand how authors and illustrators work together to tell a story.

- **Have children demonstrate understanding.** Ask volunteers to share what they have learned so far about authors and illustrators. Encourage them to give examples of authors and illustrators, using familiar classroom read-alouds.

Part 2: Modeled Instruction

Step by Step

- **Review Part 1.** Remind children that an author and illustrator work together to tell a story. The author writes the words and the illustrator draws the pictures.

- **Revisit the story.** Display *Jamaica's Blue Marker*. Page through the book, using the pictures as prompts to have children recall the story. *(RL.K.2; RL.K.7)*

- **Model naming the author and the illustrator.** Display the front cover of the book, and point to the title as you read it aloud. Then point to and read the author's name. Say:

  > **The author's name is Juanita Havill. She wrote *Jamaica's Blue Marker*. I can tell she is the author because her name is written by itself here on the page. That is one way to list an author's name.**

- Point to and read the illustrator's name. Emphasize the words *Illustrations by*. Say:

  > **The illustrator is Anne Sibley O'Brien. She drew the pictures in the story. The words *Illustrations by* tell me the difference between her name and the author, Juanita Havill.**

- Use the Close Reading activity to help children think about the pictures that an illustrator draws for the front cover of a book.

- Tell children you will model how to complete the Student Book page by naming the title, author, and illustrator of *Jamaica's Blue Marker*.

- **Model completing the Student Book page.** Have children turn to page 78. Point to and read aloud the words on the book cover. Then point to each blank box and tell what words go in the box *(story title; name of the author; name of the illustrator)*. Read aloud the answer choices. Model drawing a line from each answer choice to its place on the book cover.

> **Tip:** Point out that the picture of the blank storybook is set up like the cover of *Jamaica's Blue Marker*. Have children recall where they saw the author's and illustrator's name on the real book.

- Prompt children to explain the words *written by* and *illustrated by* as you model drawing the line between each answer and its correct place. Point out that these words are clues in the Student Book that do not appear on the real book cover.

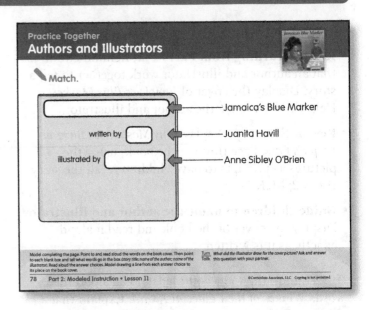

- **Have children demonstrate understanding.** Display the book cover. Read aloud the Turn and Talk activity. Model what a conversation with a partner should sound like by asking and answering the question below. *(SL.K.1; SL.K.2)*

  > **What did the illustrator draw for the cover picture? Ask and answer this question with your partner.** *(The illustrator drew the characters in the story: Jamaica and Russell. Jamaica is holding a blue marker and looking at Russell. Russell is looking at his cards.)*

- Point to details on the cover illustration as you model the Turn and Talk discussion.

Close Reading

- Tell children that one job of an illustrator is to draw a book cover that gives readers clues about the story. Display *Jamaica's Blue Marker*. Prompt:

  > **Look at the picture on the cover. What details about the characters do you see?** *(The characters are children. One is a girl and one is a boy. They seem to be in a classroom.)*

  > **Who do you think the girl is?** *(The girl is probably Jamaica. Her name is in the title, and she is holding a blue marker.)*

- Discuss that sometimes readers can use the cover illustration to predict what the story is about. Given that children know what happens in this story, have them tell what details they see on the cover that will come later in the story.

Part 3: Guided Practice

Step by Step

- **Review learning from Parts 1–2.** Remind children that an author and illustrator work together to tell a story. Display the cover of *Jamaica's Blue Marker*. Help children name the author and illustrator.

- **Revisit the story.** Display *Why Mosquitoes Buzz in People's Ears*. Page through the book, using the pictures as prompts to have children recall the story. (RL.K.2; RL.K.7)

- **Guide children to name the author and illustrator.** Display the cover of the book and read it aloud exactly as it is written.

> **Tip:** Point to the Caldecott Medal. Read aloud the words *Winner of the Caldecott Award*. Explain that this award is given each year to the illustrator(s) who drew the best pictures in a story.

- Reread the names and ask:

  Who is the author? *(Verna Aardema)*

  What did she do? *(She wrote the story.)*

  Who are the illustrators? *(Leo and Diane Dillon)*

  What clue words tell you that they are the illustrators? *("pictures by")*

- Point out that this book has two illustrators. Remind children that stories can have more than one author and/or illustrator.

- Tell children that you will work together to complete the Student Book page by naming the title, author, and illustrators of *Why Mosquitoes Buzz in People's Ears*.

- **Guide children to complete the Student Book page.** Have children turn to page 79. Point to and read aloud the words on the book cover. Then point to each blank box and have volunteers tell what words go in the box *(story title; name of the author; name of the illustrator)*. Read aloud the answer choices. Have children draw a line from each answer choice to its place on the book cover.

- Review and discuss the answers to the Student Book page together.

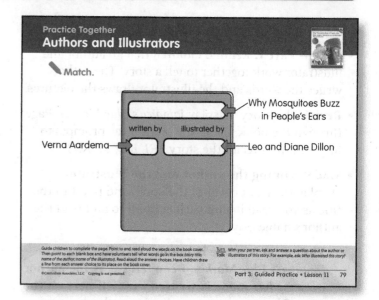

- **Have children demonstrate understanding.** Display the cover of *Why Mosquitoes Buzz in People's Ears*. Read aloud the Turn and Talk activity. (SL.K.1; SL.K.2)

  > **With your partner, ask and answer a question about the author or illustrators of this story. For example, ask: Who illustrated this story?** *(Leo and Diane Dillon)*

- Invite partners to share their questions and answers with the class.

- Use the Close Reading activity to discuss how an author can use creative words to make a story sound interesting to readers.

Close Reading

- Explain that sometimes an author writes in a way that makes a story fun to listen to. Display page 9. Tell children to listen for sounds the animals make as they move. Read aloud the page and say:

  > **The iguana makes the sound *badamin*, *badamin*. Those words are fun to say and fun to hear. Say them with me: *badamin*, *badamin*.**

- Repeat for the python's sounds *(wasawusu, wasawusu)* and the rabbit's sounds *(krik, krik)*. Point out additional examples in the story (pages 7, 10, 11, 14, 17, 25, 29).

- Invite children to tell whether the sounds make the story more fun to listen to and why.

Step by Step

- **Review learning from Parts 1–3.** Remind children that an author and illustrator work together to tell a story. Display *Why Mosquitoes Buzz in People's Ears*. Have children name the author and illustrators.

- **Revisit the story.** Display *The Art Lesson*. Page through the book, using the pictures as prompts to have children recall the story. (RL.K.2; RL.K.7)

- **Have children name the author and illustrator.** Display the cover and read aloud the title of *The Art Lesson*. Then read the name down below. Prompt:

  Who wrote this story? (*Tomie dePaola*)

  Who drew the pictures? (*Tomie dePaola*)

> **Tip:** Use the title page to reinforce that Tomie dePaola is both the author and illustrator of the story. Display the title page. Point to and read the words "Written and illustrated by Tomie dePaola."

- Tell children that they will complete the Student Book page by naming the title and author-illustrator of *The Art Lesson*.

- **Have children complete the Student Book page independently.** Have children turn to page 80. Point to and read aloud the words on the book cover. Have volunteers tell what words go in each blank box (*story title; name of the author-illustrator*). Then read aloud the answer choices. Have children draw a line from each answer choice to its place on the book cover.

- Review the answers to the Student Book page. Discuss the different jobs that Tomie dePaola did to tell the story.

- **Have children demonstrate understanding.** Display the cover of *The Art Lesson*. Read aloud the Turn and Talk activity. (SL.K.1; SL.K.2)

  Why do you think the author chose this title for the story? Ask and answer this question with your partner. (*because the story tells about art lessons that the author took as a young boy*)

- Use the Close Reading activity to help children think about how the author ends the story.

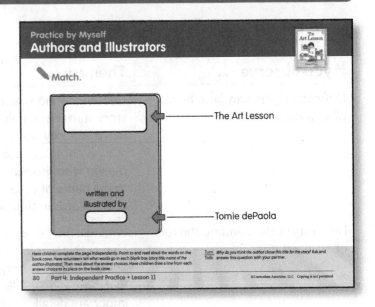

- **Have children reflect on their learning.** Invite children to tell how they can identify the author and illustrator of a story. Discuss the different ways the names of the author and illustrator can be displayed on a book cover. Have children tell how an author and illustrator work together to tell a story.

Close Reading

- Explain that an author makes certain choices about how to tell a story. Display and read aloud pages 26–32. Ask:

  Why doesn't Tommy want to do what the art teacher asks? (*He doesn't want to copy.*)

  How is the problem solved? (*Tommy copies the picture first and then draws his own picture.*)

  What work does Tommy do as a grown-up? (*He works as an illustrator.*)

- Ask children why Tomie dePaola ends the story with Tommy as a grown-up. (*to show that he became an artist*) Point out how Tomie dePaola uses the words "and he still does" along with the pictures to show this ending.

Assessment and Remediation

If you observe . . .	Then try . . .
Difficulty understanding the role of an author	Demonstrating that authors write the words of a story. Use the following story starter and help children add several sentences. *Once upon a time, there was a little boy named_____. He loved to_____. Then one day, he_____.* When the story is complete, ask: *Who wrote this story?* Point out that the author is the person who thought of the words, even if you wrote them down. Then point to the name of the author in a familiar book. Explain that this person thought of the words in that particular story.
Difficulty understanding the role of an illustrator	Writing a brief story of three to four sentences and asking children to draw a picture that would go with the story. When the drawing is finished, say: *I am the author. I wrote the story. You drew the pictures that go with the story, so what does that make you? (the illustrator)* Emphasize that an illustrator's job is to draw important details so readers can imagine and understand the story.
Difficulty naming the author and illustrator of a story	Reading the names on the cover of a book. If there is only one name, discuss whether it would be just an illustrator. *(no, because the author's name is always on the cover)* If there are two names, look for other clues such as the words *written by* or *illustrated by.* If it is still not clear, help children locate the title page to identify the names of the author and/or illustrator there.

Connect to the Anchor Standard

R6: *Assess how point of view or purpose shapes the content and style of a text.*

Throughout the grades, Standard 6 develops students' understanding of who is telling a story. From simply identifying the author, illustrator, and narrator, students progress to recognizing the points of view of different characters. They will learn to compare and contrast different points of view across stories, as well as to analyze how characters' points of view affect readers' perceptions of the text. Students might consider questions such as these: *Why did the author choose to tell the story through this character's eyes? How would the story be different if it were told from another character's point of view?* Use the following activities to help children begin this transition.

- Guide children to notice when story characters feel differently about the same thing. Read aloud pages 22–23 of *The Art Lesson*. Ask: *What does Miss Landers think about using school crayons? What does Tommy think about using school crayons?* Discuss with children why each character thinks she or he is right. Talk about why the author presents these two ways of thinking about crayons. *(SL.K.1; SL.K.2)*

- Discuss how a story would be different if it were told from another point of view. Read aloud page 6 of *Jamaica's Blue Marker*. Ask: *What does Jamaica think about sharing her markers with Russell?* Help children recall that throughout the story, the author tells Jamaica's thoughts and feelings but not Russell's. Ask: *What if the author had written more about how Russell thinks and feels? How might we feel about Russell? How might we feel about Jamaica?*

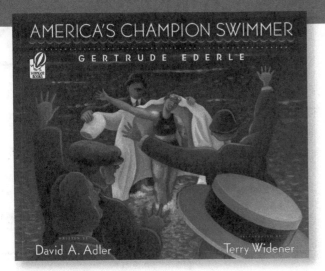

AMERICA'S CHAMPION SWIMMER

GERTRUDE EDERLE

David A. Adler   Terry Widener

Lesson Objectives

You will read aloud *America's Champion Swimmer*, which children will revisit in later lessons. With prompting and support, children will:

• Identify the main topic of an information book.

• Ask and answer questions about key details.

• Retell key details to describe sections of the book.

About the Text

Summary

Gertrude (Trudy) Ederle was the first woman to swim the English Channel. At seven, she learned to swim; at fifteen, she won her first race. Her Channel record beat the men's record by almost two hours. Trudy's determination and desire to compete have made her a model for all to follow.

Information Book: Biography

• Explain that a *biography* is a book that tells about the life of a real person, either living or no longer alive.

• Tell children that biographies are often like stories, with a beginning, middle, and end, and have events that lead to an exciting part of the person's life.

Critical Vocabulary

• Prior to reading, briefly define the following words:

determined (p. 7) having a strong wish or desire to do something

mastered (p. 7) learned something well

attempted (p. 9) tried to do

challenge (p. 13) a job or activity that is hard to do

• As you read, pause to point to the words as you encounter them, and review their definitions.

Word Bank

• Display a word bank of the Critical Vocabulary.

• Add other important words from the book, such as *current, record,* and *beat,* on subsequent readings.

New Concepts: Setting Records

• Explain that a *record* is the best performance of something, such as the longest time jumping rope or the fastest speed a car has ever gone. Talk about how people can try to *set* a record by doing better at a task, sport, or activity than anyone has done before.

• Tell children that there is a book of world records that tells about many different things people have done in order to be the very best at something. Have children listen for records that get set by Trudy in the book.

Ready *Teacher Toolbox*

Teacher-Toolbox.com

	Prerequisite Skills	RI.K.2
Ready Lessons		✓
Tools for Instruction	✓	✓
Interactive Tutorials	✓	

Step by Step

- **Introduce and explore *America's Champion Swimmer*.** Read aloud the title and subtitle (Gertrude Ederle), explaining that Gertrude Ederle is the woman whose life this biography tells about. Read aloud the name of the author, David A. Adler, and the name of the illustrator, Terry Widener. Explain that he drew the pictures in the book.

- Display the book and ask children what they see on the cover. (*a swimmer; people cheering and looking excited*)

- Turn the pages of the book, asking children what they see. Ask them to find Gertrude (Trudy) in the pictures. Discuss the different places they see Trudy swimming.

- Explain that as you read the book aloud, children should listen closely to find out about Trudy and why she is America's champion swimmer. Remind them to look closely at the illustrations as they listen.

- **Read aloud *America's Champion Swimmer*.** As you read, pause to define challenging vocabulary and give children time to look at the details of the illustrations.

> **Tip:** Use a globe or world map to show where England, France, and the English Channel are, both in relation to one another and to the United States. Explain that a *channel* is a body of water that connects two larger bodies of water. In this case, the English Channel connects the Atlantic Ocean and the North Sea.

- **Guide a review of the book.** Direct children to turn to Student Book page 33. Have them circle the picture that shows what the book *America's Champion Swimmer* is mostly about. Point to and name each picture. (*a red-eyed tree frog; an animal that lives in a shell; a swimmer; a fish*)

- Then have children draw one important thing they learned from the book. For example, they might draw people greeting Trudy after she swims the English Channel.

- **Have children discuss text evidence.** Read aloud the Turn and Talk activity. Have partners tell each other about one important thing they learned from this book. Help children use their pictures and evidence from the book to support their ideas. (*SL.K.1; SL.K.2; SL.K.4; SL.K.5*)

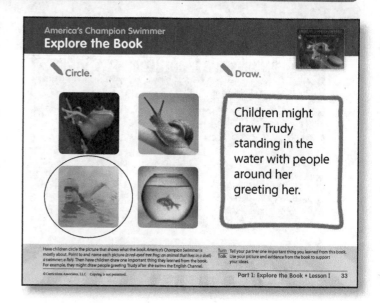

America's Champion Swimmer
Explore the Book

Circle.   Draw.

Children might draw Trudy standing in the water with people around her greeting her.

Have children circle the picture that shows what the book *America's Champion Swimmer* is mostly about. Point to and name each picture (*a red-eyed tree frog; an animal that lives in a shell; a swimmer; a fish*). Then have children draw one important thing they learned from the book. For example, they might draw people greeting Trudy after she swims the English Channel. **Turn Talk** Tell your partner one important thing you learned from this book. Use your picture and evidence from the book to support your ideas.

©Curriculum Associates, LLC Copying is not permitted.   Part 1: Explore the Book • Lesson 1   33

- Guide their discussions with prompts such as this:

  Why does Trudy want to swim across the English Channel? (*She wants to be the first woman to do so.*)

- Invite children to share other details they learned about Trudy, as well as other people in the book, in class discussion.

- Ask children if they have more questions about Trudy after listening to the text, such as, *Did anyone break the record that Trudy set crossing the English Channel?* or *Did Trudy go on to set or break any other swimming records?* Discuss where you might look to find the answers.

- Refer to the *Notes from the Author* section on page 32 as needed to answer some of children's questions.

ELL Support: Contractions

- Say these sentences: *She was not scared./She wasn't scared.* Tell children that the words *was* and *not* in the first sentence are put together as one word in the second sentence: *wasn't*. Make it clear that the meaning of the words has not changed.

- Use two blank cards. Say the words *was* and *not*, holding up one card for each word. Bring the cards together, saying *wasn't*. Have children repeat.

- Continue with *couldn't, didn't, isn't, weren't, can't, won't,* and so on, using new sentences. Provide practice so children are able to hear the contractions as common words and understand their meanings quickly and clearly.

Step by Step

- **Reread to learn about Trudy winning swimming races.** Explain that children will listen and look for details about Trudy's swimming races and challenges. Instruct them to listen closely as you reread pages 4–13.

- **Have children identify details.** Use questions such as these to guide discussion. (RI.K.1; SL.K.1; SL.K.2)

  Pages 6–7: Why does Trudy learn to swim?
  (She almost drowns so her father teaches her to swim.)

  Page 8: What does Trudy do when she is fifteen?
  (She wins her first big swimming race.)

  Pages 9–11: Why do people start to notice Trudy?
  (She beats a men's record by swimming 17 miles in just over 7 hours. She wins 3 medals at the Olympics.)

  Pages 12–13: What is Trudy determined to do?
  (be the first woman to swim the English Channel)

> **Tip:** Explain that at the time of these events, women were thought to be less strong than men, in mind and in body. Tell children that Trudy's strength and courage helped many people learn that this view was not true.

- Use the Close Reading activity to help children find evidence that tells how Trudy learns to swim.

- **Focus on a key detail.** Direct children to turn to Student Book page 34. Have them draw a picture that shows Trudy winning her first big swimming race. Reread page 8 to help them recall the details. (RI.K.3)

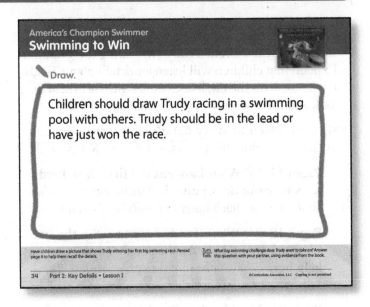

- **Have children discuss text evidence.** Read aloud the Turn and Talk activity. Guide partners to have a conversation, beginning as follows:

  What big swimming challenge does Trudy want to take on? (She wants to swim the English Channel.)

- Invite children to share their ideas with the class.

- Work with children to help them identify the most important details from this part of the book. Encourage them to use evidence from the book as well as their drawings to help explain their ideas. (SL.K.4)

Tier Two Vocabulary: *declared*

- Display the second paragraph on page 13. Read it aloud. Underline the word *declared*.

- Help children understand that a newspaper editorial *declared* something. Talk about what a newspaper does: tells news; says things about events; states or gives opinions.

- Work together to decide that the newspaper *said*, or *declared*, that Trudy wouldn't make it. Explain that *declared* means "said in a strong way."

- Provide an example: *The principal declared that we need to recycle paper.* Have children use *declared* in other examples, using complete sentences. (L.K.1.f; L.K.5.c)

Close Reading

- Help children find evidence that tells how Trudy learns to swim. Display and read aloud pages 6–7. Then prompt:

  What does Trudy's father do to teach her how to swim? (He ties a rope to her waist, puts her in a river, and tells her to "paddle like a dog.")

  What words tell that Trudy learns to swim? (The words say that Trudy "mastered the dog paddle." They also say that she copies the strokes, or swimming moves, of her sister and the other children and soon swims better than they do.)

- Discuss how quickly Trudy learns to swim, even though she starts out not knowing how.

117

Step by Step

- **Reread to learn about Trudy swimming the Channel.** Explain that children will listen for details about Trudy trying to swim the English Channel. Instruct them to look and listen closely as you reread pages 14–25.

- **Have children identify details.** Use questions such as these to guide discussion. (RI.K.1; SL.K.1; SL.K.2)

  Pages 14–15: What happens the first time Trudy tries to swim the Channel? (*Her trainer thinks she's swallowed too much water and pulls her from the sea.*)

  Pages 18–21: When Trudy tries to swim the Channel again, how do the people on the tugboat help her? (*They make sure she doesn't get lost. They help her stay safe. They sing songs. They give her food.*)

  Pages 22–25: Why does Trudy's trainer want her to come out of the water? (*The storm is strong and the waves are high. Her leg is stiff. He is frightened for her.*)

  Page 24: What do the words "swim the Channel or drown" tell about Trudy? (*She is determined to finish the swim this time even though she is scared.*)

  Tip: Children might remember the events more easily if they act out this part of the biography as you read it aloud. Have some children role-play the people on the boats while other children play Trudy.

- Use the Close Reading activity to find evidence that tells why Trudy's trainer on the tugboat wants her to stop swimming and come out of the water.

America's Champion Swimmer
Swimming the Channel

✎ Draw.

Children might draw Trudy's sister Margaret and others singing on a boat, Trudy eating in the water, the boats that go with Trudy, or another detail of the swim.

Have children draw a picture that shows one thing that helps Trudy during her swim across the Channel. Reread pages 18–23 to help them recall the details.

Turn Talk *Why does Trudy get scared during her swim across the Channel? Answer this question with your partner, using evidence from the book.*

©Curriculum Associates, LLC Copying is not permitted.

Part 3: Key Details • Lesson 1 35

- **Focus on a key detail.** Direct children to turn to Student Book page 35. Have them draw a picture that shows one thing that helps Trudy during her swim across the Channel. Reread pages 18–23 to help them recall the details. (RI.K.3)

- **Have children discuss text evidence.** Read aloud the Turn and Talk activity. Guide partners to have a conversation, beginning as follows:

  Why does Trudy get scared during her swim across the Channel? (*The storm makes the water rough and the waves high. Sometimes she can't see the tugboat and gets scared because she is all alone.*)

- Invite children to share their ideas. (SL.K.4)

Tier Two Vocabulary: *accompany*

- Display the second sentence on page 18. Read it aloud. Underline the word *accompany*.

- Review the picture on page 19. Ask children where the tugboat is as Trudy swims. (*beside her or nearby*) Ask: *Does the tugboat go with her or stay away from her?* Discuss that the tugboat goes with her as she swims.

- Work with children to decide that *accompany* means "to go with; to stay beside."

- Provide a personal example: *I like to accompany my friend when she goes to the store.*

- Have children give other examples, using complete sentences. (L.K.5.c)

Close Reading

- Help children find evidence that tells why Trudy's trainer wants her to come out of the water. Display and read aloud the first paragraph on page 23. Prompt:

  What does Trudy's trainer want her to do? (*to give up*)

- Then display and read aloud the first paragraph on page 24. Prompt:

  What does Trudy say about her leg? (*It is stiff.*)

  How does the trainer feel when Trudy tells him her leg is stiff? (*He is frightened for her.*)

  What does it mean that he is frightened for her? (*He is afraid she will drown trying to finish.*)

Step by Step

- **Reread to learn how people celebrate Trudy's record.** Explain that children will listen and look for details about what Trudy's record means to people. Instruct them to listen closely as you reread pages 26–31.

- **Have children identify details.** Use questions such as these to guide discussion. *(RI.K.1; SL.K.1; SL.K.2)*

  Pages 26–27: Who greets Trudy as she reaches the shore? *(hundreds of people; her father)*

  Page 26: Who does Trudy say will celebrate her swim? *("all the women of the world")*

  Page 29: How long did it take Trudy to swim the Channel? *(fourteen hours and thirty-one minutes)*

  Page 29: By how much time did Trudy beat the men's record? *(almost two hours)*

  Pages 30–31: Where and how does Trudy celebrate? *(in New York City with a parade)*

  Page 31: Who calls Trudy "America's Best Girl"? *(President Calvin Coolidge)*

  Tip: Discuss with children why Trudy's swim was history making and why she was called "a beacon of strength to girls and women everywhere."

- **Focus on a key detail.** Direct children to turn to Student Book page 36. Have them draw a picture that shows the way Trudy celebrates in New York City. Reread pages 30–31 to help them recall the details.

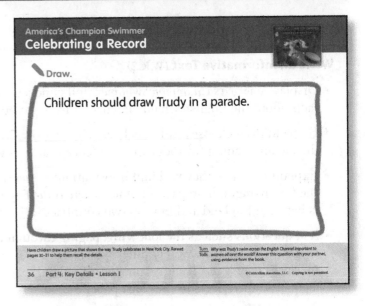

America's Champion Swimmer
Celebrating a Record

Draw.

Children should draw Trudy in a parade.

Have children draw a picture that shows the way Trudy celebrates in New York City. Reread pages 30–31 to help them recall the details.

Turn Talk: *Why was Trudy's swim across the English Channel important to women all over the world?* Answer this question with your partner, using evidence from the book.

36 Part 4: Key Details • Lesson 1   ©Curriculum Associates, LLC Copying is not permitted.

- **Have children discuss text evidence.** Read aloud the Turn and Talk activity. Guide partners to have a conversation, beginning as follows:

  Why was Trudy's swim across the English Channel important to women all over the world? *(It showed that women were just as strong, determined, and courageous as men and could accomplish great things.)*

- **Review** *American's Champion Swimmer.* Use the prompts in the Book Review to revisit and record important details from the book. Use the words and illustrations throughout the book to help children recall important details about Trudy and her historic swim across the Channel. *(RI.K.7)*

Integrating Foundational Skills

Use these activities to integrate foundational skills into your reading of *America's Champion Swimmer.*

1. Have children blend onset and rime. Say and have children blend: /b/ /ōt/, boat; /d/ /ā/, day; /s/ /ĭk/, sick; /b/ /ēt/, beat; /m/ /ĕn/, men; /s/ /īt/, sight. Have children segment the following words into onset and rime: red, cap, tide, set. *(RF.K.2.c)*

2. Write the word *dog* and read it aloud. Then write *fog.* Have children tell which letter in *fog* is different in *dog.* (f) Ask them to say the sound, (/f/), and read each word as you point to it. Continue with *cap/cup; man/map; past/fast/last; take/bake/cake; beat/meat/seat; race/face/lace; red/fed/led.* *(RF.K.3.a, b, d)*

Book Review

- As children review key details from *America's Champion Swimmer,* record their answers on chart paper. Keep the chart on hand for future revisiting.

  How does Trudy learn to swim? *(Her father teaches her to dog paddle. She copies the strokes of other people. She keeps swimming and gets better.)*

  What is Trudy's biggest challenge? *(She wants to be the first woman to swim the English Channel.)*

  What makes Trudy's Channel swim so hard? *(a storm; she can't see the boats; her leg gets stiff)*

  How does Trudy celebrate her history-making swim? *(with a parade in New York City)*

Writing Activity

Write an Informative Text (W.K.2)

- Display *America's Champion Swimmer*. Tell children that together you will write an informative text that tells facts about the English Channel: where it is, how wide it is, and where Trudy started and ended her swim.

- Help children choose a title, such as "The English Channel." Write the title on chart paper. Ask children to dictate an opening (introductory) sentence that tells what they are going to write about.

- Explain that now they will find information in *America's Champion Swimmer* about the Channel. Read aloud the first paragraph on page 13. Ask: *Where is the English Channel?* Help children understand that the Channel is between England and France, two countries in Europe. Have children dictate a sentence to tell that fact.

- Ask questions such as the following, paging through the book to find the answers. *How wide is the English Channel?* (more than twenty miles wide; page 13) *In which country did Trudy start her swim?* (France; page 14) *In which country did Trudy's swim end?* (England; page 26) Have children dictate what to write to tell these facts. Add these facts to the chart paper.

- Have children dictate a final thought to end the text.

- Read aloud the finished text with the class.

Speaking and Listening Activity

Conduct an Interview (SL.K.1; SL.K.2; SL.K.3)

- Tell children they will be reporters who are interviewing Trudy after her Channel swim. Explain that you will be Trudy. (A small group of children could also act as Trudy.)

- Have children work in small groups. Have each group discuss questions they want to ask Trudy about her swim. Help them draw or dictate these questions to refer to during the interview.

- Begin the interview, calling on children to ask questions. Have them raise their hands if they are ready to ask a question. As possible, encourage children to ask follow-up questions in response to your answers.

- Remind children to take turns, listen carefully, and make sure their questions are clear and on topic.

- Have children take turns giving a brief summary/report to pull together Trudy's responses for the "audience" after the interview.

Language Activity

Plural Nouns (L.K.1.c; L.K.4.b)

- Tell children they will talk about words that mean more than one person, place, or thing. Explain that these words are called plural nouns.

- Read aloud the last paragraph on page 29 of the book. Display the word *wings* on chart paper. Read the word aloud with children and discuss its meaning (*"more than one wing"*).

- Cover up the letter s on *wings* with a self-stick note. Read the word *wing* with children and discuss its meaning (*"one wing"*). Explain that adding the letter s to the end of a naming word makes it mean more than one of that thing.

- Continue with the words *airplanes, boats, bells, horns,* and *foghorns*. Have children change plural nouns to singular nouns and vice versa on their own, asking them to explain what they are doing.

- Have children take turns using the words in sentences, such as *I see two airplanes./Now I see just one airplane.*

Unknown Words

CCSS

RI.K.4: With prompting and support, ask and answer questions about unknown words in a text.

Required Read Alouds: F (*Red-Eyed Tree Frog*); I (*America's Champion Swimmer*)

Lesson Objectives

- Ask questions about unknown words in information books.

- Use text evidence to answer questions about unknown words and determine their meanings.

- Understand why determining the meanings of unknown words helps readers comprehend an information book.

The Learning Progression

- **Prior to K:** Children should be able to distinguish between spoken words they recognize and spoken words they do not understand.

- **Grade K: CCSS RI.K.4 expects children to ask and answer questions about unknown words in a text with prompting and support.**

- **Grade 1:** CCSS RI.1.4 advances the standard by having children ask and answer questions in order to determine or clarify the meaning of words or phrases in a text.

Tap Children's Prior Knowledge

- Remind children that they have previously used clues to figure out the meanings of words in stories they do not know.

- Explain that you will play a quick game called "Figure It Out." You will say a word, and children will try to figure out what it means based on the way it is used in an example sentence.

- Say: *The word is* humorous. *I think Bob is humorous because he is always doing funny things and he makes me laugh.*

- Ask: *What do you think the word* humorous *means? (funny)* Invite children to tell which words in the sentence helped them decide the meaning.

- Repeat with additional words such as *assist, practice, jealous,* and *comfortable.* If possible, provide opportunities for children to use word and visual clues to determine a word's meaning.

- Emphasize that good readers look for clues to the meanings of words they do not understand. Figuring out the meaning of an unknown word can help readers make sense of the information they are reading.

- Tell children that in this lesson, they will practice asking questions and using clues to find the meanings of words they do not know in information books.

Ready *Teacher Toolbox*

Teacher-Toolbox.com

	Prerequisite Skills	RI.K.4
Ready Lessons		✓
Tools for Instruction	✓ ✓	✓
Interactive Tutorials		✓

Additional CCSS

RI.K.2; RI.K.7; SL.K.1; SL.K.2 (*See page A38 for full text.*)

Step by Step

- **Introduce the standard.** Remind children that when they read or listen to information books, there may be words they do not know or understand. Explain that they will review strategies for finding the meaning of an unknown word.

- Draw or post pictures of a grasshopper and a bee. Read aloud the following text:

  An insect has three body parts. Most insects have three pairs of legs and two pairs of wings. Grasshoppers and bees are insects.

- Have children name words they heard that they do not know. (*Possible responses may include* insect, pairs, grasshoppers.)

- Explain that together you will figure out the meaning of the word *insect*. Discuss the word as follows:

  How can we figure out what the word *insect* means? The words say it has three body parts, three pairs of legs, and two pairs of wings. They also say that grasshoppers and bees are both insects. Now let's look at the pictures. I know this is a bee, so this other one must be a grasshopper. If these are both insects, what do we think the word *insect* means?

- Work with children to define *insect* as "a small animal with three body parts, three pairs of legs, and two pairs of wings." Emphasize that using the words and pictures together helped you to figure out its meaning.

- Remind children that they have used word and picture clues to find the meanings of words in stories they do not know. Tell them that in their Student Books, they will revisit questions they can ask to help them understand words they do not know in information books.

- **Read aloud the Student Book page.** Have children turn to Student Book page 81. Read aloud the page as children listen and follow along.

- Point to and discuss each question. Tell children they will practice looking for word and picture clues for another unknown word in the text, such as *pairs*.

Listen and Learn

Unknown Words

Sometimes you hear or read a word you do not know. You can ask questions about the word to find out what it means.

Here are some questions you can ask:
- What clues can I find in the other words?
- What clues can I find in the pictures?

Finding the meaning of new words can help you understand an information book.

Part 1: Introduction • Lesson 12   81

- Reread the text, having children listen carefully for sentences that contain the word *pairs*. Then invite them to repeat word clues from the text. (*pairs of legs; pairs of wings*) Next help them point to and count the legs and wings in the picture.

> **Tip:** Remind children that they can also think about where they have heard a word used in other places. For instance, ask: *What is your favorite pair of shoes? What color is the pair of socks you are wearing?*

- Work with children to define *pair* as "a set of two things that go together." Clarify that if there are "three pairs of legs," you should count six legs total.

- Tell children that often if they do not figure out the meanings of unknown words, they cannot fully understand what they read. Remind them that they can use word and picture clues to figure out what an unknown word means.

- **Have children demonstrate understanding.** Have volunteers share what they have learned so far about finding the meanings of unknown words. Ask them to tell the questions they can ask themselves when they listen to or read a word they do not know.

- Encourage children to tell how noticing words they do not know and figuring out their meanings will help them better understand an information book.

Step by Step

- **Review Part 1.** Review with children the questions they can ask to find out meanings of unknown words.

- **Revisit the book.** Display *America's Champion Swimmer.* Page through the book, using the pictures as prompts to have children recall it. (*RI.K.2; RI.K.7*)

- **Model asking questions about unknown words.** Explain that you will model figuring out the meaning of a word in this book. Display and read aloud pages 24–25. Think aloud:

  > I don't know the meaning of *trainer.* The words say that Trudy's trainer was frightened for her and yelled for her to come out. What picture clues can I find? I see three people yelling to Trudy, but one is moving his arm. I think that man is Trudy's trainer. He helps her with her swimming and tries to keep her safe. So *trainer* means "a person who coaches, or helps another person know what to do."

  Tip: Remind children they can find clues from other places in the book, too. Turn back to page 14 and reread it. Use the details on this page to reinforce that the *trainer* is responsible for keeping Trudy safe.

- Encourage children to take turns using *trainer* in a sentence to show they understand its meaning.

- Display and read aloud page 26. Model figuring out the meaning of *shore.* Think aloud:

  > I don't know the word *shore.* The words around it say Trudy is near the coast. She sees people and flares, or lights, and then her feet touch land. What picture clues can I find? Trudy is in the water and the land is right ahead of her. Using these clues, I can figure out that *shore* means "the land along the edge of the water."

- Tell children you will model completing the Student Book page by identifying pictures that show unknown words in *America's Champion Swimmer.*

- **Model completing the Student Book page.** Have children turn to page 82. For the first item, ask: *Which picture shows a trainer?* Demonstrate circling the correct picture. Continue with the second item. Ask: *Which picture shows a shore?* Discuss the evidence that helped you choose each correct picture.

- **Have children demonstrate understanding.** Display page 26 of *America's Champion Swimmer.* Read aloud the Turn and Talk activity. Model what a conversation with a partner should sound like by asking and answering the question below. (*SL.K.1; SL.K.2*)

  > **What evidence in the book tells about the word shore? Ask and answer this question with your partner.** (*The words say Trudy is near the coast, people guided her with flares, and her feet touch land. The picture shows Trudy swimming toward the land.*)

- Use the Close Reading activity to model finding the meaning of another unfamiliar word on page 26.

Close Reading

- Display page 26 and read aloud the first paragraph. Think aloud to figure out the word *gathered.*

  > I want to figure out what the word *gathered* means. The words say "thousands of people gathered" to greet Trudy. In the picture, I see a big crowd of people with lights. The people are standing on the land close together. I think the word *gathered* means "the people got together in a group."

- Discuss how using words and pictures to unlock a word's meaning helps readers better understand the information in the book.

Step by Step

- **Review learning from Parts 1–2.** Review where readers can look for clues to figure out the meaning of unknown words. Display pages 24–25 of *America's Champion Swimmer*. Have children tell the meaning of *trainer* and the clues they used to figure it out.

- **Revisit the book.** Display *Red-Eyed Tree Frog*. Page through the book, using the pictures as prompts to have children recall it. (RI.K.2; RI.K.7)

- **Guide children to ask questions about unknown words.** Display and read aloud pages 10–12. Then reread page 11 and point to the word *katydid*. Prompt:

   What do the words say about the *katydid*? *(The frog will not eat it.)*

   What does the picture show? *(It shows a green animal with thin, thorny legs and white eyes.)*

   What does the word *katydid* mean? *(It is a green animal with thin, thorny legs and white eyes.)*

- Display and reread page 12. Point to the word *poisonous*. Prompt:

   What words tell about *poisonous*? *(It is the reason why the frog will not eat the caterpillar.)*

   What does the picture show? *(a brightly-colored caterpillar with long whiskers)*

> **Tip:** Emphasize that children cannot use picture clues to figure out the meaning of *poisonous* on this page, but they can discuss why the caterpillar does not look good for the frog to eat.

- Use the Close Reading activity to help children look closely at the author's choice of punctuation.

- Tell children you will work together to complete the Student Book page by identifying pictures that show unknown words in *Red-Eyed Tree Frog*.

- **Guide children to complete the Student Book page.** Have children turn to page 83. For the first item, ask: *Which picture shows a katydid?* Guide children to circle the correct picture. Continue with the second item. Ask: *Which picture shows how someone might feel after eating something poisonous?* Discuss the clues that helped children choose each correct picture.

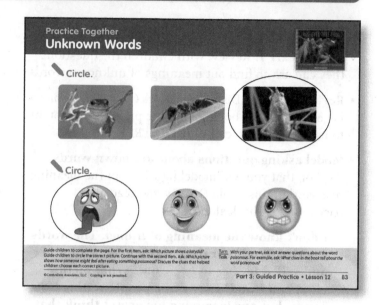

- **Have children demonstrate understanding.** Display pages 10–12 of *Red-Eyed Tree Frog*. Read aloud the Turn and Talk activity. (SL.K.1; SL.K.2)

   With your partner, ask and answer questions about the word *poisonous*. For example, ask: What clues in the book tell about the word poisonous? *(The words say the caterpillar is poisonous and the frog won't eat it. The exclamation point on No! shows that the caterpillar is not good to eat, or even dangerous.)*

- Invite partners to share their ideas with the class.

Close Reading

- Help children see that an author chooses punctuation for specific reasons. Display and read aloud page 12. Use strong expression for emphasis as you read. Then prompt:

   What question does the author ask? *("Will it eat the caterpillar?")*

   What is the answer? *("No! The caterpillar is poisonous.")*

   What does the word *No!* tell you? *(The frog really doesn't want to or shouldn't eat the caterpillar.)*

- Change your tone of voice to demonstrate the difference between *No!* and *No*. Explain that *poisonous* means "very bad for you; can make you sick." Have children tell how the exclamation point gives a clue to the word's meaning.

Step by Step

- **Review learning from Parts 1–3.** Review strategies to figure out the meanings of unknown words. Display pages 10–12 of *Red-Eyed Tree Frog*. Have children tell the meaning of *poisonous* and the clues they used to figure it out.

- **Have children ask questions about unknown words.** Display and read aloud pages 14–17 of *Red-Eyed Tree Frog*. Tell children to listen closely for clues about the word *slithers*. Reread page 14. Prompt:

  How does the snake move? (*It slips and slithers along a branch.*)

> **Tip:** Help children understand that *slips* means "slides smoothly and easily." Give examples, such as soap slipping out of your hand or feet slipping on ice.

  What does the picture show? (*A snake is curled up with its head pointing forward.*)

  What does the word *slithers* mean? (*"slides along smoothly"*)

- Display pages 16–17 and reread page 16. Point to the word *flicks*. Prompt:

  What part of the snake's body flicks? (*its tongue*)

  What does the picture show? (*The snake has its tongue out of its mouth. It is going after the frog.*)

  What does the word *flicks* mean? (*moves quickly*)

- Use the Close Reading activity to demonstrate how understanding new words helps readers better understand information in a book.

- Tell children that they will complete the Student Book page by identifying pictures that show unknown words in *Red-Eyed Tree Frog*.

- **Have children complete the Student Book page independently.** Have children turn to page 84. For the first item, ask: *Which picture shows how an animal slithers?* Have children circle the correct picture. Continue with the second item. Ask: *Which picture shows how a snake flicks its tongue?* Have children discuss the clues that helped them choose each correct picture.

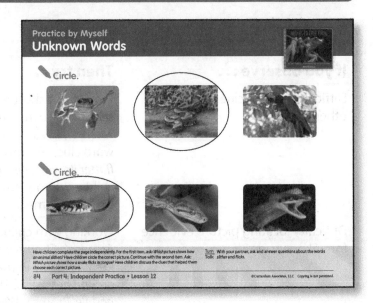

Practice by Myself
Unknown Words

Circle.

Circle.

Have children complete the page independently. For the first item, ask: *Which picture shows how an animal slithers?* Have children circle the correct picture. Continue with the second item. Ask: *Which picture show a snake flicks its tongue?* Have children discuss the clues that helped them choose each correct picture.

Turn Talk With your partner, ask and answer questions about the words *slither and flicks.*

84 Part 4: Independent Practice • Lesson 12 ©Curriculum Associates, LLC Copying is not permitted.

- **Have children demonstrate understanding.** Display pages 14–17 of *Red-Eyed Tree Frog*. Read aloud the Turn and Talk activity. (*SL.K.1; SL.K.2*)

  With your partner, ask and answer questions about the words *slithers* and *flicks*. (*What is an animal that slithers? [a snake] What part of its body does a snake flick? [its tongue]*)

- **Have children reflect on their learning.** Invite children to tell why it is important to pay attention to words they do not understand in a book. Have them discuss questions they can ask themselves when they hear or read words they do not know.

Close Reading

- Tell children that figuring out the meanings of unknown words helps them better understand the information they read. Display and read aloud pages 14–17. Ask:

  What do the words *slips and slithers* tell about? (*the way a snake moves*)

  Do you think something that slips and slithers makes a lot of noise? Explain. (*No. To slip and slither means "to move quickly and quietly."*)

  Look this picture. How does the snake get so close to the frog? (*It moves quickly and quietly.*)

- Emphasize that understanding the meaning of *slip* and *slither* helps children understand why the frog must get away from the snake quickly.

Assessment and Remediation

If you observe . . .	Then try . . .
Difficulty finding clues in the other words	Providing a short text with a single unknown word. Read aloud brief sentences such as the following: *The bird flutters its wings. The bird can fly when it moves its wings this way.* Discuss the meaning of *flutters* based on word clues. Prompt: *What is the bird fluttering? (its wings) Why does the bird flutter its wings? (so it can fly) What do birds' wings look like when birds fly?* Have children demonstrate the motion to the last question, and help them see that *flutters* means "moves, or flaps, quickly."
Difficulty locating picture evidence for unknown words	Working with children to identify details in pictures. Display pages 6–7 of *America's Champion Swimmer* and read the second paragraph. Have children identify Trudy in the picture and explain how they knew. (*She has rope around her waist.*) Then have them look for picture clues to the meaning of *paddle.* Prompt: *What is Trudy doing? What does the water around her arms look like?* Help children see that *paddle* is an action that means "to move your arms through the water." Discuss that Trudy is doing it to stay above the water; she is learning how to swim.
Difficulty defining unknown words	Having children attempt a definition and then checking a second resource. As children tell what they think a word means by pointing, gesturing, or giving an example, prompt them to describe what it is they are pointing to or telling about. Then look in a children's dictionary for an example of how to describe the word's meaning. Help children connect the words and ideas in their definition with the meaning in the dictionary.

Connect to the Anchor Standard

R4: Interpret words and phrases as they are used in a text, including determining technical, connotative, and figurative meanings, and analyze how specific word choices shape meaning or tone.

Throughout the grades, Standard 4 develops students' ability to analyze vocabulary found in both general and academic reading. At the early grades, students seek out the literal meaning of unfamiliar words. In later grades, students learn to identify the meanings of unfamiliar words and then interpret their connotations in increasingly sophisticated informational texts. They consider the role the author's word choice plays in making arguments. Students might consider questions such as these: *What is the meaning of this word as it is used in this text? Why did the author choose this word over other options? How does this word help me understand exactly what the author means?* Use the following activities to help children begin this transition.

- Help children think about a word's connotation. Read aloud page 13 of *America's Champion Swimmer.* Point to the word *determined,* and say: *A determined person makes a decision and stays with it.* Discuss whether these sentences say the same or different things: *Trudy was determined to swim the Channel. Trudy wanted to swim the Channel.* Help children see that by using *determined,* the author tells readers that Trudy would swim the Channel no matter what.

- Discuss the author's word choice in *Red-Eyed Tree Frog* and its effect on the reader. Cover the text on page 23 with this sentence strip and read it aloud: *The frog eats the moth.* Remove the strip and read aloud the text. Ask: *Do both sentences tell what the frog does? Which sentence is more fun to read? Why?* (SL.K.1; SL.K.2)

Parts of a Book

CCSS

RI.K.5: Identify the front cover, back cover, and title page of a book. **RI.K.6:** Name the author and illustrator of a text and define the role of each in presenting the ideas or information in a text.

Required Read Alouds: F (Red-Eyed Tree Frog); G (What's It Like to Be a Fish?); H (What Lives in a Shell?)

Lesson Objectives

- Identify the front cover, the back cover, and the title page of a book.

- Understand that the covers and title page of a book provide important information about the book.

- Describe and understand the roles of authors and illustrators in creating an information book.

The Learning Progression

- **Prior to K:** Children should be able to hold a book correctly and understand that it turns from right to left. They should also be able to identify the titles of familiar books by looking at their covers.

- **Grade K: CCSS RI.K.5 expects children to identify the front and back cover and title page of a book. CCSS RI.K.6 requires children to identify the author and illustrator of an information book and to describe the role of each in presenting the information in the book.**

- **Grade 1:** CCSS RI.1.5 asks children to identify and use text features (such as tables of contents, headings, glossaries) to find information in a text. CCSS RI.1.6 expects children to determine what information is provided by photos, illustrations, or other visuals, and what information is provided by words, in an information book.

Tap Children's Prior Knowledge

- Review with children that they have learned the roles of authors and illustrators in a previous lesson.

- Display the front cover of *Jamaica's Blue Marker*. Ask children to name the title of the book. Point to and read the author's name, Juanita Havill. Then repeat with the illustrator's name, Anne Sibley O'Brien.

- Have children describe the job that Juanita Havill does. *(She is the author. She writes the words in the book.)* Then have them describe the job that Anne Sibley O'Brien does. *(She is the illustrator. She draws the pictures in the book.)*

- Remind children that they can usually find the names of the author and the illustrator on the front cover of a book. Explain that sometimes they can use the words *written by* and *illustrated by* on the cover to identify the author and the illustrator.

- Display the front cover of *America's Champion Swimmer*. Discuss the title, author, and illustrator. Clarify that even though Gertrude Ederle's name is written in big letters, her name is part of the full title.

- Tell children that the front cover is one part of a book. Explain that in this lesson, they will learn how to identify other parts of a book—the back cover and the title page.

Ready *Teacher Toolbox*   Teacher-Toolbox.com

	Prerequisite Skills	*RI.K.5; RI.K.6*
Ready Lessons		✓
Tools for Instruction		
Interactive Tutorials		

Additional CCSS

RI.K.2; RI.K.7; SL.K.1; SL.K.2 *(See page A38 for full text.)*

Step by Step

- **Introduce the standard.** Tell children they will learn about different parts of a book and the information they can find in each part, including the names of the author and illustrator.

- Display a variety of information books on various topics. Include books with photographs, books with illustrations, and a few books by the same author or with the same illustrator or photographer.

- Remind children that these are all examples of information books. They are different from stories because they tell real, not made-up, information about things that exist in real life.

> **Tip:** Explain that photographs show real things because they were taken with a camera. Drawings can show real or made-up things. In information books, they show real things.

- Choose one book to display. As you look over the front cover with children, ask and answer the following questions:

  What is the name of this book?

  What clues can this picture give me about what I will learn?

  Do I know anything about this topic, or am I just learning about it for the first time?

  Who wrote this book? Have I read any books by this author before?

- Display the back cover of the same book. Ask and answer the following questions:

  If there is a summary, what will I learn from this book?

  If there is a list of other books by this author, have I heard of or read any of them?

  Is this book part of a series? If so, what do all the books have in common?

- Point out that good readers prepare to read by asking and answering these questions, using the information on both covers of the book. They think about whether they are interested in the topic, about to learn something new, or revisiting an author who tells information in a familiar way.

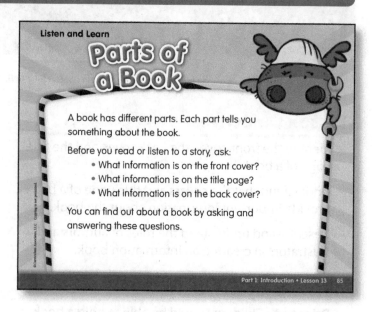

Listen and Learn

Parts of a Book

A book has different parts. Each part tells you something about the book.

Before you read or listen to a story, ask:
- What information is on the front cover?
- What information is on the title page?
- What information is on the back cover?

You can find out about a book by asking and answering these questions.

Part 1: Introduction • Lesson 13   85

- Tell children that in their Student Books, they will learn questions they can ask to find information from the different parts of a book.

- **Read aloud the Student Book page.** Have children turn to Student Book page 85. Read aloud the page as children listen and follow along.

- Display another book. Read aloud the title, author, and illustrator. Point out any phrases such as *written by* or *illustrations by* as applicable. Then ask the questions related to the front cover, and invite children to help you answer them.

- Turn to the title page and explain that this page tells the full title of the book, the names of the author and illustrator, and the name of the company that made the book. Tell children they can look at the title page for information if the front cover of a book is unclear.

- Display the back cover, and use the back-cover prompts to discuss the information found there.

- After reviewing the front and back covers, discuss with children whether they would be interested in reading this book and why.

- **Have children demonstrate understanding.** Call on volunteers to share what they have learned so far about the different parts of books. Encourage them to identify front and back covers and title pages of familiar classroom books and tell what information they could find on each part.

Step by Step

- **Review Part 1.** Remind children that they have learned about the different parts of a book. Help them recall the kinds of information they can find on the front and back covers and the title page.

- **Revisit the book.** Display *Red-Eyed Tree Frog*. Page through the book, using the pictures as prompts to have children recall what happens. *(RI.K.2; RI.K.7)*

- **Model identifying parts of a book.** Explain that you will model how to identify the information found on different parts of the book. Think aloud:

  > **This part of the book is the front cover. At the top is the title: *Red-Eyed Tree Frog*.** [Track with your finger.] **At the bottom, it says "by Joy Cowley." I know that is the author's name because of the clue word *by*. Next to the author's name it says "photographs by Nic Bishop." This tells me he took the pictures in the book.**

- Use the Close Reading activity to help children get important information from the front cover photo.

- Display the title page. Think aloud:

  > **This part of the book is called the title page. It is often the first page in the book. It has a lot of the same information as the front cover. I see the title of the book, the name of the author, and the name of the photographer. It also tells the name of the company that made the book.**

Tip: The title page says *story by*, which might confuse children. Explain that this book is a true story about a day in the life of a tree frog.

- Turn to the back cover. Point out that the summary makes the book sound exciting and fun to read.

- Tell children you will model how to complete the Student Book page by identifying different parts of the book *Red-Eyed Tree Frog*.

- **Model completing the Student Book page.** Have children turn to page 86. For the first item, display the front cover of *Red-Eyed Tree Frog*. Ask: *What part of the book is this?* Point to and name each picture (*front cover; title page; back cover*). Demonstrate circling the correct answer. Continue with the second item. Display the title page. Ask: *What part of the book is this? (front cover; title page; back cover)*

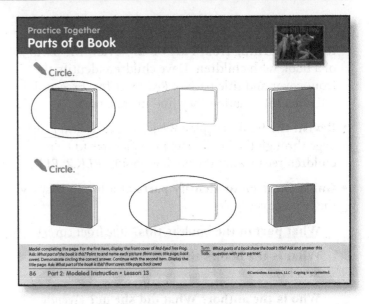

- **Have children demonstrate understanding.** Display the front cover and title page. Read aloud the Turn and Talk activity Model what a conversation with a partner should sound like by asking and answering the question below. *(SL.K.1; SL.K.2)*

  > **Which parts of a book show the book's title? Ask and answer this question with your partner.** *(the front cover and the title page)*

Close Reading

- Explain that pictures on a book cover give information about the book's contents. Display the front cover of *Red-Eyed Tree Frog*. Ask:

  > **Is this a photo or a drawing?** *(photo)*

  > **How do you know?** *(The cover says "photographs by." The picture was taken with a camera. The frog looks like a real-life frog.)*

  > **What information can you learn from this photo?** *(what the frog looks like; its red eyes show how the frog gets its name)*

- Discuss with children why they think Nic Bishop chose this photo for the book's cover. Talk about what is interesting about the photo.

Step by Step

- **Review learning from Parts 1–2.** Review the parts of a book with children. Have children identify the front cover and title page of *Red-Eyed Tree Frog* and tell what information they find in each part.

- **Revisit the book.** Display *What's It Like to Be a Fish?* Page through the book, using the pictures to help children recall what the book is about. *(RI.K.2; RI.K.7)*

- **Guide children to identify parts of a book.** Display the front cover. Ask:

  What part of the book is this? *(the front cover)*

  What is the book's title? *(What's It Like to Be a Fish?)*

  Who is the author? What did she do? *(Wendy Pfeffer; she wrote the words)*

  Who is the illustrator? What did she do? *(Holly Keller; she drew the pictures)*

> **Tip:** As needed, have children return to Student Book page 77 to recall the roles of the author and illustrator.

- Turn to the title page and have children identify all the same information that appeared on the front cover. Discuss the differences. *(The pictures are different and it names the company that made the book.)*

- Display the back cover of the book. Ask:

  What part of the book is this? *(the back cover)*

- Point to the pictures and explain that these are other books in the same series, or group of related things. These books are all about interesting science topics.

- Use the Close Reading activity to help children look closely at the summary on the back cover.

- Tell children that you will work together to complete the Student Book page by identifying different parts of the book *What's It Like to Be a Fish?*

- **Guide children to complete the Student Book page.** Have children turn to page 87. For the first item, display the back cover of *What's It Like to Be a Fish?* Ask: *What part of the book is this?* Point to and name each picture *(front cover; title page; back cover)*. Have a volunteer tell which picture to circle. Continue with the second item. Display the front cover. Ask: *What part of the book is this? (front cover; title page; back cover)*

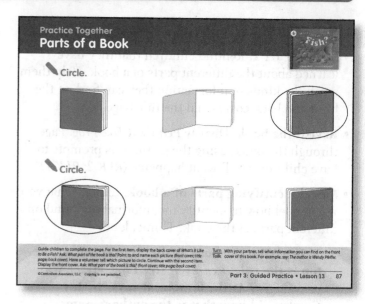

- **Have children demonstrate understanding.** Display *What's It Like to Be a Fish?* Read aloud the Turn and Talk activity. Have children identify the front cover before they begin. *(SL.K.1; SL.K.2)*

  With your partner, tell what information you can find on the front cover of this book. For example, say: *The author is Wendy Pfeffer.* (*This book is part of a series called "Let's-Read-And-Find-Out Science."*)

- Invite partners to share their ideas with the class.

Close Reading

- Display the back cover of *What's It Like to Be a Fish?* Read aloud the text at the top. Ask:

  What question does it ask? *("Could you live underwater?")*

  What does the text describe? *(the ways a fish's body is different from our bodies)*

  Why would you read this information before reading the book? *(It tells what the book is about and what you will learn by reading it.)*

- Point to the bottom part of the cover and recall that this book is part of a series called "Let's-Read-And-Find-Out Science." Discuss with children what they can find out from reading this book.

Step by Step

- **Review learning from Parts 1–3.** Remind children that a book has different parts. Have them point to the front and back covers of *What's It Like to Be a Fish?* and tell what information is on each part.

- **Revisit the book.** Display *What Lives in a Shell?* Page through the book, using the pictures to help children recall what the book is about. *(RI.K.2; RI.K.7)*

- **Have children identify parts of a book.** One at a time, display the front cover, title page, and back cover of *What Lives in a Shell?* Ask children these questions about each part in turn:

    What part of the book is this?

    What information is on this part of the book? *(Front cover: title, author's and illustrator's names; Title page: title, author's and illustrator's names, name of the company that made the book; Back cover: summary, other books to read)*

Tip: Point out that this book has information on the inside of each cover, but this is not a standard feature in all books. Briefly discuss the information there.

- Then ask:

    Who is the author? *(Kathleen Weidner Zoehfeld)*

    Who is the illustrator? *(Helen K. Davie)*

- Tell children that they will complete the Student Book page by identifying different parts of the book *What Lives in a Shell?*

- **Have children complete the Student Book page independently.** Have children turn to page 88. For the first item, display the title page of *What Lives in a Shell?* Ask: *What part of the book is this?* Point to and name each picture *(front cover; title page; back cover)*. Have children circle their answers. Continue with the second item. Display the front cover. Ask: *What part of the book is this?* *(front cover; title page; back cover)*

- Use the Close Reading activity to find similarities between two books in the same series.

- **Have children demonstrate understanding.** Display the front cover, title page, and back cover of *What Lives in a Shell?* Read aloud the Turn and Talk activity. Have children complete the activity with a partner, using the following prompt. *(SL.K.1; SL.K.2)*

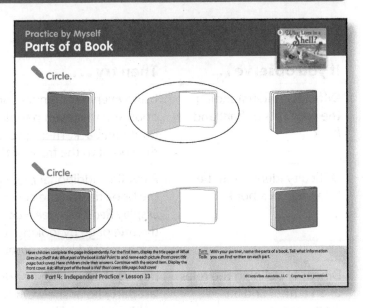

With your partner, name the parts of a book. Tell what information you can find written on each part. *(The front cover has the title and author's and illustrator's names. The title page has the title, author's and illustrator's names, and the name of the company that made the book. The back cover sometimes has a summary and names of other books to read.)*

- **Have children reflect on their learning.** Invite children to identify the different parts of a book and the questions they can ask about the information on each part. Have them share their ideas about the roles of an author and an illustrator in creating a book.

Close Reading

- Display the back cover of *What Lives in a Shell?* Read aloud the question and summary. Ask:

    What does this text tell you? *(what we can learn from reading the book)*

    Name another book we have read that has a back cover like this. *(What's It Like to Be a Fish?)*

    How are the books connected? *(They are part of the same series called "Let's-Read-And-Find-Out Science." They are both about animals.)*

- Point out that reading books from the same series helped children immediately recognize what kind of information they would find on the back cover.

Assessment and Remediation

If you observe . . .	Then try . . .
Difficulty understanding the concepts of *front* and *back*	Using everyday comparisons. Point out that a house has a front door and a back door, and that even people have a front and a back. Have children point to their front and back. Then give each child a book. Ask them to show the front cover as they point to the front of their bodies. Repeat for the back cover.
Difficulty identifying the title page of a book	Providing additional practice. Explain that one way to find the title page is to match the book title on the cover with the book title on an inside page of the book. Display *Red-Eyed Tree Frog*. Read aloud the title, tracking the print. Ask a child to find the title page by looking for the page inside the book that shows the title with the same-colored letters. Repeat with other books.
Difficulty defining the roles of an author and an illustrator	Having children practice doing each job. Invite a child to tell you a story about the last party he or she went to. Summarize the child's story in three to four sentences on chart paper. Above the story, write *Written by [name]*. Say: *You are the author of this story. What did you do?* (thought of the words to the story) Repeat by having another volunteer provide an illustration to go along with the story.

Connect to the Anchor Standard

R5: *Analyze the structure of texts, including how specific sentences, paragraphs, and larger portions of the text (e.g., a section, chapter, scene, or stanza) relate to each other and the whole.*
R6: *Assess how point of view or purpose shapes the content and style of a text.*

Throughout the grades, Standard 5 builds students' ability to gain information not just from the front and back covers of a book but from increasingly sophisticated text features. In later grades, students learn to identify the underlying text structure within a single text and across two or more texts. They may consider questions such as these: *How can I use this text feature to find information? Is this text organized by chronology? comparison? cause/effect? problem/solution?*

Meanwhile, Standard 6 develops students' understanding of how information is presented in a text, including recognizing the author's purpose and how it compares to their own point of view. Students will compare and contrast related texts, thinking about the author's distinct point of view in each text. Students might consider questions such as these: *What is the author's purpose in writing this book? How is my point of view similar to or different from that of the author?* Use the following activities to help children begin these transitions.

- Help children see the time-order structure of *Red-Eyed Tree Frog*. Display and read aloud pages 2–3. Ask: *What time of day is it at the beginning of the book?* Help children point to evidence that supports the answer. Then page through the book, having children describe what happens to the frog at night. Display and read aloud pages 26–29. Ask: *What time of day is it at the end of the book?* Discuss how the author writes about events in order from evening, throughout the night, until morning. *(SL.K.1; SL.K.2)*

- Discuss the author's purpose for writing *What's It Like to Be a Fish?* Prompt children to think about the book's title. Ask: *After reading this book, do you think you know what it's like to be a fish? Explain your answer.* Discuss with children that the author's purpose was to give information to readers who did not know much about fish.

Story Words and Pictures

CCSS

RL.K.7: With prompting and support, describe the relationship between illustrations and the story in which they appear (e.g., what moment in a story an illustration depicts).

Required Read Alouds: D (*Stone Soup*); E (*Why Mosquitoes Buzz in People's Ears*)

Lesson Objectives

- Describe what the words in a story tell.

- Describe what the pictures in a story show.

- Understand the connection between the words and pictures in a story.

- Recognize that the pictures in a story depict moments described in the words.

The Learning Progression

- **Prior to K:** Children should be able to distinguish between the words and the illustrations in a story. Children should also understand that words tell and illlustrations show what happens in a story.

- **Grade K: CCSS RL.K.7 requires that children describe the relationship between illustrations and words in a story with prompting and support. Children are expected to identify moments in a story that the illustrations depict.**

- **Grade 1:** CCSS RL.1.7 further develops the standard by having children use illustrations and story details to tell about characters, setting, or events.

Tap Children's Prior Knowledge

- Remind children that an author and an illustrator work together to tell a story. Invite volunteers to recall what the author does and what the illustrator does. (*An author writes the words. An illustrator draws the pictures.*)

- Tell children that you will work together to tell a story. Suggest a topic, such as getting a new bike, and begin the story for children. For example, say: *Max got a new bike for his birthday.*

- Invite children to continue the story. Encourage them to tell what happens next, and make notes for reference. After children have contributed three additional sentences, retell the story from the beginning.

- Repeat the story, pausing after each sentence. Ask: *If you were drawing a picture to go with this part of the story, what would you draw?* Invite children to share the details of what they would draw.

- Help children see that the pictures they described would show what the story is about. Explain that in this lesson, they will learn more about how words and pictures work together to tell a story.

Ready *Teacher Toolbox*

Teacher-Toolbox.com

	Prerequisite Skills	RL.K.7
Ready Lessons		✓
Tools for Instruction	✓	
Interactive Tutorials		✓ ✓

Additional CCSS

RL.K.2; SL.K.1; SL.K.2 (*See page A38 for full text.*)

Step by Step

- **Introduce the standard.** Tell children they will learn about how words and pictures work together to tell a story. Explain that thinking about what the words say and what the pictures show helps readers understand what happens in a story.

- Draw or post a picture of a dog sitting in a wash tub surrounded by bubbles. Also show a bottle of shampoo on the ground. Model describing what the picture shows. Think aloud:

  I see a dog sitting in a tub. I can also see bubbles all over the dog and in the tub, and a bottle of shampoo on the ground.

- Invite children to describe the picture in their own words. Then have them listen carefully as you read aloud a story that goes with the picture:

  I gave my dog, Storm, a bath in the tub. I used special dog shampoo. The shampoo made lots of bubbles. Storm loved it!

- Model describing the details you hear in the story. Think aloud:

  What do the words in the story tell about? I read that a dog named Storm got a bath in a tub. The words also tell that the dog was washed with special shampoo that made lots of bubbles.

- Help children find the details that appear in both the words and the picture. Then look for details that appear in just the words or just the picture, such as the dog's name.

- Tell children that in their Student Books, they will learn questions they can ask about words and pictures to help them understand what is happening in a story.

- **Read aloud the Student Book page.** Have children turn to Student Book page 89. Read aloud the page as children listen and follow along.

- Point to the first bullet and reread the question. Tell children that to find out what happens in a story, they think about what the characters do and say.

Tip: Clarify that in this story, the character is the person telling about giving Storm a bath. The story does not tell readers the character's name.

- Point to the second bullet and reread the question. Have children listen carefully as you reread the story. Prompt them to recall what the words tell about:

  What is Storm doing? (*getting a bath*)

  Where is Storm? (*in the tub*)

  What does Storm's owner use for the bath? (*special dog shampoo*)

  What does the shampoo make? (*lots of bubbles*)

  How does Storm feel about the bath? (*He loved it.*)

- Point to the third bullet and reread the question. Prompt children to tell what the picture shows as you point to the details:

  (Point to the dog.) **Who is this?** (*the dog, Storm*)

  (Point to the tub.) **What is this?** (*a tub*)

  (Point to the bubbles.) **What is this all over the dog?** (*bubbles*)

  What made the bubbles? (*special dog shampoo*)

- Ask a volunteer to point to the shampoo.

- Tell children that words and pictures work together to tell what happens in a story. The pictures show what the words describe, or tell about.

- **Have children demonstrate understanding.** Ask children to share what they have learned so far about words and pictures in a story. Encourage them to share questions they can ask about the words and pictures when they read a new story.

Step by Step

- **Review Part 1.** Remind children that words and pictures work together to tell a story. Review the questions they can ask about words and pictures to help them understand what happens in a story.

- **Revisit the story.** Display *Why Mosquitoes Buzz in People's Ears.* Page through the book, and review important events with children. (RL.K.2)

- **Model connecting words and pictures.** Explain that you will model thinking about what words tell and what pictures show in a story. Display pages 16–17 and read aloud page 17. Then think aloud:

  First I ask: *What do the words tell about?* **The words say that King Lion asks the monkey why he killed one of the owl babies. Then the monkey tells the King it was the crow's fault.**

  Next I ask: *What does the picture show?* **In this picture, I see many animals. Here is King Lion and here is the monkey. I see that the monkey's mouth is open, like he is talking to King Lion. I also see that the monkey is pointing his thumb at the birds behind him.**

  > **Tip:** Make sure every child can see the illustration clearly. If projecting is not an option, walk around the room and give each child a chance to point to the details you named.

  So now I ask: *How do the words and pictures work together to tell what happens?* **They both tell that the monkey talks to King Lion. The words say that the monkey tells King Lion it was the crow's fault, and the picture shows the monkey pointing at the crows.**

- Tell children you will model how to complete the Student Book page by connecting the words and picture in this part of *Why Mosquitoes Buzz in People's Ears.*

- **Model completing the Student Book page.** Have children turn to page 90. Ask children to look closely at the picture. Then read aloud the three sentences. Ask: *Which sentence tells what is happening in the picture?* Demonstrate circling the correct answer. Point to the picture again and reread the sentence that tells what is happening in the picture.

- **Have children demonstrate understanding.** Display pages 16–17. Read aloud the Turn and Talk activity. Model what a conversation with a partner should sound like by asking and answering the question below. (SL.K.1; SL.K.2)

  What moment in Why Mosquitoes Buzz in People's Ears *does the picture show?* Ask and answer this question with your partner. (*The picture shows the monkey talking to King Lion.*)

- Use the Close Reading activity to help children understand that a picture can show details that are not described in the words of a story.

Close Reading

- Display pages 16–17, and ask children to look closely at the picture. Prompt:

  What do you see in this picture? (*the monkey talking to King Lion and pointing at the crows; the other animals watching*)

- Point out that the words do not tell the names of all the council animals that the picture shows. Ask:

  Why do you think the author did not name the rest of the animals in the picture? (*The other animals are not saying or doing anything in this part of the story.*)

- Discuss with children how describing every detail in a picture could make a story very long and difficult to follow. Emphasize that authors choose the most important details for the words on a page.

Step by Step

- **Review learning from Parts 1–2.** Remind children that words and pictures work together to tell a story. Display pages 16–17 of *Why Mosquitoes Buzz in People's Ears.* Ask children to recall what the words and pictures tell about King Lion and the monkey.

- **Revisit the story.** Display *Stone Soup.* Page through the book, and review important events with children. *(RL.K.2)*

- **Guide children to connect words and pictures.** Display pages 10–11 of *Stone Soup.* Tell children to look closely at the pictures and listen carefully to the words as you read aloud the pages. Then prompt:

  What do the words tell about what the peasants are doing? *(The peasants are hiding their food from the soldiers.)*

  Tip: This page has a lot of potentially unfamiliar vocabulary, such as *sacks, barley, hay, lofts,* and *wells.* Provide brief definitions for each word, and help children point to those that appear in the picture.

  (Point to page 10.) **What do you see in this picture?** *(Two men are lifting a sack up into the loft and trying to hide it under the hay.)*

  (Point to page 11.) **What do you see in this picture?** *(Two kids are watching a woman hide cabbage and potatoes under a bed.)*

  How are the words and the pictures connected? *(They tell about and show the peasants hiding the food.)*

- Use the Close Reading activity to help children use pictures to deepen their understanding of the story.

- Tell children you will work together to complete the Student Book page by connecting words and pictures in this part of *Stone Soup.*

- **Guide children to complete the Student Book page.** Have children turn to page 91. Ask them to look closely at the picture. Then read aloud the three sentences. Ask: *Which sentence tells what is happening in the picture?* Have a volunteer tell which sentence to circle. Point to the picture again and reread the sentence that tells what is happening in the picture.

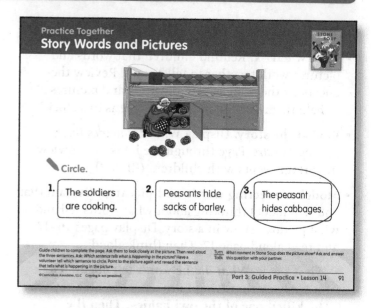

- Review and discuss the answers to the Student Book page. Help volunteers point to evidence in the story that supports the correct answer.

- **Have children demonstrate understanding.** Display pages 10–11 of *Stone Soup.* Read aloud the Turn and Talk activity. *(SL.K.1; SL.K.2)*

  What moment in Stone Soup *does the picture show?* Ask and answer this question with your partner. *(The peasant is hiding cabbages under a bed.)*

Close Reading

- Remind children that story pictures can deepen their understanding of what is happening. Display and reread pages 10–11 of *Stone Soup.* Prompt:

  Who is in these pictures? *(the peasants)*

  Are they all men? All women? Explain. *(No. There are men, a woman, and some children.)*

  What is everyone doing? *(hiding the food)*

- Reread the following sentence on page 10: "And they hurried to hide their food." Ask children what evidence they see of the peasants hurrying.

- Discuss how the men, women, and children all working at the same time shows that everyone available needed to help hide the food quickly.

Step by Step

- **Review learning from Parts 1–3.** Remind children that words and pictures work together to tell a story. Display pages 10–11 of *Stone Soup*. Invite children to tell how the picture shows what the words describe.

- **Have children connect words and pictures.** Tell children they will describe and connect words and pictures in another part of the story. Display and read aloud pages 26–27 of *Stone Soup*.

> **Tip:** Some children may need help understanding who is talking on page 26. Explain that on the previous page, the soldiers began talking about what the soup needs. They continue talking on page 26.

- Prompt children:

  What do the words describe? (*The soldiers want salt, pepper, and carrots for the soup. The children run to fetch the salt and pepper. The woman brings an apron full of carrots.*)

  (Point to page 26.) **Describe what you see in this picture.** (*two children each carrying a cup*)

  (Point to page 27.) **Describe what you see in this picture.** (*a woman with lots of carrots in her apron*)

  What details do both the words and pictures describe? (*children getting salt and pepper; a woman carrying carrots in her apron*)

- Use the Close Reading activity to help children see that sometimes they need details in the words to understand what a picture shows.

- Tell children that they will complete the Student Book page by connecting words and pictures in this part of *Stone Soup*.

- **Have children complete the Student Book page independently.** Have children turn to page 92. Ask them to look closely at the picture. Then read aloud the three sentences. Ask: *Which sentence tells what is happening in the picture?* Have children circle their answers.

- Review and discuss the answers to the Student Book page. Have children tell why the other sentences do not tell what is happening in the picture.

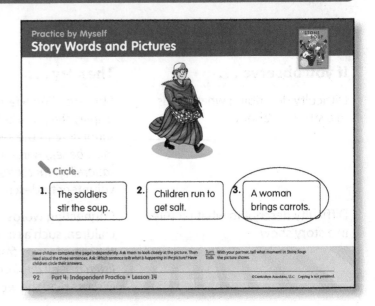

- **Have children demonstrate understanding.** Display pages 26–27 of *Stone Soup*. Read aloud the Turn and Talk activity. (SL.K.1; SL.K.2)

  With your partner, tell what moment in *Stone Soup* the picture shows. (*The woman is bringing carrots for the soup.*)

- **Have children reflect on their learning.** Invite children to tell how recognizing the way words and pictures work together helps them understand what is happening in a story. Emphasize that the words and the pictures each offer distinct details as well.

Close Reading

- Explain to children that words give important details that help readers make sense of pictures. Display and reread page 26. Prompt:

  What do you see in the picture? (*a boy and a girl running, carrying large cups in their arms*)

  What do the words say the children are carrying? (*salt and pepper*)

  Which words explain why the children are carrying salt and pepper? (*The soldiers said that "any soup needs salt and pepper."*)

- Emphasize that pictures alone cannot always give readers enough information. The words and pictures together tell what is happening.

Assessment and Remediation

If you observe . . .	Then try . . .
Difficulty describing what words in a story tell about	Close-reading a familiar story. Read aloud page 35 of *Stone Soup,* but do not display the picture. Reread the first paragraph and ask: *What was ready? (the soup)* Reread the second paragraph and ask: *What must be done first? (A table must be set.)* Reread the third paragraph and ask: *What was placed in the square? (great tables)* When all of the questions have been answered, ask a volunteer to describe what is happening in this part of the story.
Difficulty describing what pictures in a story show	Connecting words and pictures. Display a picture of something unfamiliar to children, such as a record player. Then read the following sentences: *I got this record player from my grandfather. It plays the most beautiful music. I can listen to it all day long.* Ask children what the picture shows. *(a record player)* Discuss how the words helped them understand the picture.
Difficulty identifying moments in a story that illustrations depict	Playing "Freeze Frame." Tell children that you will give directions telling them to act out a scene, such as playing a game or getting ready for school. Once they start an action, you will say "freeze." They will stop moving at that moment. When the children are "frozen," have a volunteer describe what they are doing in that precise moment. Explain that a picture can similarly "freeze" a specific moment in a story.

Connect to the Anchor Standard

R7: *Integrate and evaluate content presented in diverse media and formats, including visually and quantitatively, as well as in words.*

Throughout the grades, Standard 7 develops students' understanding of how content is presented in various formats. At the early grades, students identify and describe literal connections between words and illustrations in stories. In later grades, students progress to analyzing the relationship between text and illustrations to understand content more fully. In learning how to evaluate this relationship in more depth, students might consider questions such as these: *How do the illustrations support key details in a story? Do the illustrations help me better understand the characters, setting, or events in the story? What details discussed in the text have been left out of the illustrations? What details are included in the illustrations? Are these details critical to understanding the story?* Use the following activities to help your students begin this transition.

- Display and read aloud pages 18–19 of *Stone Soup.* Have children look closely at how the peasants are depicted in the picture. Ask: *Who are the peasants facing? (the soldiers) How did the illustrator draw the peasants' eyes? (wide open) From details in the picture, how did the peasants feel about stone soup? (curious)* Discuss how the picture helps children better understand the peasants' attitude. *(SL.K.1; SL.K.2)*

- Display pages 31–32 of *Why Mosquitoes Buzz in People's Ears.* Review that at this point, all the animals think the mosquito should be punished. Have children use the pictures to figure out how the mosquito is punished. Display page 31. Ask: *What does the picture show? (the mosquito talking into a person's ear; the person looking annoyed)* Display page 32. Ask: *What details in the picture show how the mosquito is punished? (The person smacks the mosquito.)* Have children discuss why this picture is so important to the story.

Comparing Characters

CCSS

RL.K.9: With prompting and support, compare and contrast the adventures and experiences of characters in familiar stories.

Required Read Alouds: *A (Jamaica's Blue Marker); C (Chrysanthemum)*

Lesson Objectives

- Identify what story characters do, say, and feel.
- Identify the similarities and differences between the experiences of characters in a story.
- Understand how comparing and contrasting characters' experiences helps readers learn more about the characters.

The Learning Progression

- **Prior to K:** Children should be able to tell about familiar stories, including naming the characters and some of the events. They should also have a basic understanding of what it means to be the same or different.
- **Grade K: CCSS RL.K.9 expects children to compare and contrast characters' adventures and experiences in familiar stories, with prompting and support.**
- **Grade 1:** CCSS RL.1.9 advances the standard by having children compare and contrast story characters' adventures and experiences more independently in less familiar stories.

Tap Children's Prior Knowledge

- Tell children they are going to talk about experiences they have. Explain that an *experience* is something that someone does. Offer simple examples such as reading a story at bedtime or going to a friend's house.
- Discuss with children the different ways they all get to school each day. Ask: *Who rides the bus to school? Who rides in a car? Who walks?* Have children form groups based on the way they get to school.
- Discuss the groups. Ask: *Does everybody in class get to school the same way? Does everybody have the same experience each morning?*
- Ask a volunteer from each group to describe his or her trip to school. Then have children in that group tell what is the same about how they get to school. Point out that children are *comparing* their trips when they tell how the trips are the same.
- Ask another volunteer from each group to tell how his or her way of getting to school is different from that of another group. Explain that children are *contrasting* their trips when they tell how they are different.
- Tell children that in this lesson, they will learn how to compare and contrast the experiences of story characters, just as they compared and contrasted their own experiences of getting to school.

Ready *Teacher Toolbox*		*Teacher-Toolbox.com*
	Prerequisite Skills	**RL.K.9**
Ready Lessons		✓
Tools for Instruction		✓ ✓
Interactive Tutorials		✓ ✓

Additional CCSS

RL.K.2; RL.K.7; SL.K.1; SL.K.2 *(See page A38 for full text.)*

Step by Step

- **Introduce the standard.** Tell children they will compare and contrast characters by thinking about what they do, say, and feel. Explain that this helps readers better understand the characters.

- Remind children that a *character* can be a person, an animal, or a life-like object. Invite them to tell questions they can ask to find out about characters. (*What do the characters do? What do the characters say? How do the characters feel?*)

- Have children listen carefully as you read aloud the following story:

  Mick and Mack go to the amusement park. Mick is excited, but Mack is a little nervous. They go on rides. Mick rides the roller coaster. Mack rides the Ferris wheel. Mick says he wants to go on the same ride again. Mack says he wants to try a new ride.

- Remind children that they previously compared and contrasted the ways they get to school. Explain that they can compare and contrast the experiences of characters in a story the same way.

- Have children identify the characters and the setting in the story you just read. (*Mick, Mack; an amusement park*) Then ask:

  What do Mick and Mack do that is the same? (*They both go to the amusement park. They both go on rides.*)

  What do Mick and Mack do that is different? (*Mick rides the roller coaster. Mack rides the Ferris wheel.*)

- Remind children that they *compared* the characters by telling what was the same and *contrasted* them by telling what was different.

- Tell children that in their Student Books, they will learn additional questions they can ask to compare and contrast characters in a story.

- **Read aloud the Student Book page.** Have children turn to Student Book page 93. Read aloud the page as children listen and follow along.

- Point to the first bullet and reread the question. Then reread the story. Review with children what Mick and Mack do that is the same. Then review what they do that is different.

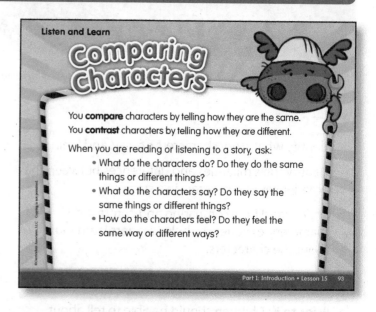

Tip: Create a T-Chart with the headings *Mick* and *Mack*, and write details related to each character in the appropriate column. Help children look for words that match. Explain that these matches show something about the characters that is the same. Rows of words that do not match show things that are different.

- Point to the second and third bullets and reread the questions. Reread the story (or refer to the T-Chart) and ask:

  Do Mick and Mack say the same things or different things? (*different things; Mick says he wants to go on the same ride, but Mack wants to try a new ride*)

  Do Mick and Mack feel the same way or different ways? (*different; Mick is excited, but Mack is nervous*)

- Help children frame their responses in ways that reflect similarities and differences, such as these:

  Both Mick and Mack _____.

  Mick rides the _____, but Mack rides the _____.

- Explain that comparing and contrasting characters helps readers get to know more about the characters.

- **Have children demonstrate understanding.** Call on volunteers to share what they have learned so far about comparing and contrasting story characters. Encourage them to give examples of how characters are alike and different, using familiar classroom read-alouds.

Step by Step

- **Review Part 1.** Remind children that it is important to think about whether characters' experiences are the same or different. This helps readers get to know the characters better.

- **Revisit the story.** Display *Jamaica's Blue Marker*. Page through the book, using the pictures as prompts to have children recall the story. (RL.K.2; RL.K.7)

- **Model comparing characters' experiences.** Explain that you will model comparing characters in this part of the story. Display and read aloud pages 26–29. Think aloud:

  Let's compare how the characters feel about Russell moving. (Turn to page 29) **On this page, Russell says: "You're lucky. You get to stay here." If Russell thinks Jamaica is lucky to stay, I think he wishes he didn't have to move; he feels sad about moving away. So what does Jamaica say? She says: "I wish you didn't have to move." This tells me she feels sad about Russell moving away, too.**

  > **Tip:** These exchanges between Jamaica and Russell require children to make several inferences about the characters' feelings. Provide practice as needed, having children state your feelings based on things you say. For example: *I'm never going to her house again! (mad)*

  So do the characters feel the same way or different ways about Russell moving? They both feel sad that he is moving, so they feel the same way.

- Tell children you will model how to complete the Student Book page by comparing and contrasting characters' experiences in this part of *Jamaica's Blue Marker*.

- **Model completing the Student Book page.** Have children turn to page 94. For the first item, ask: *How does Russell feel about moving away?* Point to and describe each picture (*surprised; happy; sad*). Demonstrate circling the correct answer. Continue with the second item. Ask: *In this part of the story, how does Jamaica feel about Russell moving away?* (*surprised; happy; sad*)

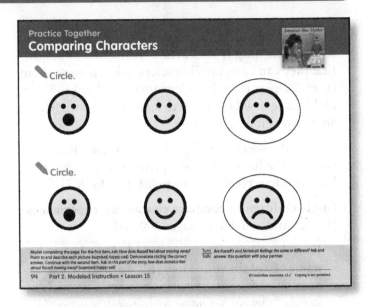

- **Have children demonstrate understanding.** Display pages 26–29 of *Jamaica's Blue Marker*. Read aloud the Turn and Talk activity. Model what a conversation with a partner should sound like by asking and answering the question below. (SL.K.1; SL.K.2)

  Are Russell's and Jamaica's feelings the same or different? Ask and answer this question with your partner. (*Their feelings are the same. They both feel sad about Russell moving away.*)

- Use the Close Reading activity to help children contrast characters' behavior toward each other at different points in the story.

Close Reading

- Help children compare characters at different points in the story. Reread pages 10–11. Ask:

  Do you think Russell and Jamaica get along? Why or why not? (*No. He draws all over her picture, and she yells at him to stop.*)

- Read aloud pages 26–28. Prompt:

  What does Jamaica give to Russell? (*her blue marker*)

  What does Russell say about Jamaica's pictures? (*She draws the best pictures in the class.*)

  How are Jamaica and Russell behaving toward each other? (*They are both being nice.*)

- Help children recall what Jamaica now understands that causes her to be nice to Russell.

Step by Step

- **Review learning from Parts 1–2.** Remind children that they can compare characters to learn more about them. Display page 29 of *Jamaica's Blue Marker*. Have children review how Jamaica and Russell each felt about Russell moving away.

- **Revisit the story.** Display *Chrysanthemum*. Page through the book, using the pictures as prompts to have children recall the story. (RL.K.2; RL.K.7)

- **Guide children to compare characters' experiences.** Display and read aloud pages 7–9. Ask:

    How does Chrysanthemum feel about her name? Explain your answer. (*She loves it. She loves the way it looks written on things. The words say she "thought her name was absolutely perfect."*)

    What happens when Chrysanthemum's classmates hear her name? (*They all giggle.*)

    Tip: Tell children that *giggling* is a way of laughing. Explain that people giggle when they think something is silly or funny.

    Why do they giggle? How do they feel about her name? (*They think it is funny.*)

    Do Chrysanthemum and her classmates feel the same way or differently about her name? Why? (*They feel differently. Chrysanthemum loves her name, but her classmates think it is funny.*)

- Use the Close Reading activity to demonstrate using picture details to compare characters in a story.

- Tell children that you will work together to complete the Student Book page by comparing characters' experiences in this part of *Chrysanthemum*.

- **Guide children to complete the Student Book page.** Have children turn to page 95. For the first item, ask: *How does Chrysanthemum feel about her name?* Point to and describe each picture (*she loves it; she thinks it is funny; it makes her sad*). Have a volunteer tell which picture to circle. Continue with the second item. Ask: *How do Chrysanthemum's classmates feel about her name?* (*they love it; they think it is funny; it makes them sad*)

- Discuss the answers to the Student Book page. Help children point to story evidence that supports the correct answers.

- **Have children demonstrate understanding.** Display pages 7–9 of *Chrysanthemum*. Read aloud the Turn and Talk activity. (SL.K.1; SL.K.2)

    With your partner, talk about how Chrysanthemum feels about her name. Then talk about how her classmates feel about her name. For example, say: *Chrysanthemum loves her name, but her classmates think her name is funny.*

- Invite partners to share their discussions with the class.

Close Reading

- Tell children they can also use picture clues to compare and contrast characters. Display page 9. Help children find Chrysanthemum. Ask:

    What do you notice about Chrysanthemum's name? (*It does not fit in the box.*)

    Is that the same as or different from the other kids? (*different; their names are shorter and fit in the box*)

    How does Chrysanthemum's face look? (*worried and sad*)

    Is that the same as or different from the other kids? (*different; the other kids are laughing*)

- Discuss how the picture clues emphasize how Chrysanthemum's name is different from the rest of her classmates' names.

Step by Step

- **Review learning from Parts 1–3.** Remind children that they can compare and contrast what characters do and say and how they feel. Ask children to give an example of how characters feel differently in *Chrysanthemum*.

- **Have children compare characters' experiences.** Display and read aloud pages 26–29 of *Chrysanthemum*. Tell children they will compare and contrast characters in this part of the story. Ask:

  What do the girls say about Chrysanthemum's name? (*It's "so long. It scarcely fits on her name tag. She's named after a flower."*)

  What does Mrs. Twinkle say about her own name, Delphinium? (*It's long. It would scarcely fit on a name tag. She's named after a flower.*)

  What is the same about Chrysanthemum and Mrs. Twinkle? (*They are both named after flowers.*)

  How does Chrysanthemum feel about her name now? (*She loves it again.*)

  > **Tip:** Remind children that they can look at pictures to understand how characters feel. Encourage them to use the pictures on page 29 to decide that Chrysanthemum loves her name again.

- Tell children that they will complete the Student Book page by comparing characters' experiences in this part of *Chrysanthemum*.

- **Have children complete the Student Book page independently.** Have children turn to page 96. For the first item, ask: *What is Chrysanthemum named after?* Point to and describe each picture (*a flower; her grandmother; a character in a story*). Have children circle their answers. Continue with the second item. Ask: *What is Mrs. Twinkle named after?* (*a flower; her grandmother; a character in a story*)

- Discuss the answers to the Student Book page. Help children find evidence that supports the answers.

- Use the Close Reading activity to help children compare characters' feelings before and after an event.

- **Have children demonstrate understanding.** Display pages 26–29 of *Chrysanthemum*. Read aloud the Turn and Talk activity. (*SL.K.1; SL.K.2*)

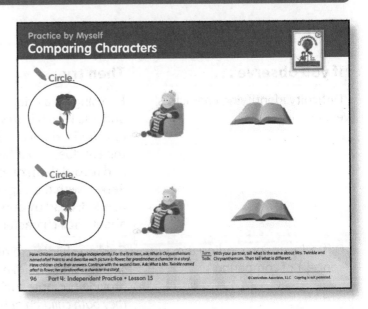

With your partner, tell what is the same about Mrs. Twinkle and Chrysanthemum. Then tell what is different. (*They are both named after a flower. They both like Chrysanthemum's name. Mrs. Twinkle is named after a delphinium, but Chrysanthemum is named after a chrysanthemum.*)

- **Have children reflect on their learning.** Invite children to discuss how they can compare and contrast characters in a story. Prompt them to share the questions they can ask and reflect on how comparing and contrasting characters' experiences helps readers better understand the characters.

Close Reading

- Guide children to compare a character's feelings before and after an important event. Read page 26.

  What does Chrysanthemum think about her name at this point? (*It's "absolutely dreadful."*)

  (Read pages 28–29.) **What does Mrs. Twinkle say about the name?** (*It's "absolutely perfect."*)

  How does Chrysanthemum feel now? Why? (*happy, because she hears Mrs. Twinkle's words; proud that someone she looks up to likes her name*)

- Help children name word and picture evidence to compare how Chrysanthemum feels before and after Mrs. Twinkle's appearance in the story.

Assessment and Remediation

If you observe . . .	Then try . . .
Difficulty identifying characters' experiences	Focusing on a brief fable, such as *The Ant and the Grasshopper*. Read it aloud and ask: *Who is in this story? Who are the two characters? (the ant and the grasshopper)* Tell children to listen as you read again for details about what the ant does, what he says, and how he feels. Invite them to share the details, and record them on chart paper beneath the title *The Ant's Experiences*. Repeat with the experiences of the grasshopper, rereading the story as needed. Read through the complete list and encourage children to tell more about each character's experiences.
Difficulty understanding the concept of comparing	Guiding children to notice similarities. Display photographs of two people side-by-side. Ask: *What is the same about these people?* For additional support, provide prompts such as these: *Are these people both boys or both girls? Are they both children or both grown-ups?* Emphasize that children are comparing the people by telling what is the same about them.
Difficulty understanding the concept of contrasting	Using a topic that is familiar to children, such as sports. Invite children to name two sports. Talk briefly about what the sports have in common. Then invite children to offer ways that the sports are different. Record their answers in a T-Chart. As you review each row on the chart, point out that children contrasted the sports by telling how they are different from one another.

Connect to the Anchor Standard

R9: *Analyze how two or more texts address similar themes or topics in order to build knowledge or to compare the approaches the authors take.*

Throughout the grades, Standard 9 guides students from comparing and contrasting characters' experiences to looking more broadly at entire books and comparing and contrasting their plots and themes. Students will learn to consider the author's impact on a story by thinking about how two authors treat a similar topic, or about how one author treats themes across books in a series. Students will ask questions such as these: *What characters in other stories have problems similar to the character's problem in this story? How do different authors treat the same theme in different stories? How are the characters, settings, and plots similar in this series by the same author?* Use the following activities to help children begin this transition.

- Remind children that the main parts of *Jamaica's Blue Marker* and *Chrysanthemum* take place at school. Help children recall the other important setting in both stories. Turn to pages 20–21 in *Jamaica's Blue Marker* and ask: *Where is Jamaica? What happens in this part of the story?* Turn to pages 20–21 in *Chrysanthemum* and ask: *Where is Chrysanthemum? What happens in this part of the story?* Guide children to compare the characters' experiences at home. Discuss how they are similar to each other, and different from the characters' experiences at school.

- Point out that in both *Jamaica's Blue Marker* and *Chrysanthemum*, the main characters have a problem at school. Ask: *What problem does Jamaica have at school? What problem does Chrysanthemum have at school?* Help children recall that classmates make being at school an unhappy experience for both Jamaica and Chrysanthemum. Then discuss what is different about each character's problem.

Words and Pictures

CCSS

RI.K.7: With prompting and support, describe the relationship between illustrations and the text in which they appear (e.g., what person, place, thing, or idea in the text an illustration depicts).

Required Read Alouds: H (*What Lives in a Shell?*); I (*America's Champion Swimmer*)

Lesson Objectives

- Describe the information given in the words of an information book.

- Describe the information given in the pictures of an information book.

- Understand the connection between the words and pictures in an information book.

- Understand how using both words and pictures in an information book can help readers learn more about a topic.

The Learning Progression

- **Prior to K:** Children should be able to distinguish between the words and the illustrations or photos in a book. With prompting and support, they should be able to describe the information they get from each.

- **Grade K: CCSS RI.K.7** requires that children describe the relationship between illustrations and words in a text with prompting and support. Children are expected to identify the person, place, thing, or idea from the book that an illustration shows.

- **Grade 1:** CCSS RI.1.7 further develops the standard by having children use illustrations and details in a text to describe its key ideas.

Tap Children's Prior Knowledge

- Remind children that both words and pictures can give them information. Sometimes the information is the same, and other times they can find additional details in the words or in the pictures.

- Display a photograph of a familiar animal, such as a cat. Then provide a few details about the cat, some visible and some not. For example, say: *This is my cat, Toby. He is orange with white stripes. He is small, but he has a lot of energy for playing!*

- On a piece of chart paper, create a T-Chart with the column heads *Words* and *Pictures*. Invite children to tell what they learned about the cat from the words you said. Record their responses. Repeat by prompting them to tell what they learned from the pictures.

- Point to the details that appear in both columns, such as the cat's color. Point out that the words and pictures work together to give this information. Then review one detail that the picture does not show, such as the cat's name. Help children see that it is important to look for information in both places.

- Tell children that in this lesson, they will learn how to connect the information in the words of a book to the information in the pictures. Explain that thinking about the information in the words and the pictures will help them better understand the topic of the book.

Ready *Teacher Toolbox*   *Teacher-Toolbox.com*

	Prerequisite Skills	RI.K.7
Ready Lessons		✓
Tools for Instruction	✓	
Interactive Tutorials		✓ ✓

Additional CCSS

RI.K.2; SL.K.1; SL.K.2 (*See page A38 for full text.*)

Step by Step

- **Introduce the standard.** Tell children they will learn that words and pictures work together to give information in a book. Explain that readers use the words and the pictures in an information book to learn about people, places, things, events, and ideas.

- Draw or post a picture of a large cactus in a dry setting. Have children look it over silently for a moment. Then read aloud the following text:

  A cactus is a type of plant. It grows in very dry places like the desert. A cactus doesn't look like most other plants: it is covered with lots of sharp points called spines that will prick your finger if you touch them.

- Prompt children to share what they have learned about a cactus:

  What is a cactus? *(It is a plant.)*

  Where does a cactus grow? *(in dry places like the desert)*

  What is unusual about a cactus? *(It is covered with sharp spines that hurt to touch.)*

- Point to details in the picture. First point to the whole cactus and ask: *What is this?* Then point to the land around the cactus and ask: *Where is the cactus growing?* Finally, ask: *What are these sharp spikes all over the cactus?*

- Help children see that the same information they learned in the words you read is also represented in the picture. Explain that in information books, words and pictures work together in this way to help readers understand important details.

Tip: Review Lesson 11 to remind children that an illustrator's job is to draw pictures that show the details in the words of a story. Explain that illustrators or photographers of information books do this same job.

- Tell children that in their Student Books, they will learn questions they can ask about the words and pictures in an information book.

- **Read aloud the Student Book page.** Have children turn to Student Book page 97. Read aloud the page as children listen and follow along.

- Reread the bold list at the top of the page and tell children the words and picture they just discussed were about a thing—a cactus. Reiterate that the words and picture gave them information about the cactus.

- Point to the first bullet and reread the question. Have children listen carefully again as you reread the passage. Using the same prompts, review the information children learned from the words.

- Point to the second bullet and reread the question. Invite volunteers to point to details in the picture and describe what they see.

- Point to the third bullet and reread the question. Remind children that *connected* means they go together. Discuss which details in the picture match what children heard in the words. As needed, reread the passage one sentence at a time, and look for specific details in the picture.

- Tell children that when they listen carefully to the words and look closely at the pictures in an information book, they can learn a lot about a topic.

- **Have children demonstrate understanding.** Call on volunteers to share what they have learned so far about words and pictures in an information book. Have them tell how pictures support the information provided in the words of a book.

Step by Step

- **Review Part 1.** Remind children that they can find important information in the words and pictures of an information book. Review the questions they should ask as they read to connect the words and pictures.

- **Revisit the book.** Display *What Lives in a Shell?* Page through the book, using the pictures as prompts to help children recall information. *(RI.K.2; RI.K.7)*

- **Model connecting words and pictures.** Explain that you are going to model looking for information in the words and pictures of this book. Display pages 18–19. Read aloud page 18, and think aloud:

  > **The words say that at the seashore, or the beach, you might see different kinds of shells and even a crab. They also say that a crab has ten legs, two claws on its front legs, and a hard shell that covers its whole body.**

  > **In the picture on this page** (page 18), **I see a girl in the sand and some seashells, but in this picture** (page 19), **I see a crab. Let me count the legs.** (Point and count to 10.) **These front legs are different. These must be the claws. And the crab looks shiny; that must be its hard shell.**

- Reread each sentence, and invite children to point to details in the picture that match the words. Emphasize that the words and picture are connected because the picture shows what the words describe.

> **Tip:** Use this example to emphasize that words and pictures that go together are not always on the same page. The picture that illustrates the words on page 18 is actually on page 19.

- Use the Close Reading activity for additional practice with connecting information in words and pictures.

- Tell children you will model how to complete the Student Book page by connecting the words and pictures in this part of *What Lives in a Shell?*

- **Model completing the Student Book page.** Have children turn to page 98. For the first item, ask: *What information do you get from the words?* Point to and name each picture (*a crab; a girl at the beach; seashells*). Demonstrate circling two correct answers. Continue with the second item. Ask: *What information do you get from the pictures?* (*a crab; a girl at the beach; seashells*)

- **Have children demonstrate understanding.** Display pages 18–19 of *What Lives in a Shell?* Read aloud the Turn and Talk activity. Model what a conversation with a partner should sound like by asking and answering the question below. *(SL.K.1; SL.K.2)*

  > **How are the words and the picture connected? Ask and answer this question with your partner.** *(The picture shows what the words tell about: the crab's legs, claws, and shell. I see ten legs—the front two are claws—and a hard, shiny shell.)*

- Discuss any places where the picture gives more detail than the words, such as the color of the crab's shell.

Close Reading

- Reread the following sentences: "A crab has ten legs. On its front legs are two claws." Display the picture on page 19, and ask:

  > **How many legs does the crab have?** *(ten)*

  > **But in the picture I only count eight legs. Where are the other two?** *(The words tell that the front legs are claws. They count as part of the ten legs.)*

- Discuss how the words and the picture work together to give information about the crab and to help make a confusing detail clearer for readers.

Step by Step

- **Review learning from Parts 1–2.** Remind children that they can find important information in words and pictures. Display pages 18–19 of *What Lives in a Shell?* Help children review the connections between the words and the picture.

- **Revisit the book.** Display *America's Champion Swimmer.* Page through the book, using the pictures as prompts to help children recall information. *(RI.K.2; RI.K.7)*

- **Guide children to connect words and pictures.** Display pages 16–17 and tell children to listen carefully for information as you read aloud page 16. Prompt:

  > **What do the words say Trudy is wearing?** (*a red bathing cap, a two-piece bathing suit, and goggles*)

  > **Look at the picture. What does Trudy's swimsuit look like?** (*It is a black, two-piece suit. The top has the American flag on it.*)

  > **What can you see on Trudy's head?** (*a red bathing cap and goggles*)

  > **How are the words and the picture connected?** (*They tell and show what Trudy is wearing.*)

- Revisit the remaining sentences and help children practice matching words to details in the picture, such as Margaret rubbing grease on Trudy's arm or the water that Trudy steps into.

- Use the Close Reading activity to help children distinguish between information found in the words and in the picture.

- Tell children that you will work together to complete the Student Book page by connecting the words and the picture in this part of *America's Champion Swimmer.*

- **Guide children to complete the Student Book page.** Have children turn to page 99. For the first item, ask: *What information do you get from the words?* Point to and name each picture (*a rowboat; a bathing cap and goggles; a bathing suit*). Have volunteers tell which pictures to circle. Continue with the second item. Ask: *What information do you get from the pictures?* (*a rowboat; a bathing cap and goggles; a bathing suit*)

- Discuss the circled images. Help children point to evidence in the story that supports each one.

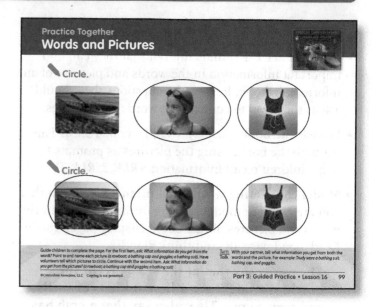

Practice Together
Words and Pictures

Circle.

Circle.

Guide children to complete the page. For the first item, ask: *What information do you get from the words?* Point to and name each picture (*a rowboat; a bathing cap and goggles; a bathing suit*). Have volunteers tell which pictures to circle. Continue with the second item. Ask: *What information do you get from the pictures?* (*a rowboat; a bathing cap and goggles; a bathing suit*)

Turn Talk. With your partner, tell what information you get from both the words and the picture. For example: *Trudy wore a bathing suit, bathing cap, and goggles.*

©Curriculum Associates, LLC   Copying is not permitted.

Part 3: Guided Practice • Lesson 16   99

- **Have children demonstrate understanding.** Display pages 16–17 of *America's Champion Swimmer.* Read aloud the Turn and Talk activity. *(SL.K.1; SL.K.2)*

  > **With your partner, tell what information you get from both the words and the picture. For example:** *Trudy wore a bathing suit, bathing cap, and goggles.* (*Margaret coated Trudy with grease. Trudy was near water.*)

- Invite partners to share their connections with the class. Help children point to the evidence in the words and the picture that supports their ideas.

Close Reading

- Remind children that pictures sometimes give more information than words. Display the picture on pages 16–17. Prompt:

  > **What else do you see besides Trudy and Margaret?** (*a man standing next to a rowboat; two men standing in the background; some ships out on the water*)

- Help children use what they know about the book to discuss who each person might be and why he would be standing there. (*The man with the rowboat will take Margaret to the tugboat. The men in the back are her trainer and her father.*)

- Explain that including these details in the picture helps the author focus the words on the most important details and events.

Step by Step

- **Review learning from Parts 1–3.** Remind children that words and pictures work together to provide information. Display pages 16–17 of *America's Champion Swimmer*. Help children review the connections between the words and the picture.

- **Have children connect words and pictures.** Display and read aloud pages 18–19 of *America's Champion Swimmer*. Tell children they will practice connecting words and pictures in this part of the book.

> **Tip:** Tell children that looking at a picture first can give readers a clue about what they will find out or what to pay close attention to in the words.

- Prompt children:

  What information do you get from the words? (*Trudy's father, sister, and trainer are on a tugboat. The tugboat will help protect Trudy and keep her from getting lost. Reporters and photographers are on another boat. Margaret puts the words "This way, Ole Kid" and an arrow on the side of the tugboat.*)

  What does the picture show? (*It shows Trudy swimming and people on two boats, one with writing.*)

  How are the words and picture connected? (*They both give information about Trudy's swim, including where she was, who was with her, and what the writing on the tugboat says.*)

- Use the Close Reading activity to explain that pictures sometimes include words that give information.

- Tell children that they will complete the Student Book page by connecting the words and pictures in this part of the book.

- **Have children complete the Student Book page independently.** Have children turn to page 100. For the first item, ask: *What information do you get from the words?* Point to and name each picture (*a tugboat; choppy water; an arrow*). Have children circle their answers. Continue with the second item. Ask: *What information do you get from the pictures?* (*a tugboat; choppy water; an arrow*)

- Discuss the answers to the Student Book page. Help children point to evidence in the book that supports the correct answers.

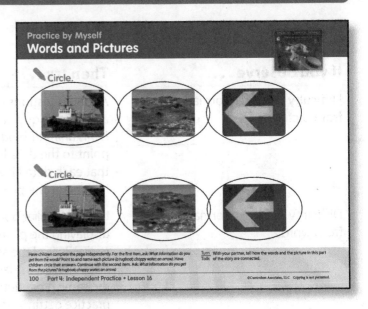

- **Have children demonstrate understanding.** Display pages 18–19 of *America's Champion Swimmer*. Read aloud the Turn and Talk activity. (*SL.K.1; SL.K.2*)

  With your partner, tell how the words and picture in this part of the story are connected. (*They both give information about the boats and Margaret writing on the side of the tugboat.*)

- **Have children reflect on their learning.** Invite children to tell why it is important to use both words and pictures to get information from a book. Emphasize that connecting the words and the pictures helps readers better understand the information they read.

Close Reading

- Explain that pictures may show words that give information. Have children look closely at page 19 as you read the last paragraph on page 18. Say:

  What does Margaret do with chalk? (*She writes an arrow and "This way, Ole Kid" on the boat.*)

  How many boats in the picture have writing on them? (*just one*)

  What does the writing on the boat help readers understand? (*It shows which boat is the tugboat that Margaret and others are on.*)

- Emphasize that connecting the words and pictures helps readers keep track of important details.

Assessment and Remediation

If you observe . . .	Then try . . .
Difficulty getting information from pictures	Asking questions about the picture. Display a photograph of a familiar animal. Ask questions such as these based on details in the picture: *How big is this animal? What color is it? How many legs does it have?* Invite children to point to the details in the picture as they give each answer. Help them see that each detail is a piece of information about the topic that they got from looking at the picture.
Difficulty getting information from words	Using a familiar book. Read aloud page 13 of *What Lives in a Shell?* without displaying the picture. Then reread the first sentence. Ask: *What likes to eat snails?* Reread the second sentence. Ask: *What is the snail unable to run away from?* Reread the last two sentences. Ask: *What does the snail do to stay safe?* Use the same procedure with another page or two in the book to help children practice getting information from words they hear.
Difficulty understanding the connection between words and pictures	Practicing with flashcards. Draw or paste pictures of familiar foods on one set of index cards. Write sentences to identify each type of food on another set of index cards. For example: *This is a [name of food].* Display the picture cards and have children identify each food item. Then, one at a time, read a sentence from a card. Call on a volunteer to match the words and pictures by placing the sentence card with its corresponding picture card. Continue until all words and pictures have been matched.

Connect to the Anchor Standard

R7: *Integrate and evaluate content presented in diverse media and formats, including visually and quantitatively, as well as in words.*

Throughout the grades, Standard 7 advances students from making connections between words and illustrations to interpreting information presented through more complex visuals within texts. Students will learn to use such visuals, as well as digital sources, to enhance their understanding of what they read. They will develop proficiency in locating information through various media. As they develop these skills, students might consider questions such as these: *How do the text and illustrations work together to deliver key ideas? How does this information presented visually contribute to my understanding of the text? Where can I find the information I am looking for?* Use the following activities to help children begin this transition.

- Guide children to use a diagram to get information. Display page 9 of *What Lives in a Shell?* Explain that a *diagram* is a picture that shows the parts of something—in this case, a snail. Point to each part and read its label. Check children's understanding of the diagram by asking: *Where is the snail's head? Where is its mouth?* (Point to the shell.) *What is this part called?* (Point to the foot.) *What is this part called? Who can find the eyes? Where are the tentacles?* (SL.K.1; SL.K.2)

- Help children understand that the events in *America's Champion Swimmer* take place in the past. Read aloud page 5 and point out that Trudy was born in 1906, over one hundred years ago. Use details in the illustrations to reinforce children's understanding of the time period. Throughout the book, point out the old-fashioned styles of clothing. In particular, point out the typewriter (page 13) and the car (page 30).

Identifying Reasons

CCSS

RI.K.8: With prompting and support, identify the reasons an author gives to support points in a text.

Required Read Alouds: *Projectable 3 (Eat Better!); I (America's Champion Swimmer)*

Lesson Objectives

- Recognize that an author presents important ideas in an information book.

- Identify reasons that support important ideas in an information book.

- Understand that identifying reasons helps readers comprehend an author's important ideas.

The Learning Progression

- **Prior to K:** Children should have a basic understanding of the concepts of questions and answers, particularly *why* questions. They should also be able to name some details from a familiar information book.

- **Grade K: CCSS RI.K.8 requires children to identify reasons that support points in a text, with prompting and support.**

- **Grade 1:** CCSS RI.1.8 builds on the Grade K standard by having children work more independently to identify reasons that support points in a text.

Tap Children's Prior Knowledge

- Choose a topic on which children likely have strong opinions, such as extending recess time. Ask children to tell how they feel about a longer recess period. Give sample responses as needed: *We should have a longer recess. Recess is just right the way it is.*

- Repeat one opinion about the topic, such as *We should have a longer recess.* Explain that this opinion is an *important idea* because it tells something that children think is important for others to understand.

- Ask: *Why should we have a longer recess period?* Invite several children to respond. Then explain that when children answer a *why* question, they are giving reasons that explain why their idea is important.

- Point out that just as children have opinions, or important ideas, so do authors. Tell children that thinking about the reasons an author gives to explain an important idea helps them better understand the idea.

- Tell children that in this lesson, they will learn how to find reasons that explain, or support, an author's important ideas.

Ready *Teacher Toolbox*

Teacher-Toolbox.com

	Prerequisite Skills	RI.K.8
Ready Lessons		✓
Tools for Instruction		✓
Interactive Tutorials		

Additional CCSS

RI.K.2; RI.K.7; SL.K.1; SL.K.2 *(See page A38 for full text.)*

Step by Step

- **Introduce the standard.** Tell children that authors often include important ideas in information books. Explain that children will learn to look for reasons the author gives to support important ideas.

- Ask children to listen carefully as you read aloud about where the class should go on a field trip. Have them imagine that a student is the author of this text.

  For our next field trip, we should go to the petting zoo. The petting zoo has many animals we have never seen. We can draw pictures of the animals. We can show the pictures during science time.

- Reread the first sentence. Ask:

  Where does the author think they should go for their field trip? (*to the petting zoo*)

- Point out that this is the author's important idea, or what she wants readers to understand.

  Tip: Explain that most books have more than one important idea, but in this short text there is just one.

- Talk about the reasons the author gives to support, or explain, this idea. Prompt:

  Why does the author think the class should go to the petting zoo? (*The petting zoo has many animals they have never seen. The class can draw the animals and show the pictures during science time at school.*)

- Remind children that earlier they gave reasons to explain their important idea of having a longer recess. Explain that they should think of this text in a similar way: when the author tells why the class should go to the petting zoo, she is giving reasons.

- Tell children that in their Student Books, they will learn questions they can ask to find reasons that support, or explain, an author's important idea.

- **Read aloud the Student Book page.** Have children turn to Student Book page 101. Read aloud the page as children listen and follow along.

- Point to the first bullet and reread the question. Reread the first sentence from the passage. Remind children that this is the important idea the author wants readers to know: the class should go to the petting zoo for their field trip.

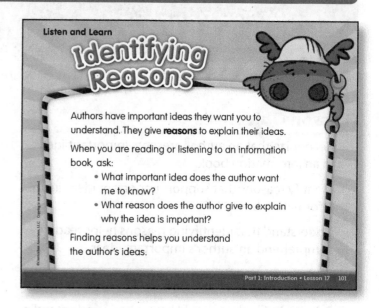

- Point to the second bullet and reread the question. Reread the rest of the passage. Model how to decide whether or not each sentence has a reason that supports the important idea. Think aloud:

  I ask myself: *Does this tell me* why *the author thinks the class should go to the petting zoo?* The first sentence tells me the zoo has many animals they have never seen. Is this a reason to go? Yes it is. This reason supports the important idea.

- Review that when an author tells *why*, the author is giving a reason to support an important idea. Discuss that thinking about reasons helps readers understand the author's important ideas.

- **Have children demonstrate understanding.** Call on volunteers to share what they have learned so far about finding reasons in order to understand important ideas. Emphasize that finding reasons often means looking for answers to questions that ask *why* about the important idea.

Part 2: Modeled Instruction

Step by Step

- **Review Part 1.** Remind children that authors give reasons to explain important ideas. Help them recall how finding reasons can help readers understand the important ideas.

- **Revisit the book.** Display *America's Champion Swimmer*. Page through the book, using the pictures as prompts to have children recall what happens. *(RI.K.2; RI.K.7)*

- **Model identifying reasons.** Display and read aloud pages 4–5. Reread this important idea: *"Gertrude Ederle's place was in the water."* Tell children that you will look for reasons that explain this important idea.

> **Tip:** Explain that someone's "place" means where they do their best at something. Gertrude's place was in the water because she performed at her best when she was swimming in the water.

- Display and read aloud page 8. Think aloud:

  What is a reason that tells why Trudy's place was in the water? Here is one detail: "She loved to swim." That tells why her place was in the water. And down here I read "At fifteen Trudy won her first big race." If Trudy is winning races, that certainly tells me she belongs in the water.

- Display and read aloud page 11. Think aloud:

  On this page, I read that Trudy won three medals in the Olympic games. Does that tell more about why her place was in the water? I think so, because it shows that she is a great swimmer. This is another reason.

- Tell children that you will model how to complete the Student Book page by identifying the reasons an author gives to support an important idea.

- **Model completing the Student Book page.** Have children turn to page 102. Read aloud the important idea: *Gertrude Ederle's place was in the water.* Explain that children will circle each reason that explains this idea. Point to each picture and name the reason (*she loved to swim; she won a race at age fifteen; she won three Olympic medals*). Model deciding whether each reason explains the important idea, and circle the pictures. Revisit the text as needed.

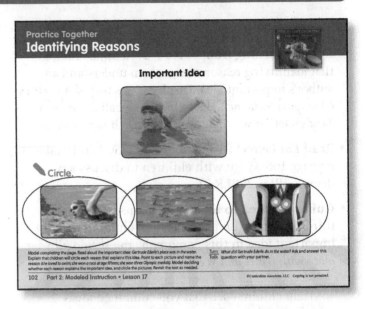

- **Have children demonstrate understanding.** Display pages 5–11 of *America's Champion Swimmer*. Read aloud the Turn and Talk activity. Model what a conversation with a partner should sound like by asking and answering the following question. *(SL.K.1; SL.K.2)*

  What did Gertrude Ederle do in the water? Ask and answer this question with your partner.
  (She swam. She won races. She won Olympic medals.)

- Help children point to evidence in the words and pictures that supports each reason.

- Use the Close Reading activity to explain that reasons can come before an idea as well as after it.

Close Reading

- Explain that an author may give reasons before or after an important idea. Display page 7. Say: *Raise your hand when you hear a reason for this idea: "Trudy's father was determined to teach her to swim."*

- Read aloud the first two paragraphs. Ask:

  What reason did you hear? Why was Trudy's father determined to teach her to swim?
  (Trudy nearly drowned.)

  Why is that a good reason to teach her to swim? *(If she didn't learn, she might drown.)*

- Remind children to look for reasons by identifying the important idea and asking *why*.

Step by Step

- **Review learning from Parts 1–2.** Remind children that identifying reasons helps them understand an author's important idea. Display pages 6–7 of *America's Champion Swimmer.* Have children recall the reason Trudy's father was determined to teach her to swim.

- **Read *Eat Better!*** Display and read aloud Projectable 3 on page 166. Work with children to discuss key details. *(RI.K.2; RI.K.7)*

- **Guide children to identify reasons.** Reread the third paragraph on page 166. Tell children the important idea in this paragraph: *You should fill your plate with fruits and vegetables.*

> **Tip:** Help children see that you combined ideas in the first two sentences to produce the author's important idea. Explain that sometimes the idea is stated directly and sometimes readers can restate it.

- Guide children to look for reasons that support the important idea.

  What will help you grow? *(the vitamins and minerals you get from fruits and vegetables)*

  What helps you play and have fun? *(the energy you get from fruits and vegetables)*

  What will make you feel good? *(healthy foods like fruits and vegetables)*

  Why should you fill your plate with fruits and vegetables? *(They give you vitamins and minerals to grow. They give you energy to play. They make you feel good.)*

- Tell children that you will work together to complete the Student Book page by identifying reasons that explain an important idea in *Eat Better!*

- **Guide children to complete the Student Book page.** Have children turn to page 103. Read aloud the important idea: *Fill your plate with fruits and vegetables.* Point to each picture and name the reason *(you will get vitamins and minerals to grow; you will have energy to play; you will feel better).* Help children decide whether each reason explains the important idea. Have them circle each reason that does.

- Discuss the answers to the Student Book page. Help children find evidence that supports the answers.

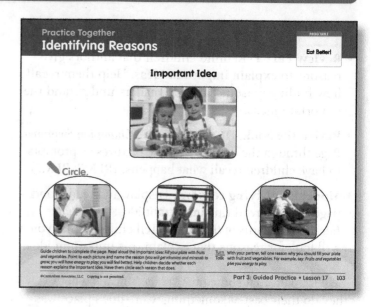

- Use the Close Reading activity to show how an author may give reasons more than once to stress their importance.

- **Have children demonstrate understanding.** Display *Eat Better!* Read aloud the Turn and Talk activity. Revisit the text as needed. *(SL.K.1; SL.K.2)*

  With your partner, tell one reason why you should fill your plate with fruits and vegetables. For example, say: *Fruits and vegetables give you energy to play.* *(Fruits and vegetables give you vitamins and minerals to grow.)*

- Invite children to share their ideas with the class.

Close Reading

- Explain that sometimes an author will give reasons more than once. Reread the first paragraph of *Eat Better!* Say:

  The important idea is: "It's a good idea to eat foods that are good for you." What reasons does the author give to explain why it's a good idea? *(They will help you grow. They will keep you healthy. They will make you feel better.)*

- Point out that these are the same reasons the author gives to explain why you should fill your plate with fruits and vegetables. By using the same reasons twice, the author shows that she thinks they are very important.

Step by Step

- **Review learning from Parts 1–3.** Remind children that finding reasons will help them understand important ideas. Display page 166 of *Eat Better!* Have children recall the reasons the author gives for filling their plate with fruits and vegetables.

- **Have children identify reasons.** Display and read aloud page 167 of *Eat Better!* Point to the first paragraph and tell children the important idea: *You should not eat "sometimes" foods every day.* Prompt children to tell reasons that support the important idea.

  What are some examples of "sometimes" foods? *(burgers, fries, and donuts)*

  Why shouldn't you eat "sometimes" foods every day? *("They have high fat, lots of salt, or too much sugar." They don't have the nutrients you need to grow.)*

- Continue reading the page, and briefly discuss how "sometimes" foods differ from "anytime" foods.

- Tell children that they will complete the Student Book page by identifying reasons that support the important idea in this part of *Eat Better!*

- **Have children complete the Student Book page independently.** Have children turn to page 104. Read aloud the important idea: *Don't eat these types of food every day.* Point to each picture and name the reason *(they are high in fat; they have lots of salt; they have too much sugar)*. Have children decide whether each reason explains the important idea. Have them circle each reason that does.

> **Tip:** You may need to help children understand the connection between high fat content in a bacon cheeseburger, high salt content in french fries, and high sugar content in frosted donuts, as shown in the pictures on the Student Book page.

- Discuss the answers to the Student Book page. Reread the paragraph and have children tell when they hear the evidence that supports each answer.

- **Have children demonstrate understanding.** Display *Eat Better!* Read aloud the Turn and Talk activity. Reread parts of *Eat Better!* as needed to guide children's discussions. *(SL.K.1; SL.K.2)*

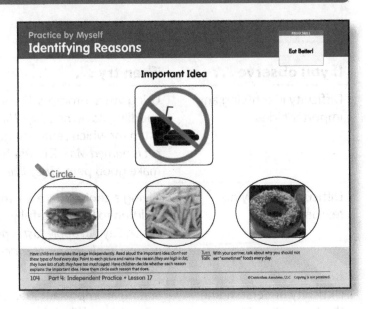

With your partner, talk about why you should not eat "sometimes" foods every day. *(They are high in fat. They have a lot of salt in them. They have too much sugar.)*

- Use the Close Reading activity to help children notice repeated words or phrases that emphasize an important idea.

- **Have children reflect on their learning.** Invite children to discuss why readers look for reasons that explain an author's important ideas. Encourage them to tell the questions they can ask to find supporting reasons for important ideas.

Close Reading

- Guide children to see that sometimes authors repeat words or phrases to emphasize important ideas. Tell children to listen for words the author uses more than once as you reread the first and last paragraphs of *Eat Better!* Ask:

  What are the important words you heard more than once? *("make healthy choices")*

  Why do you think the author used these words more than once? *(to show that it is important to make healthy choices)*

- Discuss how the key details in *Eat Better!* are connected to the important idea of making healthy choices.

Assessment and Remediation

If you observe . . .	Then try . . .
Difficulty identifying an important idea	Using visual prompts. Display two pictures, one of a dog playing and one of a dog cuddling its owner. Say: *This dog is playing. This dog is cuddling.* Then have children listen for which sentence goes best with the pictures. Say: *Dogs make good pets. My cat is named Max.* Discuss how the two pictures give reasons that explain why dogs make good pets. *(They like to play. They are nice to cuddle with.)*
Difficulty identifying reasons	Giving a choice. State an important idea such as this: *An apple is a great snack.* Tell children to listen carefully for a sentence that explains why an apple is a great snack. Say: *An apple tastes good. An apple has a stem.* Then ask: *Which sentence tells why an apple is a great snack?* Point out that the second sentence does not tell why an apple is a great snack; it just tells a detail about the apple.
Difficulty understanding the connection between an important idea and supporting reasons	Stating an important idea as a question. For example, say: *It is a good idea to share with a friend. Why is it a good idea to share with a friend?* Call on volunteers to answer the question. Repeat each response by saying: *It is a good idea to share with a friend because [reason].* Point out that each child's reason supports the important idea of why it is a good idea to share with a friend.

Connect to the Anchor Standard

R8: Delineate and evaluate the argument and specific claims in a text, including the validity of the reasoning as well as the relevance and sufficiency of the evidence.

Throughout the grades, Standard 8 develops students' understanding of how authors present evidence to support arguments. Students learn how to tie specific reasons and other evidence to corresponding points. They learn to recognize how an author connects ideas and reasons through compare-and-contrast, cause-and-effect, and sequence relationships. Students learn to evaluate authors' arguments and determine whether they have merit and sufficient evidence. Students might consider these questions: *What argument is the author making? What supporting reasons does the author provide? Is the evidence reliable and sufficient? Is the argument convincing? What relationships between ideas and reasons make the argument convincing?* Use the following activities to help children begin this transition.

- Guide children to evaluate an author's argument. Read aloud the last paragraph on page 31 of *America's Champion Swimmer.* Point out that the President of the United States felt that Trudy was "America's Best Girl." Since the author didn't challenge this, he probably would also argue that "Trudy was America's Best Girl." Ask: *Did the author provide enough evidence in the book to support this argument?* Discuss the evidence the author provides to support the claim. *(SL.K.1; SL.K.2)*

- Discuss the connections between ideas and reasons in *Eat Better!* Read aloud page 166. Begin with a cause-and-effect connection. Have children complete the statement: *The author writes that you should make healthy food choices because _____.* Continue with some comparison connections. Have children complete these statements: *The author compares "anytime" foods to _____ foods. "Anytime" foods are _____. "Sometimes" foods are _____.*

CCSS

RI.K.9: With prompting and support, identify basic similarities in and differences between two texts on the same topic (e.g., in illustrations, descriptions, or procedures).

Required Read Alouds: F (Red-Eyed Tree Frog); G (What's It Like to Be a Fish?); H (What Lives in a Shell?)

Lesson Objectives

- Identify details in the words and illustrations of a book.

- Identify basic similarities and differences between the words in two books.

- Identify basic similarities and differences between the illustrations in two books.

- Understand that comparing and contrasting books on the same topic helps readers learn more about the topic.

The Learning Progression

- **Prior to K:** Children should be able to distinguish between the illustrations or photographs and the words in a book. They should also have a basic understanding of what it means to be the same or different.

- **Grade K: CCSS RI.K.9 expects children to identify basic similarities and differences between two texts on the same topic with prompting and support.**

- **Grade 1:** CCSS RI.1.9 advances the standard by having children identify basic similarities and differences between two texts on the same topic more independently.

Tap Children's Prior Knowledge

- Guide children to compare and contrast classroom objects, or tell how they are alike and different. Review that they have compared and contrasted characters' experiences in a previous lesson.

- Hold up a piece of white chalk and a red crayon. Ask: *How are these things the same? (They are the same size. They are both used to write or draw.)* Record children's responses beneath the heading *Same*.

- Then ask: *How are these things different? (The chalk is white, but the crayon is red. The chalk is used on a chalkboard, but the crayon is used on paper.)* Record children's responses beneath the heading *Different*.

- Provide the following sentence frames to help children verbalize what is the same and different. Refer to the list to help them recall their comparisons.

  The chalk and the crayon are alike because _____.

  The chalk and the crayon both _____.

  The chalk and the crayon are different because _____.

  The chalk is _____, but the crayon is _____.

- Tell children that in this lesson, they will learn how to compare and contrast two books on the same topic.

Ready *Teacher Toolbox*   Teacher-Toolbox.com

	Prerequisite Skills	**RI.K.9**
Ready Lessons		✓
Tools for Instruction	✓	✓
Interactive Tutorials		

Additional CCSS

RI.K.2; RI.K.7; SL.K.1; SL.K.2 (See page A38 for full text.)

Part 1: Introduction

Step by Step

- **Introduce the standard.** Tell children they will compare and contrast two books about the same topic. Explain that this will help them to get a better understanding of the topic.

- Display the books *Red-Eyed Tree Frog* and *What's It Like to Be a Fish?* Tell children you will work together to tell what is the same and what is different about the books. Prompt:

  Let's compare, or think about what is the same about both books. What kind of books are these: stories or information books? (information books)

  How can you tell? (Red-Eyed Tree Frog *has photographs and tells facts about a frog.* What's It Like to Be a Fish? *is a science book that tells facts about fish.*)

  What science topic do both books tell about? (animals)

- Invite children to make additional observations about what is the same. Then continue prompting:

  Now let's contrast, or think about how the two books are different. What is different about the topic of each book? (Red-Eyed Tree Frog *tells about a frog, but* What's It Like to Be a Fish? *tells about fish.*)

  What is different about the kinds of pictures in each book? (Red-Eyed Tree Frog *has photos, but* What's It Like to Be a Fish? *has drawings.*)

  What is different about what you see on each cover? (Red-Eyed Tree Frog *just shows one frog, but* What's It Like to Be a Fish? *shows three different types of fish.*)

Tip: Children may be tempted to point out visual similarities and differences in the size and shape of the book or the lettering of each title. Acknowledge them, but explain that they should mainly focus on details related to what the book is about.

- Tell children that in their Student Books, they will learn questions they can ask to help them compare and contrast books about the same topic.

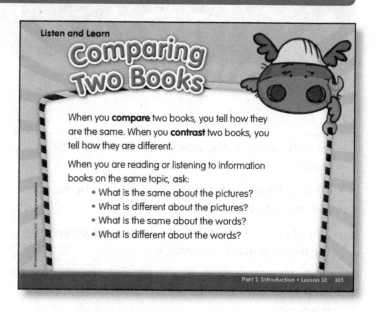

Listen and Learn

Comparing Two Books

When you **compare** two books, you tell how they are the same. When you **contrast** two books, you tell how they are different.

When you are reading or listening to information books on the same topic, ask:
- What is the same about the pictures?
- What is different about the pictures?
- What is the same about the words?
- What is different about the words?

Part 1: Introduction • Lesson 18   105

- **Read aloud the Student Book page.** Have children turn to Student Book page 105. Read aloud the page as children listen and follow along.

- Display pages 6–7 of *Red-Eyed Tree Frog* and page 20 of *What's It Like to Be a Fish?* Emphasize that even though the books are about different animals, the shared topic on these pages is eating.

- Ask children what they first notice about the words on each page. (What's It Like to Be a Fish? *has a lot more words.*) Then discuss what is different about the pictures. (Red-Eyed Tree Frog *shows a photo of one thing at a time.* What's It Like to Be a Fish? *has a drawing of many things that fish eat.*)

- Read aloud from each book and discuss the differences in the way each book talks about eating. (Red-Eyed Tree Frog *only tells one fact.* What's It Like to Be a Fish? *gives many facts.*)

- Help children understand that when readers compare and contrast details in books, they can learn more about a topic. Invite them to share what they learned about frogs and fish eating.

- **Have children demonstrate understanding.** Call on volunteers to share what they have learned so far about comparing and contrasting books on the same topic. Invite them to use the questions they have learned to describe similarities and differences between pairs of classroom information books.

Step by Step

- **Review Part 1.** Remind children that they can compare and contrast information books. Have them recall similarities and differences between *Red-Eyed Tree Frog* and *What's It Like to Be a Fish?*

- **Revisit the books.** Display *What's It Like to Be a Fish?* and *What Lives in a Shell?* Page through each book, using the pictures as prompts to have children recall what they are about. (*RI.K.2; RI.K.7*)

- **Model comparing two books.** Explain that you are going to model how to compare and contrast pages from these books. Tell children that the topic of the pages is "where animals live."

- Display and read aloud pages 5–7 of *What's It Like to Be a Fish?* Then display and reread pages 7–9 of *What Lives in a Shell?* Think aloud:

  > **I want to compare the information in these two books. First I will ask: *What do the words in both books tell about?* The words in both books tell names of animals and where they live. It is easy to tell what is different: this book tells about where fish live and this book tells about where many animals live, including a land snail.**

  > **Next I will ask: *What is the same about the pictures in each book?* Well even though they don't look the same, I know that the pictures in both books show animals in places where they live. They are different because these pictures show different fish homes and this picture shows a snail; the snail only has one home.**

> **Tip:** Children may struggle to see that the pictures have something in common because they do not look the same. Provide additional practice with familiar visuals, such as pictures of seasons or holiday symbols.

- Tell children you will model how to complete the Student Book page by comparing information from two books about where animals live.

- **Model completing the Student Book page.** Have children turn to page 106. For the first item, ask: *Where do fish live?* Point to and describe each picture (*in water; in a nest; in a shell*). Demonstrate circling the correct picture. Continue with the second item. Ask: *Where do land snails live?* (*in water; in a nest; in a shell*)

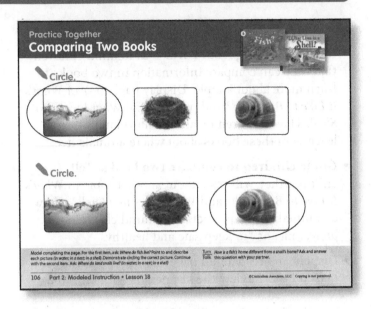

- **Have children demonstrate understanding.** Display pages 5–7 of *What's It Like to Be a Fish?* and page 8 of *What Lives in a Shell?* Read aloud the Turn and Talk activity. Model what a conversation with a partner should sound like by asking and answering the question below. (*SL.K.1; SL.K.2*)

  > ***How is a fish's home different from a snail's home?* Ask and answer this question with your partner.** (*A fish lives in the water. A snail lives in a shell on land.*)

- Use the Close Reading activity to help children compare information provided in pictures.

Close Reading

- Guide children to compare information presented in pictures. Display page 6 of *What's It Like to Be a Fish?* and page 9 of *What Lives in a Shell?* Read aloud the labels. Ask:

  > **What is the same about these pictures?** (*They both have labels that name details.*)

  > **What do the labels tell about in each picture?** (*the names of each kind of fish; the parts of the land snail's body*)

- Help children understand that they should look for pictures with labels in information books. Some labels give general information like the names of the different fish, and some give specific information like the parts of a snail's body.

Step by Step

- **Review learning from Parts 1–2.** Remind children that they can compare information in two books to learn more about a topic. Display pages 5–7 of *What's It Like to Be a Fish?* and pages 7–9 of *What Lives in a Shell?* Have children recall the information they learned in these books about where animals live.

- **Guide children to compare two books.** Tell children they will read about another topic in *What's It Like to Be a Fish?* and *What Lives in a Shell?*—how an animal's body protects it. Remind children that *protect* means "to keep safe and healthy."

- Display and read aloud pages 12–13 of *What's It Like to Be a Fish?* Review the key details with children.

> **Tip:** Clarify the phrase "like shingles on a roof." Draw or provide another visual to help children see how roof shingles overlap to keep water out of a house.

- Display and read aloud page 13 of *What Lives in a Shell?* Review the key details.

- Guide children to compare and contrast the two books. Prompt:

    What is the same about how a fish and a snail are *protected*, or how they stay safe and healthy?
    (Both animals have body parts that protect them.)

    What does a fish's body have to protect it? How does it work? *(scales; the hard plates overlap and protect the fish's body from cuts and scrapes)*

    What does a snail's body have to protect it? How does it work? *(a shell; the snail can hide inside of the shell to escape from enemies)*

- Use the Close Reading activity for additional practice with comparing information in two books.

- Tell children that you will work together to complete the Student Book page by comparing information from two books.

- **Guide children to complete the Student Book page.** Have children turn to page 107. For the first item, ask: *What part of a fish's body helps to protect it?* Point to and describe each picture *(shell; scales; fur).* Have a volunteer tell which picture to circle. Continue with the second item. Ask: *What part of a snail's body helps to protect it?* *(shell; scales; fur)*

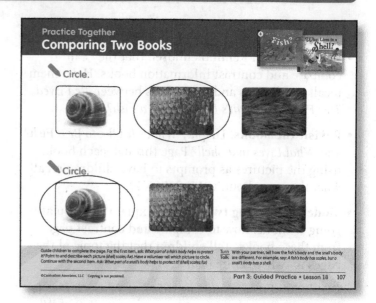

Practice Together
Comparing Two Books

Circle.

Circle.

Guide children to complete the page. For the first item, ask: *What part of a fish's body helps to protect it?* Point to and describe each picture *(shell; scales; fur).* Have a volunteer tell which picture to circle. Continue with the second item. Ask: *What part of a snail's body helps to protect it? (shell; scales; fur)*

Turn Talk: With your partner, tell how the fish's body and the snail's body are different. For example, say: *A fish's body has scales, but a snail's body has a shell.*

©Curriculum Associates, LLC   Copying is not permitted.   **Part 3: Guided Practice • Lesson 18** 107

- Discuss the answers to the Student Book page. Help children point to evidence that supports the answers.

- **Have children demonstrate understanding.** Display page 13 of *What Lives in a Shell?* and pages 12–13 of *What's It Like to Be a Fish?* Read aloud the Turn and Talk activity. *(SL.K.1; SL.K.2)*

    With your partner, tell how the fish's body and the snail's body are different. For example, say: *A fish's body has scales, but a snail's body has a shell.* *(A snail can hide inside of its body, but a fish can't.)*

- Invite partners to share their ideas with the class.

Close Reading

- Display page 13 of *What Lives in a Shell?* and pages 12–13 of *What's It Like to Be a Fish?* Ask:

    Which book has more words? *(What's It Like to Be a Fish?)*

- Reread page 12, and work with children to connect words and pictures. Discover together that many of the words like *clear slime, water,* and *germs* are hard to show in the picture and must be described in the words instead.

- Reread page 13 of *What Lives in a Shell?* Ask:

    What information can you get from this picture? *(the way a snail hides in its shell when a bird is trying to get it)*

- Discuss how authors and illustrators decide when to mostly show or tell information.

Step by Step

- **Review learning from Parts 1–3.** Remind children that comparing books helps them learn more about a topic. Display pages 12–13 of *What's It Like to Be a Fish?* and page 13 of *What Lives in a Shell?* Ask children to review how fish and snails protect themselves.

- **Have children compare two books.** Tell children they will compare another topic in *What's It Like to Be a Fish?* and *What Lives in a Shell?*—how animals swim. Display and read aloud pages 14–15 of *What's It Like to Be a Fish?* Ask:

    How do fish swim? Use the information in the words and the picture. (*They swim by swinging their tail fins and waving their other fins.*)

- Display and read aloud page 27 of *What Lives in a Shell?* Ask:

    How do scallops swim? Use the information in the words and the picture. (*They quickly open and close their shells.*)

> **Tip:** Guide children to identify the body parts in the pictures. Be sure they recognize the tail fin and other fins of the fish and the two shells of the scallop.

- Guide children to compare and contrast the information from both books. Ask:

    What is the same about how fish and scallops move? (*They both swim.*)

    What is different about how fish and scallops move? (*Fish swing their tail fins and wave other fins. Scallops open and close their shells.*)

- Tell children that they will complete the Student Book page by comparing information from two books.

- **Have children complete the Student Book page independently.** Have children turn to page 108. For the first item, ask: *What do fish use to swim?* Point to and describe each picture (*claws; shell; tail*). Have children circle their answers. Continue with the second item. Ask: *What do scallops use to swim?* (*claws; shell; tail*)

- Discuss the answers to the Student Book page. Help children point to evidence that supports the answers.

- Use the Close Reading activity to show how authors contrast things to emphasize important details.

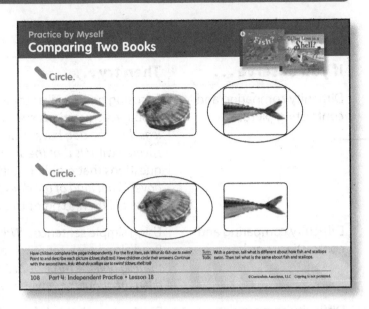

- **Have children demonstrate understanding.** Display pages 14–15 of *What's It Like to Be a Fish?* and page 27 of *What Lives in a Shell?* Read aloud the Turn and Talk activity. (*SL.K.1; SL.K.2*)

    With a partner, tell what is different about how fish and scallops swim. Then tell what is the same about fish and scallops. (*Fish use their fins to swim, but scallops use their shells. Both live in water, and both swim.*)

- **Have children reflect on their learning.** Invite children to discuss what questions they can ask to compare and contrast books. Emphasize that comparing the information in books can help them learn more about a topic.

Close Reading

- Tell children that sometimes an author will contrast two things to help describe a key detail. Display page 27 of *What Lives in a Shell?* and read aloud the second sentence. Ask:

    What does the author contrast the scallop's swimming with? (*a fish's swimming*)

    How does a fish swim? (*It swings its tail fin back and forth.*)

    How is a scallop's swimming different? (*It opens and closes its shells quickly.*)

- Discuss how picturing both types of swimming helps children understand more about the topic.

Assessment and Remediation

If you observe . . .	Then try . . .
Difficulty comparing and contrasting pictures	Focusing on a familiar topic. Display pictures of two pets, such as a dog and a rabbit. Ask questions such as these to help children identify similarities: *How many legs does the dog have? How many legs does the rabbit have? What is the dog's body covered with? Is that the same as or different from the rabbit's body?* Then ask questions that highlight differences, such as these: *What kind of tail does the dog have? What kind of tail does the rabbit have? How big is the dog? How big is the rabbit?* Invite children to point to details in the pictures as they give their answers.
Difficulty comparing and contrasting words	Using simple sentences. Write two sentences such as these: *A frog hops. A turtle crawls.* Read aloud each sentence, and invite children to act out the motions. Ask: *What are the frog and the turtle both doing? Are they sitting still? (No. They are moving.) What is different about the way the frog and the turtle move? (The frog hops, but the turtle crawls.)*
Difficulty comparing and contrasting two books on the same topic	Display two simple information books on the same topic, such as dinosaurs. Read aloud each title, and have children focus on the cover art. Then have them complete these sentences: Both of these books have pictures of _____. *[Book 1]* has a picture of _____, but *[Book 2]* has a picture of _____. Both of these books tell about _____. *[Book 1]* tells about _____, but *[Book 2]* tells about _____.

Connect to the Anchor Standard

R9: *Analyze how two or more texts address similar themes or topics in order to build knowledge or to compare the approaches the authors take.*

Throughout the grades, Standard 9 develops students' ability to compare and contrast texts on similar topics. Starting from identifying basic similarities and differences in texts, students advance to focusing on the most important points and key details in each text. In later grades, they gather information from two or more texts in order to write or speak knowledgeably about a topic. They also learn to analyze and assess authors' presentations of information. Students might consider questions such as these: *How does each author present the topic? Which text presents the information in a way that is easiest to understand? What information did I learn from one text that I did not learn from another?* Use the following activities to help children begin this transition.

- Help children compare the way information is presented. Display and read aloud pages 10–11 of *What's It Like to Be a Fish?* including the labels. Ask: *Where do you find out the names of the fish's fins?* Do the same for the names of the snail's body parts on pages 8–9 of *What Lives in a Shell?* Compare how both authors present details about the fish and the snail. Ask: *Which helps you learn the information: words or pictures with labels? Why? (SL.K.1; SL.K.2)*

- Compare and contrast the way authors conclude books. Display and read aloud pages 30–32 of *What's It Like to Be a Fish?* Ask: *What does the author write about at the end of the book?* Do the same for pages 28–32 of *What Lives in a Shell?* Point out that both books end with directions about how to handle the animals described in the books. Discuss the differences in the way each author gives instructions to readers.

The Owl and the Pussy-Cat

adapted from the poem by Edward Lear,
Nonsense Songs, Stories, Botany, and Alphabets

I

The Owl and the Pussy-Cat went to sea
   In a beautiful pea green boat:
They took some honey, and plenty of money
   Wrapped up in a five-pound note.
The Owl looked up to the stars above,
   And sang to a small guitar,
"O lovely Pussy-Cat! O Pussy-Cat my love,
   What a beautiful Pussy-Cat you are,
     You are,
     You are!
   What a beautiful Pussy-Cat you are!"

II

Pussy-Cat said to the Owl, "You elegant fowl,
   How charmingly sweet you sing!
Oh! let us be married; too long we have tarried:

But what shall we do for a ring?"
They sailed away, for a year and a day,
　To the land where the bong-tree grows;
And there in a wood a Piggywig stood
　With a ring at the end of his nose,
　　His nose,
　　His nose,
　With a ring at the end of his nose.

III

"Dear Pig, are you willing to sell for one shilling
　Your ring?" Said the Piggy, "I will."
So they took it away, and were married next day
　By the Turkey who lives on the hill.

They dined on mince, and slices of quince,
　Which they ate with a runcible spoon;
And hand in hand, on the edge of the sand,
　They danced by the light of the moon,
　　The moon,
　　The moon,
　They danced by the light of the moon.

How to Make Play Dough

You will need:

measuring cups

4 plastic containers

Ingredients:

1 cup warm water

3 cups flour

1 ½ cups salt

¼ cup vegetable oil

food coloring

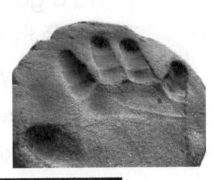

Steps:

1. Work with an adult. Mix these ingredients together in a bowl—water, flour, salt, and oil.

2. Add more flour if the mixture is too sticky. Knead the dough until it feels soft and smooth.

3. Divide the dough into four parts. Add 4 to 6 drops of food coloring to each part. Knead the coloring into the dough.

4. Store the play dough in airtight containers. It will keep for several weeks.

Eat Better!

by Linda Gold

Make healthy choices! It's a good idea to eat foods that are good for you. They will help you grow, keep you healthy, and make you feel better.

ChooseMyPlate.gov

Healthy foods are "anytime" foods. You can eat them anytime! Enjoy them as a snack or pack them for lunch.

Healthy foods, like fruits and vegetables, are also colorful. Fill your plate with different colors. Then you will have lots of vitamins and minerals to help you grow. You will have energy to play and have fun. You will feel good!

Watch out for "sometimes" foods, like burgers, fries, and donuts. You should not eat them every day. They have high fat, lots of salt, or too much sugar. They don't have the nutrients you need to help you grow.

When you go to the supermarket with your family, make healthy choices. Choose lots of "anytime" foods.

Choose "Anytime" Foods

Make Healthy Lunches

Pack your lunch with different foods that you like and are *good for you*.

- Make half your meal fruits and vegetables. Eat red, orange, purple, yellow, and dark green fruits and vegetables.

- Make sure you eat protein. Try one of these sandwiches: tuna salad, turkey and tomato, hummus and cucumber.

- Add new and interesting things to your salads: try spinach, orange, or avocado.

- Have yogurt and berries.

- Have 3-bean vegetarian chili.

Grab Smart Snacks

Go for snacks that contain whole grains, low-fat dairy products, fruits, vegetables, and lean protein.

- Mix it up! Make a healthy fruit smoothie.

- Grab an apple for a quick snack.

- Drink low-fat milk.

- Spread almond butter on whole-grain crackers.

- Have a slice of watermelon.

- Reach for water, not sugary drinks.